Guide to the CEQA Initial Study Checklist

By
Ernest Perea

Ceqainfo.com

Printed in the United States of America

ISBN-13: 978-1460948750
ISBN-10: 1460948750

PlanTech Publishing
www.ceqainfo.com

Thanks to the following that provided the author with valuable feedback during the course of writing this book.

Barbara Carson, AICP

Gustavo Romo, Principal,
Romo Planning Group, Inc.

Mat Evans, AICP

Roger Scherer, AICP, Principal,
Advanced Development Solutions

Table of Contents

Chapter

Appendices

Introduction

The Environmental Checklist Form (i.e. Initial Study Checklist) is the backbone of the CEQA process.

The Initial Study Checklist will determine what type of CEQA document will be required for a project, whether it be a Negative Declaration, a Mitigated Negative Declaration, or an Environmental Impact Report.

The determination of what type of CEQA document is required for a project is based on the responses to **89 questions covering 18 environmental issues** contained in *Appendix G of the Guidelines to the California Environmental Quality Act*, prepared by the California Natural Resources Agency.

According to the California Natural Resources Agency, Appendix G is a sample form that may be modified as necessary to suit the lead agency and to address the particular circumstances of the project under consideration. In addition, the Third District Court of Appeal recently issued an opinion that clarified that all substantial evidence regarding potential impacts of a project must be considered, even if the particular potential impact is not listed in Appendix G. (*Protect the Historic Amador Waterways*, *supra*, 116 Cal.App.4th at 1109.)

In practice, Appendix G serves as the basis for the majority of Initial Study Checklists prepared by a lead agency. Even if a lead agency uses a modified form, the information contained in this book can be useful.

Each of the 18 environmental issues described in Appendix G are covered in standalone chapters for easy reference. The Initial Study Checklist preparer can select what environmental issue they are interested in and find all of the information in that chapter.

This is not a book that has to be read cover to cover to be understood, but instead can be used as a quick reference source for whatever environmental topic the Initial Study Checklist preparer is interested in.

This book suggests a framework for completing the Environmental Checklist Form for each of the 89 questions. This framework was developed by the author based on over 28 years of preparing and reviewing Initial Study Checklists. It has evolved from the days of the "naked" checklist in which the questions were just marked without any justification to support the answer to today's practice of substantiating each answer with factual data.

This framework does not have to be followed precisely to prepare an adequate Initial Study Checklist as there are many people who prepare legally adequate Checklists everyday using their own methodology. This is just the methodology the author uses and that others have found to be helpful.

The framework is described as follows

- ***Determining the Scope of the Question.***

The author, in the process of reviewing Initial Studies, often times found that only part of a question was answered or that it was answered out of the context of its meaning.

This section assists in determining an appropriate scope for the question so that the question can be answered comprehensively and in an appropriate context.

If the questions posed in the Initial Study Checklist Form are not answered in an appropriate context then the process for determining what type of CEQA document is required for a project will be flawed.

- ***Where to Find the Factual Data to Answer the Question.***

This section directs the Initial Study Checklist preparer to sources of information that can help in answering the question. With the advance of the Internet, many sources of information are readily available. The book provides references to websites that contain information relative to the question.

- *Example Answers.*

  Example answers are provided for each of the 89 questions. The example answers provide one or more examples of a question that is answered comprehensively and one that is not. The example answers are intended to assist the Initial Study Checklist preparer with framing an appropriate response to each question.

  The example answers were based on answers to questions that are contained in documents the author has prepared or reviewed. In many cases, the example answers are based on real world situations. Because there are so many different circumstances unique to a project and its environmental setting, it is impossible to provide an example answer that addresses every conceivable situation.

  The example answers should be used to frame the Initial Study Checklist preparers own answers based on the circumstances of the project under review.

  For each question, there are four possible answers:

Potentially Significant Impact	Less Than Significant With Mitigation Incorporated	Less Than Significant	No Impact
☐	☐	☐	☐

For any question that is answered with a "Potentially Significant Impact" an Environmental Impact Report will be required.

- ***Determining Significance.***

  Determining significance can be one of the more complicated steps in the CEQA process and is dependent on many variables specific to the unique circumstances of a project. This section contains some general factors to consider in the process of determining significance.

***

This book is written in a manner that strives to implement *Article 10. Considerations in Preparing EIRs and Negative Declarations* of the CEQA Guidelines.

CEQA Guidelines Section 15140 states: "*EIRs [Negative Declarations] shall be written in plain language and may use appropriate graphics so that the decision makers and the public can rapidly understand the documents.*"

In reviewing various CEQA documents, the author has encountered pages devoted to the definitions of acronyms used in the document. In many instances, there were paragraphs that contained numerous acronyms that made understanding the document difficult, even for an experienced planner.

Therefore, in order to encourage the use of "plain language" the use of acronyms is limited in this book and the author encourages Initial Study Checklist preparers to limit the use of acronyms in writing CEQA documents.

Chapter I

Aesthetics

Introduction

Aesthetics deals with how the appearance or views to or from an area are impacted by a project and the resulting visual change that occurs. Anytime land (whether developed or undeveloped) is altered the aesthetic character of the site and its surroundings changes to some degree depending on the type of project.

Aesthetics is one of the more difficult topics to address in the Initial Study Checklist because it can be so subjective. For example, a vacant lot with no unique features that is adjacent to a residential area is viewed by some as being preferable to development of a multi-family project or shopping center.

There have been many instances where the proposed development, although consistent with a general plan, zoning code, and design requirements is nonetheless perceived as degrading the aesthetic quality of the neighborhood because residents don't like the proposed land use.

The questions posed in this Chapter involve Scenic Vistas, State Scenic Highways, Visual Character, and Light and Glare.

1

I. AESTHETICS

Would the project:

(a) Have a substantial adverse effect on a scenic vista?

1. Determining the Scope of the Question

There is no clear cut definition of what constitutes a scenic vista. What some may consider a scenic vista may not be considered a scenic vista by others. A general plan, specific plan, zoning code or other planning document may provide guidance.

For example, a general plan may contain a policy that states "*Locate and site development to preserve public and private views of hillside areas and the Santa Victoria Mountains.*" In this case, the Santa Victoria Mountains are considered a scenic vista because the general plan states so.

In another example, the zoning code may have provisions for ridgeline protection and contain a map that identifies certain ridgelines that are considered to be important to the community's identity. These ridgelines would be considered a scenic vista.

Determining whether or not a scenic vista exists can become very subjective if there is no guidance in a general plan, specific plan, zoning code, or other planning documents.

In general, in answering this question it is best to apply a broad approach to what constitutes a scenic vista. Not all scenic vistas relate to ocean

2

views, mountains, hills, lakes, rivers, canyons, open spaces or other natural features.

A scenic vista can include an urban setting that is important on a communitywide basis and helps define the aesthetic character of a community. For example, areas of the community that contain unique types of development (e.g. a cluster of historic buildings) or areas that define a gateway to the community (e.g. a bridge, building, or other structure).

2. Where to Find the Factual Data to Answer the Question

- The lead agency's general plan, zoning code, or other planning documents.

- Before and after photo simulations, story poles, viewshed studies, balloon flights, sight line analyses, etc.

- It is recommended that the California Environmental Resources Evaluation System website be consulted to see if there is any information related to this question. The website is located at:

  ceres.ca.gov or enter "ceres evaluation" in an Internet search engine.

3. Example Answers

The following example answers the question comprehensively:

The most significant views in the area focus on streetscapes along major arterials, long-range views from high-rise towers, and short-range views of the generously landscaped grounds and plazas of certain office tower and business park developments.

The project site is located along Main Street, which has a landscaped median and parkway landscaping which is designed to enhance the image of the community (i.e. water features, heritage trees). The existing surface parking lot (the location of the proposed hotel structure) is surrounded by the adjoining 12-story office building to the east, the on-site nine-story parking structure to the south, and an 11-story parking structure to the west.

Project implementation would replace existing views of the site (surface parking structure) with views of a hotel development. Project implementation would not have a substantial adverse effect on a scenic vista identified by the General Plan. Additionally, views of streetscapes along Main Street would not be obstructed due to the proposed setbacks and the heights of the surrounding structures/buildings.

This response frames the discussion in the context of its locale and identifies what constitutes a scenic vista (in this case the landscaped palette along Main Street). It then discusses why the project won't impact a scenic vista. It also states whether or not there are any scenic vistas identified in the general plan.

The following example does not answer the question comprehensively:

The project site and surrounding area are relatively flat and have been developed with urban uses. The project consists of six (6) single-story single-family residences and other facilities typically appurtenant to residential development. The project is located within a residential area, and is compatible with the surrounding land uses. As such, the project will not produce any uncommon or aesthetically offensive sights.

This response makes the assumption that "flat land" and "urban uses" do not constitute a scenic vista when in fact they might in a certain setting. Although it considers the project's compatibility with surrounding land uses and makes a point that the project will not produce any uncommon or aesthetically offensive sights, it does not address whether or not scenic vistas, if any, will be adversely impacted by the project.

4. Determining Significance

Following are some general factors to consider for determining significance:

- Are there any Thresholds of Significance that were formally adopted by the lead agency that are applicable to the project?

- Has the lead agency set a precedent in previously approved CEQA documents in responding to the question? If so, the Initial Study Checklist preparer should be aware of

how other CEQA documents have responded to the question.

- Are there policies in a planning document, such as a general plan, specific plan, or the zoning code which identify scenic vistas or requires the protection of features that could contribute to a scenic vista such as hillsides, knolls, ridgelines, buildings, or structures?

- Does the project significantly impair the public view of a feature(s) that is typically considered to be a scenic vista such as ocean views, mountains, hills, lakes, rivers, canyons, open spaces or other natural features?

However, note that features other than the above can be considered a scenic vista if they have a scenic value to the community. For example, areas of the community that contain unique types of development (e.g. a cluster of historic buildings) or serve as a gateway to a community (e.g. bridge, building, or other structure).

I. AESTHETICS (cont.)

Would the project:

(b) Substantially damage scenic resources, including, but not limited to, trees, rock outcroppings, and historic buildings within a state scenic highway?

1. Determining the Scope of the Question

This question is asking about scenic resources that are located *within* a State Scenic Highway. State Scenic Highways are regulated by the California Department of Transportation under the California Scenic Highway Program. If the project site is not located within a State Scenic Highway then there would be no impact.

However, it is important to note that the California Scenic Highway System has two categories for highways, those that are "officially designated" and those that are "eligible."

According to the California Department of Transportation, the status of a proposed state scenic highway changes from "eligible" to "officially designated" when the local governing body applies to the California Department of Transportation for scenic highway approval, adopts a Corridor Protection Program, and receives notification that the highway has been officially designated a Scenic Highway.

If a project site is located within a State Scenic Highway then development will be guided by a Corridor Protection Program adopted by the local jurisdiction in which the segment of the State Scenic Highway is located.

If the project site is within an "eligible" state scenic highway then the author suggests this be evaluated in the Initial Study Checklist even though the project is not technically within an "officially designated" State Scenic Highway. This is even more so the case if the lead agency's general plan contains a policy to pursue designation of a highway as an official State Scenic Highway.

2. Example Answers

The following examples answer the question comprehensively:

Example 1

According to the California Department of Transportation Scenic Highway Program, Interstate 10, which runs adjacent to the project site, is not identified as "Officially Designated" or an "Eligible State Scenic Highway-Not Officially Designated". Therefore, there will be no impact.

This response identifies that the highway adjacent to the project site is not classified as "Officially Designated" or "Eligible State Scenic Highway-Not Officially Designated" and therefore there is no impact.

Example 2

Interstate 10 adjacent to the project site is classified as an "Eligible State Scenic Highway-Not Officially Designated" by the California Department of Transportation Scenic Highway Program. However, the City has not applied to the California Department of Transportation for official Scenic Highway status nor does the City's General Plan (or other policies or directives) require the City to do so.

Therefore, there is no Corridor Protection Plan in place. In addition, there are no trees, rock outcroppings, historic buildings or other scenic resources on the site that would be considered to add the scenic quality of this section of Interstate 10.

This response takes into account the although the highway is eligible for State Scenic Highway status the local jurisdiction has not applied for such status and has not adopted a Corridor Protection Plan nor does its general plan or other policies require it to do so. In addition, the response indicates that there are no scenic resources or historic buildings on the site.

The following example does not answer the question comprehensively:

The project proposes the development of office buildings. The buildings are all single-story in height. The new construction is compatible in height and architectural design and with existing uses in the area. Therefore, no aesthetic impacts will occur from the proposed development.

This response makes no reference as to the project's location relative to a State Scenic Highway. It was not answered in an appropriate context.

3. Where to Find Factual Data to Answer the Question

- California Department of Transportation Landscape Architecture website located at:

  www.dot.ca.gov/hq/LandArch/scenic/cahisys.htm or enter "caltrans landscape architecture" in an Internet search engine.

- A list and map of officially designated scenic highways can be located at:

  www.dot.ca.gov/hq/LandArch/scenic_highways/index.htm or enter "caltrans scenic highways" in an Internet search engine.

- It is recommended that the California Environmental Resources Evaluation System website be consulted to see if there is any information related to this question. The website is located at:

  ceres.ca.gov or enter "ceres evaluation" in an Internet search engine.

4. Determining Significance

Following are some general factors to consider for determining significance:

- Are there any Thresholds of Significance that were formally adopted by the lead agency that are applicable to the project?

- Has the lead agency set a precedent in previously approved CEQA documents in responding to the question? If so, the Initial Study Checklist preparer should be aware of how other CEQA documents have responded to the question.

- If the project site is located adjacent to an officially designated State Scenic Highway, is the project consistent with the Corridor Protection Program?

- Is the project site is located adjacent to an Eligible State Scenic Highway? If so, has the lead agency applied for the highway to be officially designated? Is the project consistent with any proposed Corridor Protection Plan?

I. AESTHETICS (cont.)

Would the project:

(c) Substantially degrade the existing visual character or quality of the site and its surroundings?

1. Determining the Scope of the Question

Visual character is also one of the more difficult issues to analyze because like a scenic vista, it is often times subjective. In practice, visual character is generally defined as "human perceptions of combining form, bulk, scale, texture, color, and viewing range of a site, relative to the context of its locale."

In answering the question, it is important to consider the existing visual character of the site and how the project may change that. For example, the site may be located in a hillside area where the grading or cutting of slopes would alter the appearance of the hillside area significantly.

If the site contains trees, riparian areas, wetlands or other natural features the project could affect these resources in terms of visual character. If the site is located in an area that has a distinct character (e.g. rural) then this should considered in answering the question.

2. Where to Find Factual Data to Answer the Question

- Before and after photo simulations.

- Slope analysis.

- Grading plans.

- Architectural elevations.

- It is recommended that the California Environmental Resources Evaluation System website be consulted to see if there is any information related to this question. The website is located at:

  ceres.ca.gov or enter "ceres evaluation" in an Internet search engine.

3. Example Answers

The following example answers the question comprehensively:

The existing visual character of the project site and its surroundings is dominated by high-rise office developments, presenting a mix of architectural styles. The area is further defined by multi-story commercial and office uses, paved roadways, landscaping, and parking lots/structures.

The northern portion of the site consists of an asphalt surface parking lot and ornamental landscaping.

The southern portion of the site contains an eleven-level parking structure. Additionally, the southeast portion of the site contains (in part) an open space feature that includes a fountain, pond, seating areas, walkways, and ornamental landscaping. There are no unique or scenic visual resources on the project site or in its vicinity.

Short-Term Construction:

During the construction phase, views across the project site from surrounding areas would be disrupted. Graded surfaces, construction debris, construction equipment, and truck traffic would be visible. Additionally, soil would be stockpiled and equipment for grading activities would be staged at various locations throughout the site. Construction-related activities would be visible from the surrounding office and commercial uses and motorists traveling along Main Street.

Mitigation Measure AES-1 requires the project to use appropriate screening (e.g., temporary opaque fencing material) at equipment staging areas. With implementation of Mitigation Measure AES-1, construction related impacts to the site's visual character would be reduced to less than significant levels.

Long-Term Operations:

The project would permanently alter the appearance of the site by replacing the existing surface parking lot with a four-story hotel, approximately 50 feet in height. Based on the context of its surroundings, the proposed development would be visually compatible with existing uses.

This response addresses all aspects of visual character such as identifying the existing setting, describing what type of development is proposed, and discussing both short-term and long-term impacts.

The following example does not answer the question comprehensively:

The project would alter the existing visual character of the site and its surroundings through various means including the demolition of 5 single-story residential structures and the construction of a self-storage facility.

However, the project would not significantly degrade the existing visual character of the site in that the project would be required to undergo architectural and site design review by the Planning Commission to ensure compatibility with the surrounding neighborhood.

The response does not evaluate the change in visual character from single-family residences to a self-storage facility. It assumes that undergoing future architectural review will suffice in addressing the change in visual character.

However, it does not state what the architectural standards will be or how they deal with the change in terms of form, bulk, scale, texture, color, landscaping, site improvements etc. and their compatibility with the project's surroundings.

4. Determining Significance

Following are some general factors to consider for determining significance:

- Are there any Thresholds of Significance that were formally adopted by the lead agency that are applicable to the project?

- Has the lead agency set a precedent in previously approved CEQA documents in responding to the question? If so, the Initial Study Checklist preparer should be aware of how other CEQA documents have responded to the question.

- A project is generally considered to have a significant impact on visual character if it substantially changes the character of the project site such that it becomes visually incompatible or visually unexpected when viewed in the context of its surroundings.

I. AESTHETICS (cont.)

Would the project:

(d) Create a new source of substantial light or glare which would adversely affect day or nighttime views in the area?

1. Determining the Scope of the Question

Glare occurs when bright, direct light or indirect bright sunlight hits the eye. It can be caused by lighting (both interior and exterior), or reflective glare from building surfaces (e.g. glass, metal).

In determining the scope of the question, consider that there may be several sources of light and glare such as:

- ✓ Building surfaces that reflect sunlight (e.g. glass, metal roofs, etc.).

- ✓ Interior lighting that creates glare during nighttime (e.g. bright lights that are visible through windows).

- ✓ Outdoor lighting, such as for parking lots, sports fields, street lights, buildings.

- ✓ Signs.

- ✓ Skyglow (the "glow" effect that can be seen over populated areas).

In responding to this question, many Initial Study Checklist preparers only deal with outdoor lighting, however as shown above, there are several sources of light and glare other than from just outdoor lighting.

2. Where to Find Factual Data for Answering the Question

- Architectural plans.

- Lighting plans.

- Photometric lighting study (i.e. measurement of lighting levels at property lines).

- It is recommended that the California Environmental Resources Evaluation System website be consulted to see if there is any information related to this question. The website is located at:

  ceres.ca.gov or enter "ceres evaluation" in an Internet search engine.

3. Example Answers

The following example answers the question comprehensively:

Lighting associated with the use of the building would be that of a typical office building. Any outdoor lighting would be directed downward and shielded to avoid spillover onto adjacent properties.

The project site is frequently subject to fog and low cloud cover that tend to increase light dispersion from buildings and glare can be generated from reflective building materials. The project could therefore increase the amount of light and glare in the area. Mitigation Measure AES-1 is recommended to minimize light and glare from development through use of primary façade materials with low-glare potential.

This response takes into account several sources of light and glare such as from outdoor lighting and reflective building materials.

The following example does not answer the question comprehensively:

Implementation of the project would contribute additional lighting within the area. The project site is located within an urban area that presently generates similar lighting sources. Illumination is provided by a variety of building and pole-mounted outdoor lighting on the project site and the immediate vicinity.

The project will incorporate external lighting for visibility and safety; however, the project site is not located adjacent to housing or other land uses considered sensitive to night lighting. In addition, night lighting would generate illumination within a confined area and would not create glare beyond the immediate project site.

This response only discusses glare from outdoor lighting. It does not consider other potential sources of light and glare such as from building surfaces.

4. Determining Significance

Following are some general factors to consider for determining significance:

- Are there any Thresholds of Significance that were formally adopted by the lead agency that are applicable to the project?

- Has the lead agency set a precedent in previously approved CEQA documents in responding to the question? If so, the Initial Study Checklist preparer should be aware of how other CEQA documents have responded to the question.

- Is outdoor lighting shielded so that light spillover onto adjacent properties is avoided? If not, impacts may be significant.

- Does the amount of light, however measured, exceed any identified thresholds identified in a general plan or zoning code? If so, impacts may be significant.

- Does the building or structure contain materials that reflect sunlight such as glass or metal that would create glare? If so, impacts may be significant.

Chapter II

Agriculture and Forestry Resources

Introduction

The California Natural Resources Agency adopted amendments to *Appendix G of the CEQA Guidelines* on December 30, 2009. The amendments were effective as of March 18, 2010. The title of this section was changed from "Agriculture Resources" to "Agriculture and Forestry Resources" and two (2) questions pertaining to forest and timberland (Questions c and d) were added. In addition, guidance on where information could be found with respect to forest and timberland resources was added.

The reasons for revising this section of Appendix G are described below.

According to the California Natural Resources Agency's *Final Statement of Reasons for Regulatory Action, December 2009*, "*The amendments would add several questions addressing forest resources in the section on Agricultural Resources. Forestry questions are appropriately addressed in the Appendix G checklist for several reasons. First, forests and forest resources are directly linked to both GHG emissions and efforts to reduce those emissions. For example, conversion of forests to non-forest uses may result in direct emissions of GHG emissions. (See, e.g., California Energy Commission Baseline GHG Emissions for Forest, Range, and Agricultural Lands in California (March, 2004) at p. 19.)*

"Such conversion would also remove existing carbon stock (i.e., carbon stored in vegetation), as well as a significant carbon sink (i.e., rather than emitting GHGs, forests remove GHGs from the atmosphere). (Scoping Plan, Appendix C, at p. C-168.) Thus, such conversions are an indication of potential GHG emissions. Changes in forest land or timberland zoning may also ultimately lead to conversions, which could result in GHG emissions, aesthetic impacts, impacts to biological resources and water quality impacts, among others.

"Thus, these additions are reasonably necessary to ensure that lead agencies consider the full range of potential impacts in their initial studies. In the same way that an EIR must address conversion of prime agricultural land or wetlands as part of a project (addressing the whole of the action requires analyzing land clearance in advance of project development), so should it analyze forest removal. Agriculture and Forest Resources deals with project impacts that may affect agricultural land, forest land, and timberland either directly (through removal of such lands by project development) or indirectly (by contributing to factors that result in the conversion of such land to other uses)."

II. AGRICULTURE and FORESTRY RESOURCES:

In determining whether impacts to agricultural resources are significant environmental effects, lead agencies may refer to the California Agricultural Land Evaluation and Site Assessment Model (1997) prepared by the California Department of Conservation as an optional model to use in assessing impacts on agriculture and farmland. In determining whether impacts to forest resources, including timberland, are significant environmental effects, lead agencies may refer to information compiled by the California Department of Forestry and Fire Protection regarding the state's inventory of forest land, including the Forest and Range Assessment Project and the Forest Legacy Assessment Project; and the forest carbon measurement methodology provided in the Forest Protocols adopted by the California Air Resources Board.

Would the project:

(a) Convert Prime Farmland, Unique Farmland, or Farmland of Statewide Importance (Farmland), as shown on the maps prepared pursuant to the Farmland Mapping and Monitoring Program of the California Resources Agency, to non-agricultural use?

1. Determining the Scope of the Question

This question is asking about three (3) types of farmland as described below according to information provided by the California Department of Conservation.

Prime Farmland: In order to be shown on the Farmland Mapping and Monitoring Program maps as Prime Farmland, land must meet both the following criteria:

(1) Has been used for irrigated agricultural production at some time during the four years prior to the Important Farmland Map date. Irrigated land use is determined by the Farmland Mapping and Monitoring Program staff by analyzing current aerial photos, local comment letters, and related GIS data, supplemented with field verification, and

(2) The soil must meet the physical and chemical criteria for Prime Farmland as determined by the United States Department of Agriculture, Natural Resources Conservation Service. The Natural Resources Conservation Service compiles lists of which soils in each survey area meet the quality criteria.

Unique Farmland: Farmland of lesser quality soils used for the production of the state's leading agricultural crops. This land is usually irrigated, but may include nonirrigated orchards or vineyards as found in some climatic zones in California. Land must have been cropped at some time during the four years prior to the mapping date.

Farmland of Statewide Importance: Farmland similar to Prime Farmland but with minor shortcomings, such as greater slopes or less ability to store soil moisture. Land must have been used for irrigated agricultural production at some time during the four years prior to the mapping date.

If the project site is not mapped then the response to the question would generally be "no impact."

However, please note that if a site is not mapped as "*Prime Farmland*", "*Unique Farmland*", or "*Farmland of Statewide Importance*" by the Farmland Mapping and Monitoring Program, it still may be considered as agricultural land (i.e. farmland) for the purposes of assessing environmental impacts pursuant to Public Resources Code 21060.1 (b).

Public Resources Code 21060.1(b) makes reference to Government Code Section 51201(c) which defines agricultural land as follows:

(1) All land that qualifies for rating as class I or class II in the Natural Resource Conservation Service land use capability classifications. (*Note: See link to Natural Resource Conservation Service webpage in Section 2 below*).

(2) Land which qualifies for rating 80 through 100 in the Storie Index Rating. (*Note: See link to Land Evaluation and Site Assessment webpage in Section 2 below*).

(3) Land which supports livestock used for the production of food and fiber.

(4) Land planted with fruit or nut bearing trees, vines, bushes, or crops.

(5) Land which has returned from the production of unprocessed agricultural plant products an annual gross value of not less than two hundred dollars ($200) per acre for three of the previous five years.

The Initial Study Checklist preparer should be aware of conditions that may qualify the land as agriculture land even though it is not mapped by the Farmland Mapping and Monitoring Program.

If the project site is mapped and the project would convert the land to a non-agricultural use then this needs to be analyzed in detail in the Initial Study Checklist to determine the significance of the impact.

The California Agricultural Land Evaluation and Site Assessment Model is often used to conduct this analysis, but it is an optional requirement. However, in practice, it is being considered more and more as the standard method of analysis. Most environmental firms have persons who prepare assessments using the model.

2. Where to Find Factual Data for Answering the Question

- The Farmland Mapping and Monitoring Program has an excellent website which addresses this topic. It contains interactive maps that can be used to determine if a site is mapped as agricultural land. The website is located at:

www.consrv.ca.gov/dlrp/FMMP *or enter* "farmland mapping and monitoring program" in an Internet search engine.

- The Natural Resource Conservation Service Web Soil Survey provides soil data and information produced by the National Cooperative Soil Survey. The website can be located at:

http://websoilsurvey.nrcs.usda.gov/app/ or enter "nrcs web soil survey" in an Internet Search engine.

- The Land Evaluation Site Assessment Model is recommended by the California Department of Conservation to determine the suitability of land for agriculture use. The website can be located at:

www.consrv.ca.gov/DLRP/Pages/qh_lesa.aspx or enter "land evaluation site assessment" in an Internet search engine.

- The local agency general plan may also contain information about farmland and soil types suitable for agriculture use.

- It is recommended that the California Environmental Resources Evaluation System website be consulted to see if there is any information related to this question. The website is located at:

ceres.ca.gov or enter "ceres evaluation" in an Internet search engine.

3. Example Answers

The following example answers the question comprehensively:

According to the California Department of Conservation Farmland Mapping and Monitoring Program the site has not been mapped as Prime Farmland, Unique Farmland, or Farmland of Statewide Importance and falls within the classification of Urban Built-Up Land.

The project site does not contain suitable soils for agriculture use based on the Natural Resources Conservation Service Web Soil Survey.

In addition, the small size of the site (5 acres) and location (surrounded by residential development) makes the site not suitable for agricultural production.

This response cites the Farmland Mapping and Monitoring Program and indicates that other factors make it unsuitable for agriculture use (e.g. size, soils type, and location).

Author's Note: _As noted above, Public Resources Code 21060.1(b) also considers land that is not mapped by the Farmland Mapping and Monitoring Program as agricultural land. Therefore, the author recommends that a response to this question be more comprehensive and consider factors other than whether or not the site is mapped by the Farmland Mapping and Monitoring Program, especially in areas where agricultural production is common._

The following example does not answer the question comprehensively:

No agricultural uses are located on the project site. The project would not result in conversion of any farmland or have a significant impact on agricultural resources.

This response assumes that because there is no agricultural activity then the land does not contain suitable characteristics for farmland. It also does not reference if the Farmland Mapping and Monitoring Program was consulted.

4. Determining Significance

Following are some general factors to consider for determining significance:

- Are there any Thresholds of Significance that were formally adopted by the lead agency that are applicable to the project?

- Has the lead agency set a precedent in previously approved CEQA documents in responding to the question? If so, the Initial Study Checklist preparer should be aware of how other CEQA documents have responded to the question.

- Any project which converts or rezones agricultural or farmland to other uses may have a significant impact.

II. AGRICULTURE and FORESTRY RESOURCES (cont.)

Would the project:

(b) Conflict with existing zoning for agricultural use, or a Williamson Act contract?

1. Determining the Scope of the Question

In order to determine the scope of the question, it is separated into the following parts:

<u>Existing Zoning</u>

Agricultural zoning strives to protect the viability of agriculture in a region and is generally used by communities that are concerned about maintaining the economic viability of their agricultural industry.

Generally, a conflict with existing zoning for agriculture use would occur if a project would intrude into agricultural areas and create conflicts between agriculture uses and non-agriculture uses.

Following are some typical activities associated with an agriculture use:

- ✓ Tractors operating during early- morning or late-night hours;

- ✓ Livestock operations that produce odors from livestock waste;

- ✓ Chemical applications that are used for controlling insects and diseases in high-value crops; and

✓ Machinery moving slowly on the roads from farm to farm.

Many agriculture zones allow non-agriculture uses to be located in an agriculture zone such as one - family dwellings, churches, schools, or real estate offices to name a few. These uses may conflict with the agriculture activities described above.

The Initial Study Checklist preparer should be aware what potential conflicts a project could create on agriculture uses and address them in the Initial Study Checklist.

Finally, when answering this question always use the general plan land use designation as the basis in answering this question because by law zoning must be consistent with the general plan.

Often times in areas of transition, the general plan land use map designation may show a non-agricultural use but the existing zoning may still be agricultural. If there is a conflict, note this in the Initial Study Checklist and address how it will be rectified. The point is that although the question uses the term "zoning" the general plan land use designation takes precedence.

Williamson Act Contract

The California Department of Conservation describes a Williamson Act Contract as follows: *"The California Land Conservation Act of 1965-- commonly referred to as the Williamson Act-- enables local governments to enter into contracts with private landowners for the purpose of restricting specific parcels of land to agricultural or* _related open space use. In return, landowners receive property tax assessments which are much lower than normal because they are based upon farming and open space uses as opposed to full market value."_

As long as a Williamson Act Contract is in effect, the land can only be used for agricultural uses (including appurtenant structures) or related open space uses. In many cases, a property owner may be in the process of petitioning the local agency for cancellation of the contract because of the desire to develop the land for non-agricultural uses. Typically if a development application is submitted the cancellation is in process.

2. Where to Find Factual Data for Answering the Question

- The existence of a Williamson Act Contract can be found on a title report or by contacting the County Assessor's office in which the land is located.

- The California Department of Conservation has an excellent website which addresses this topic. The website is located at:

  www.conservation.ca.gov/dlrp/lca or enter "williamson act contract" in an Internet search engine.

- It is recommended that the California Environmental Resources Evaluation System website be consulted to see if there is any information related to this question. The website is located at:

ceres.ca.gov or enter "ceres evaluation" in an Internet search engine.

3. Example Answers

The following example answers the question comprehensively:

The project site is located within the R-3 Residential Zone and agricultural uses are not permitted in this zone. There is no Williamson Act contract that affects the project site according to the County Assessor's Office.

This response answers both parts of the question, first about existing zoning by identifying the zone and whether or not agriculture use is allowed and secondly by stating that the county assessor's office confirmed that there is not a Williamson Act Contract that applies to the project site.

The following example does not answer the question comprehensively:

There are no agricultural elements associated with the proposed project. The site is presently vacant with little or no vegetation.

Although this response states there are "no agricultural elements associated with the project" it does not specifically address the zoning question nor the presence or absence of a Williamson Act Contract.

4. Determining Significance

Following are some general factors to consider for determining significance:

- Are there any Thresholds of Significance that were formally adopted by the lead agency that are applicable to the project?

- Has the lead agency set a precedent in previously approved CEQA documents in responding to the question? If so, the Initial Study Checklist preparer should be aware of how other CEQA documents have responded to the question.

- Any project that would create land use compatibility conflicts with an existing agriculture use may have a significant impact.

- Any project that would conflict with a Williamson Act contract may have a significant impact.

II. AGRICULTURE and FORESTRY RESOURCES (cont.)

(c) Conflict with existing zoning for, or cause rezoning of, forest land (as defined in Public Resources Code section 12220(g)) or timberland (as defined in Public Resources Code section 4526)?

1. Determining the Scope of the Question

In order to determine the scope of the question, it is separated into the following parts:

Forest Land

Public Resources Code 12220(g) defines "Forest land" as follows:

"Forest Land is land that can support 10-percent native tree cover of any species, including hardwoods, under natural conditions, and that allows for management of one or more forest resources, including timber, aesthetics, fish and wildlife, biodiversity, water quality, recreation, and other public benefits."

Forest land zoning is applied to lands where the protection of forest land is the primary objective.

Many forest land zones allow non-forest land uses to be located in a forest land zone such as one - family dwellings, recreational uses (e.g. boating, equestrian facilities, parks, and playgrounds), and lodging facilities to name a few. These uses may conflict with the preservation of forest land by affecting the ecosystem the forest land depends upon.

The Initial Study Checklist preparer should be aware what potential conflicts a project could create on forest land and address them in the Initial Study Checklist.

Forest Land Zoning Conflicts or Rezoning

In addition, the question is asking if the project would cause rezoning of forest land. In the opinion of the author, the context of the question relates to an application for rezoning forest land to non-forest land use and not to impacts that would require the forest land to be rezoned because it is no longer viable.

When answering this question always use the general plan land use designation as the basis in answering this question because by law zoning must be consistent with the general plan.

Often times in areas of transition, the general plan land use map designation may show a non-forest land use but the existing zoning may still be forest land. If there is a conflict, note this in the Initial Study Checklist and address how it will be rectified. The point is that although the question uses the term "zoning" the general plan land use designation takes precedence.

Timberland

Public Resources Code 4525 defines timberland as follows:

"Timberland" *means land, (other than land owned by the federal government and land designated by the State Board of Forestry and Fire Protection as experimental forest land), which is available for, and capable of, growing a crop of trees of any commercial species used to produce lumber and other forest products, including Christmas trees. Commercial species shall be determined by the State Board of Forestry and Fire Protection on a forest district basis after consultation with the forest district technical advisory committees and others."*

Land that is zoned as timberland is usually done so under the Forest Taxation Reform Act. Such lands are specially zoned for timber production and compatible uses.

These lands are assessed based on their ability to grow trees. In exchange for this tax benefit, landowners have to be willing to dedicate their timberland to timber growing and compatible uses for a period of at least ten years. Unless terminated by the County with jurisdiction over the land or the landowner, these ten years renew each year, thus creating a rolling minimum or self-perpetuating ten-year commitment.

Lands zoned in this manner are identified as "Timberland Production Zone." Landowners still pay an annual property tax, but the assessed value of Timberland Production Zone land is valued for the cultivation of timber. This results in a lower tax assessment than customary "highest and best use" valuation.

Timberland Zoning Conflicts or Rezoning

The immediate rezoning of land identified as Timberland Production Zone requires the submittal of an application for a Timberland Conversion Permit and Timberland Conversion Plan. (ref. 14 CCR §1109, 14 CCR §§1100(j), and 1100(g) (2)). This process is administered by the Department of Forestry and Fire Protection.

Many timberland zones allow non-timberland uses to be located in a timberland zone such as one - family dwellings, recreational uses (e.g. boating, equestrian facilities, parks, and playgrounds), and lodging facilities to name a few. These uses may conflict with the preservation of timberland by affecting the ecosystem the timberland depends upon.

The Initial Study Checklist preparer should be aware what potential conflicts a project could create on timberland and address them in the Initial Study Checklist.

In addition, the question is asking if the project would cause rezoning of timberland. In the opinion of the author, the context of the question relates to an application for rezoning timberland to non-timberland use and not to impacts that would require the timberland to be rezoned because it is no longer viable.

When answering this question always use the general plan land use designation as the basis in answering this question because by law zoning must be consistent with the general plan.

Often times in areas of transition, the general plan land use map designation may show a non-timberland use but the existing zoning may still be timberland. If there is a conflict, note this in the Initial Study Checklist and address how it will be rectified. The point is that although the question uses the term "zoning" the general plan land use designation takes precedence.

2. Where to Find Factual Data for Answering the Question

- The general plan land use map and zoning map.

- The California Department of Forestry and Fire Protection has an excellent website which addresses this topic. The website is located at:

  www.fire.ca.gov/ and click on the "Resource Management" link or enter "california department of forestry" in an Internet search engine.

- It is recommended that the California Environmental Resources Evaluation System website be consulted to see if there is any information related to this question. The website is located at:

  ceres.ca.gov or enter "ceres evaluation" in an Internet search engine.

3. Example Answers

The following example answers the question comprehensively:

The project site is located within the R-3 Residential Zone and proposes residential development and is therefore not in conflict with forest or timberland zoning. The project does not propose a zone change that would convert existing forest or timberland zoning.

This response answers both parts of the question, first about a conflict with existing zoning and secondly by stating that no rezoning is proposed.

The following example does not answer the question comprehensively:

There are no forest or timberland elements associated with the proposed project. The site is presently vacant with little or no vegetation.

This response does not specifically address the zoning conflict part of the question or the rezoning part of the question.

4. Determining Significance

Following are some general factors to consider for determining significance:

- Are there any Thresholds of Significance that were formally adopted by the lead agency that are applicable to the project?

- Has the lead agency set a precedent in previously approved CEQA documents in responding to the question? If so, the Initial Study Checklist preparer should be aware of how other CEQA documents have responded to the question.

- Any project that converts or rezones forest land or timberland to other uses or would create land use compatibility conflicts with an existing forest land or timberland uses may have a significant impact.

- Changes in forest land or timberland may also affect Greenhouse Gas Emissions, Aesthetics, Biological Resources and Water Quality, among others.

  These resources should be discussed in the appropriate section of the Initial Study Checklist analysis. Depending on various factors, these impacts may be significant unless the Initial Study Checklist demonstrates otherwise.

II. AGRICULTURE and FORESTRY RESOURCES (cont.)

(d) Result in the loss of forest land or conversion of forest land to non-forest use?

1. Determining the Scope of the Question

The question is asking if the project will remove or convert forest land to the extent that such land will no longer be available for forest use in the future.

The key point in responding to this question is to recognize that the loss or conversion of forest land does not only mean that such land is being converted to urban uses, but that conversion also includes the use of the land for agricultural uses (for example vineyards or crop production). This is an important distinction that the Initial Study Checklist preparer needs to be aware of.

2. Where to Find Factual Data to Answer the Question

- Field inspection.

- The California Department of Forestry and Fire Protection has an excellent website which addresses this issue. The webpage is located at:

  www.fire.ca.gov/or enter "timberland conversions" or "california department of forestry" in an Internet search engine.

- It is recommended that the California Environmental Resources Evaluation System website be consulted to see if there is any information related to this question. The website is located at:

ceres.ca.gov or enter "ceres evaluation" in an Internet search engine.

3. Example Answers

The following example answers the question comprehensively:

The proposed improvements would occur within the existing Carson Park area which contains a campground and related facilities. There are no forest lands within this area so the loss of forest land or conversion of forest land to non-forest use would not occur.

This response clearly states that the project improvements are not located in an area that would impact forest land.

The following example does not answer the question comprehensively:

There are no forest land elements associated with the proposed project.

This response is too vague and does not explain the existing conditions of the site with respect to forest land.

4. Determining Significance

Following are some general factors to consider for determining significance:

- Are there any Thresholds of Significance that were formally adopted by the lead agency that are applicable to the project?

- Has the lead agency set a precedent in previously approved CEQA documents in responding to the question? If so, the Initial Study Checklist preparer should be aware of how other CEQA documents have responded to the question.

- Always consider both direct impacts (i.e. conversion or rezoning) and indirect impacts (i.e. impacts caused by projects in the vicinity or adjacent to forest land that may be detrimental the environment that supports such land). These types of changes may have a significant impact.

II. AGRICULTURE and FORESTRY RESOURCES (cont.)

(e) Involve other changes in the existing environment which, due to their location or nature, could result in conversion of Farmland to non-agricultural use or conversion of forest land to nonforest use?

1. Determining the Scope of the Question

"Other changes in the existing environment" as stated in this question vary but are typically associated with such factors as:

- ✓ Urbanization of land near forest or agriculture land;

- ✓ Division of adjacent land into smaller parcels which encourages the conversion to other non-compatible uses;

- ✓ Altering the habitat suitability of land and other ecosystems in close proximity to farmland or forest land; and

- ✓ Changes in the surrounding hydrology of an area which impacts farmland or forest land.

In summary, consider what impacts a proposed project may have on adjacent or nearby land used as farmland or forest land.

2. Where to Find Factual Data to Answer the Question

- • Field reconnaissance.

45

- The California Department of Forestry and Fire Protection has an excellent website about forest lands. The website can be located at:

  www.fire.ca.gov/. Click on the link "Forestry Assistance" or enter "california department of forestry" in an Internet search engine.

- The California Department of Conservation has an excellent website about farmland. The website can be located at:

  www.conservation.ca.gov/. Click on the link "Land Protection" or enter "california department of conservation" in an Internet search engine.

- It is recommended that the California Environmental Resources Evaluation System website be consulted to see if there is any information related to this question. The website is located at:

  ceres.ca.gov or enter "ceres evaluation" in an Internet search engine

3. Example Answers

The following example answers the question comprehensively:

The project site is not located in close proximity to forest land or farmland as shown on the maps prepared by the California Department of Conservation and based on a field reconnaissance.

46

The project would not involve the disruption or damage of the existing environment that would result in the loss of farmland to nonagricultural use or conversion of forest land to non-forest use because its location is not in the vicinity of farmland or forest land. Therefore, no impact is anticipated.

This response states that the location of the proposed site is not within the vicinity of forest or agriculture land and will therefore have no impact on these resources.

The following example does not answer the question comprehensively:

The project would not involve other changes in the existing environment, which, could result in the conversion of forest land or farmland.

This response does not give the reasons why this conclusion was reached.

4. Determining Significance

Following are some general factors to consider for determining significance:

- Are there any Thresholds of Significance that were formally adopted by the lead agency that are applicable to the project?

- Has the lead agency set a precedent in previously approved CEQA documents in responding to the question? If so, the Initial Study Checklist preparer should be aware of

how other CEQA documents have responded to the question.

- Always consider both direct impacts (i.e. conversion or rezoning) and indirect impacts (i.e. impacts caused by projects in the vicinity or adjacent to farmland land or forest land that may be detrimental the environment that supports such land). These types of changes may have a significant impact.

Chapter III

Air Quality

Introduction

Air Quality is one of the more technical environmental topics addressed in an Initial Study Checklist. Analyzing Air Quality impacts requires familiarity with the numerous air quality regulations and typically requires the use of computer models to estimate air pollution emissions. Therefore, for larger or more complex projects an air quality report is usually a prerequisite for completing this section of the Initial Study Checklist.

In order to determine the scope of the questions posed in this Chapter, it is useful to understand the regulatory framework for air quality.

Air pollutants are regulated at the federal, state, and local level. The U.S. Environmental Protection Agency regulates at the federal level. The California Air Resources Board regulates at the state level. The applicable Air Pollution Control District/Air Quality Management District (of which there are 35) regulates at the local level.

49

The U.S. Environmental Protection Agency:

At the federal level, the U.S. Environmental Protection Agency is charged with reducing emissions from federally controlled sources such as commercial aircraft, trains, marine vessels, and other sources. The Federal Clean Air Act requires the U.S. Environmental Protection Agency to set outdoor air quality standards for the nation. These are known as National Ambient Air Quality Standards (called "Federal Standards" in this Chapter).

The U.S. Environmental Protection Agency also oversees approval of all State Implementation Plans which are comprehensive plans that describe how an area will attain National Ambient Air Quality Standards.

The California Air Resources Board:

At the state level, the California Air Resources Board is responsible for reducing emissions from motor vehicle and consumer products. The Board has the overall responsibility for statewide air quality maintenance and air pollution prevention.

The Federal Clean Air Act also allows states to adopt additional or more stringent air quality standards if necessary. California has adopted a set of standards known as California Ambient Air Quality Standards (called "State Standards" in this Chapter).The State Standards differ from the Federal Standards in some instances.

According to the California Air Resources Board, California has set standards for certain pollutants, such as particulate matter and ozone, which are more protective of public health than the Federal Standards. California has also set standards for some pollutants that are not addressed by Federal Standards, such as Visibility Reducing Particles, Sulfates, Hydrogen Sulfide, and Vinyl Chloride.

In addition, The California Air Resources Board reviews and approves State Implementation Plan elements prepared by local air districts and submits them to the U.S. Environmental Protection Agency for approval and publication in the Federal Register.

Air Pollution Control District/Air Quality Management District:

California is divided into 35 districts. These districts are responsible for controlling emissions primarily from stationary sources (e.g. power plants, chemical plants, oil refineries, manufacturing facilities, and other industrial facilities).

The District's also set standards (often times referred to as "significance thresholds") for various air pollutant emissions that occur during the construction and/or operation of a project. Significance thresholds vary from District to District.

The Districts also maintain air quality plans that serve to implement the State Implementation Plan.

Author's Note*: Questions III (a), (b), and (c) by their nature overlap to some degree. In many CEQA documents these questions are answered together or the answers are cross-referenced with each other. For purposes of clarity, the author has addressed these questions individually so there will be some repetition of the information.*

III. AIR QUALITY - Where available, the significance criteria established by the applicable air quality management or air pollution control district may be relied upon to make the following determinations.

Would the project:

(a) Conflict with or obstruct implementation of the applicable air quality plan.

1. Determining the Scope of the Question

In order to determine the scope of this question, it is separated into the following parts:

Applicable Air Quality Plan

An air quality plan is a plan prepared by an Air Pollution Control District/Air Quality Management District for a geographic region designated as a "Non-attainment" area for the purpose of bringing the area into compliance with the requirements of the Federal and /or State Ambient Air Quality Standards.

Non-attainment areas do not meet either Federal or State Ambient Air Quality Standards for what are called "criteria pollutants." Following is a list of all the criteria pollutants in California:

Ozone (O3)
Respirable Particulate Matter (PM10)
Fine Particulate Matter (PM2.5)
Carbon Monoxide (CO)
Nitrogen Dioxide (NO2)
Sulfur Dioxide (SO2)
Lead
Sulfates*
Hydrogen Sulfide*
Visibility Reducing Particles*
Vinyl Chloride*

Not a Federal Criteria Pollutant.

Authors Note: *The California Air Resources Board has identified Lead and Vinyl Chloride as "toxic air contaminants" with no threshold level of exposure for adverse health effects determined. These actions allow for the implementation of control measures at levels below the ambient concentrations specified for these pollutants.*

In summary, the "applicable air quality plan" in the context of the question is a plan prepared by an Air Pollution Control District/Air Quality Management District for an identified Non-attainment area for both Federal and State Ambient Air Quality Standards.

The Initial Study Checklist preparer is advised to contact the applicable Air Pollution Control District/Air Quality Management District to determine what the applicable air quality plan is for the project area being analyzed.

<u>Conflict with or Obstruct the Air Quality Plan</u>

In practice, there are two commonly used criteria to consider when answering this question.

- ✓ A project is consistent with an air quality plan if it will not result in an increase in the frequency or severity of existing air quality violations or cause or contribute to new violations with respect to criteria pollutants or delay timely attainment of air quality standards or the interim emission reductions specified in an air quality plan.

- ✓ A project is consistent with an air quality plan if it is compliance with the air pollution control measures identified in the air quality plan.

In order to answer the question, an analysis of air pollution emissions is necessary. Depending on the characteristics of a project and which Air Pollution Control District/Air Quality Management District the project is located in, the methodology used for analysis will vary. Often times this requires the preparation of an air quality report.

The Urban Emissions Model (URBEMIS) is a modeling tool used to estimate air quality impacts from land use projects. Many Air Quality Control Districts/Air Quality Management Districts recommend using URBEMIS. URBEMIS is a user friendly and can be used by the Initial Study Checklist preparer.

Update: *Subsequent to the publication of this book in July 2010, ENVIRON International Corporation* announced that starting in February 2011 ,that the new *California Emissions Estimator Model*(CalEEMod) *Software would be available for use free of charge to provide a uniform platform for conducting an air quality analysis by government agencies, land use planners, and environmental professionals. CalEEMod was developed by Environ in collaboration with the South Coast Air Quality Management District and other California Air Quality Districts and can be used to calculate the criteria pollutant and greenhouse gas emissions associated with land-use development projects throughout California.*

The model quantifies direct emissions from construction and operation (including vehicle use), as well as indirect emissions, such as GHG emissions from energy production, solid waste handling, vegetation planting and/or removal, and water conveyance.

Information about the CalEEMod Software is available from the following website:

www.caleemod.com/

TIP. If an Air Quality Report is required, ask that the report be formatted to answer all of the Air Quality questions posed in Appendix G of the CEQA Guidelines. This will make completing the Initial Study

How to conduct an air quality analysis is beyond the scope of this book. Many District's have guidance documents on how to prepare an air quality analysis that meets CEQA requirements. These documents are often times available on each District's website or can be obtained in hard copy format from the District.

2. Where to Find the Factual Data to Answer the Question

- The best source of information is the Air Quality Control District/Air Quality Management District in which the project is located in. A list of Districts can be found at:

  www.arb.ca.gov/capcoa/roster.htm or enter "california local air district directory" in an Internet search engine.

- The Urban Emissions Model" (URBEMIS) is a modeling tool used to estimate air quality impacts from land use projects. Many Air Quality Control Districts/Air Quality Management Districts recommend using URBEMIS. The most recently updated version of the model (URBEMIS, Version 9.2.4), can be downloaded from the following sites:

  www.aqmd.gov/ceqa/urbemis.html and **www.urbemis.com** or enter "urbemis 2007" in an Internet search engine.

- ICF Jones and Stokes (now ICF International) has prepared an excellent guide called *Software User's Guide: URBEMIS 2007 for Windows* that can help in using URBEMIS. The guide can be located at:

**www.urbemis.com/support/manual.ht
ml** or enter "urbemis users manual" in an
Internet search engine.

- The *California Emissions Estimator Model*
  (CalEEMod) was developed by Environ in
  collaboration with the South Coast Air
  Quality Management District and other
  California Air Quality Districts and can be
  used to calculate the criteria pollutant and
  greenhouse gas emissions associated with
  land-use development projects throughout
  California.

  The model quantifies direct emissions from
  construction and operation (including vehicle
  use), as well as indirect emissions, such as
  GHG emissions from energy production, solid
  waste handling, vegetation planting and/or
  removal, and water conveyance.

  Information about the CalEEMod Software is
  available from the following website:

  www.caleemod.com/

- It is recommended that the California
  Environmental Resources Evaluation System
  website be consulted to see if there is any
  information related to this question. The
  website is located at:

  ceres.ca.gov or enter "ceres evaluation" in
  an Internet search engine.

3. Example Answers

The following example answers the question comprehensively:

The project is located in a portion of the Air Quality Management District ("District") which has been identified by the California Air Resources Board as being in Nonattainment for Ozone, Respirable Particulate Matter (PM10), and Fine Suspended Particulate Matter (PM2.5).

The applicable air quality plan is the 2009 Air Quality Improvement Plan ("Plan"). The project was evaluated for consistency with the Plan based on the following criteria:

1. *The first criteria is if the project's air pollutant emissions with respect to the Federal and State Ambient Air Quality Standards will not result in an increase in the frequency or severity of existing air quality violations, cause or contribute to new violations, delay their timely attainment, or interfere with the interim emission reductions specified in the Plan.*

   Based on the air quality report prepared for the project which used the Urban Emissions Model, the air pollution emissions do not exceed the Federal or State Ambient Air Quality Standards. Therefore, the project meets the first criteria for compliance with the Plan.

2. *The second criteria is compliance with the control measures in the Plan. The Plan contains a number of land use and transportation control measures that are intended to reduce air pollution emissions. The project will comply with*

the control measures identified in the Plan in addition to all of the District's applicable rules and regulations. Therefore, the project complies with the second criteria.

This response identifies the applicable air quality plan and states that based on the air quality report prepared for the project, both the first and second criteria for compliance will be met.

The following example does not answer comprehensively:

In general, the project area is already exposed to emissions that are in excess of State and Federal Air Quality Standards for a majority of the year. Standard construction conditions have been included to control fugitive dust and to ensure that dust emissions are kept to a minimum during the construction period.

This response does not identify the applicable air quality plan and it does not address whether or not the project is in compliance with the plan based on the two criteria described above. In addition, it only focuses on dust and not the other pollutants which are part of the Federal and State Ambient Air Quality Standards.

4. Determining Significance

Following are some general factors to consider for determining significance:

- Are there any Thresholds of Significance that were formally adopted by the lead agency that are applicable to the project?

- Has the lead agency set a precedent in previously approved CEQA documents in responding to the question? If so, the Initial Study Checklist preparer should be aware of how other CEQA documents have responded to the question.

- A project is consistent with an air quality plan if the project will not result in an increase in the frequency or severity of existing air quality violations or cause or contribute to new violations with respect to criteria pollutants or delay timely attainment of air quality standards or the interim emission reductions specified in the air quality plan. If a project does not satisfy these criteria, then impacts may be significant.

- A project is consistent with an air quality plan if it is compliance with the air pollution control measures identified in the plan. If a project is not consistent with the air pollution control measures, then impacts may be significant.

III. AIR QUALITY (Cont.)

(b) Violate any air quality standard or contribute substantially to an existing or projected air quality violation?

1. Determining the Scope of the Question

In order to determine the scope of the question, it is separated into the following parts:

Violate Air Quality Standards

According to the California Air Resources Board, an air quality standard is *"The prescribed level of a pollutant in the outside air that should not be exceeded during a specific time period to protect public health. The standards are established by both federal and state governments."*

In the context of this question, air quality standards typically means the Federal and State Ambient Air Quality Standards and the standards established by the applicable Air Quality Pollution Control District/Air Quality Management District.

Federal and State Standards

The Federal and/or State Ambient Air Quality Standards are health and welfare based standards for outdoor air which identify the maximum acceptable average concentrations of air pollutants during a specified period of time. (See Table 1 on Pages 65-66 for an example).

Air Quality Management District/Air Pollution District Standards

In addition to Federal and State Ambient Air Quality Standards, Air Pollution Control Districts/Air Quality Management Districts have air quality standards that apply to project's within their jurisdiction.

Depending on the District, these standards may be identified as "air quality significance thresholds" or they may be contained in various rules that in effect serve as thresholds.

The Initial Study Checklist preparer should verify what the applicable significance thresholds are for the District in which the project is located. These standards typically apply to the construction and operation of a project.

A project would be in violation of an air quality standard if the air pollution emissions generated by the project exceed either the Federal and/or State Ambient Air Quality Standards or the standards/thresholds established by the applicable Air Pollution Control District/Air Quality Management District.

Contributing Substantially to an Existing or Projected Air Quality Violation

This part of the question relates directly to the project's characteristics and the air quality environment in the vicinity or area in which the project is located. In order to answer the question an analysis of air pollution emissions is necessary. Depending on the characteristics of a project and which Air Pollution Control District/Air Quality Management District the project is located in, the methodology used for analysis will vary. Often times this requires the preparation of an air quality report.

The Urban Emissions Model (URBEMIS) is a modeling tool used to estimate air quality impacts from land use projects. Many Air Quality Control District/Air Quality Management District's recommend using URBEMIS. URBEMIS is a user friendly and can be used by the Initial Study Checklist preparer.

Update: *Subsequent to the publication of this book in July 2010, ENVIRON International Corporation announced that starting in February 2011 ,that the new* California Emissions Estimator Model*(CalEEMod) Software would be available for use free of charge to provide a uniform platform for conducting an air quality analysis by government agencies, land use planners, and environmental professionals. CalEEMod was developed by Environ in collaboration with the South Coast Air Quality Management District and other California Air Quality Districts and can be used to calculate the criteria pollutant and greenhouse gas emissions associated with land-use development projects throughout California.*

The model quantifies direct emissions from construction and operation (including vehicle use), as well as indirect emissions, such as GHG emissions from energy production, solid waste handling, vegetation planting and/or removal, and water conveyance.

Information about the CalEEMod Software is available from the following website:

www.caleemod.com/

How to conduct an air quality analysis is beyond the scope of this book. Many District's have guidance documents on how to prepare an air quality analysis that meets CEQA requirements. These documents are often times available on each District's website or can be obtained in hard copy format from the District.

2. Where to Find the Factual Data to Answer the Question

- Information on Federal and State Ambient Air Quality Standards can be found on the California Air Resources Board webpage located at:

  www.arb.ca.gov/research/aaqs/aaqs.htm or enter "california ambient air quality standards (aaqs)" in an Internet search engine.

- The Air Quality Control District or the Air Quality Management District in which the project site is located. A list of Districts can be found at:

  www.arb.ca.gov/capcoa/roster.htm or enter "california local air district directory" in an Internet search engine.

- The Urban Emissions Model" (URBEMIS) is a modeling tool used to estimate air quality impacts from land use projects. Many Air Quality Control District/Air Quality Management District's recommend using URBEMIS. The most recently updated version of the model (URBEMIS, Version

9.2.4), can be downloaded from the following sites:

www.aqmd.gov/ceqa/urbemis.html and **www.urbemis.com** or enter "urbemis 2007" in an Internet search engine.

- ICF Jones and Stokes (now ICF International) has prepared an excellent guide called *Software User's Guide: URBEMIS 2007 for Windows* that can help in using URBEMIS. The guide can be located at:

www.urbemis.com/support/manual.html or enter "urbemis users manual" in an Internet search engine.

- The *California Emissions Estimator Model* (CalEEMod) was developed by Environ in collaboration with the South Coast Air Quality Management District and other California Air Quality Districts and can be used to calculate the criteria pollutant and greenhouse gas emissions associated with land-use development projects throughout California.

The model quantifies direct emissions from construction and operation (including vehicle use), as well as indirect emissions, such as GHG emissions from energy production, solid waste handling, vegetation planting and/or removal, and water conveyance.

Information about the CalEEMod Software is available from the following website:

www.caleemod.com/

- It is recommended that the California Environmental Resources Evaluation System website be consulted to see if there is any information related to this question. The website is located at:

   ceres.ca.gov or enter "ceres evaluation" in an Internet search engine.

3. Example Answers

The following example answers the question comprehensively:

The project is a 65 unit condominium complex on a 4.6 acre site.

Federal and State Standards

Table 1 below identifies the Federal and State Standards for Ambient Air Quality.

Table 1: Ambient Air Quality Standards

Pollutant	Averaging Time	State Standard	Federal Standard
Ozone (O3)	1-hour	0.09 ppm	None
	8-hour	0.070 ppm	0.07 ppm
Carbon Monoxide (CO)	1-hour	20 ppm	35 ppm
	8-hour	9.0 ppm	9 ppm
Nitrogen	1-hour	0.18 ppm	None

Pollutant	Averaging Time	State Standard	Federal Standard
Dioxide (NO$_2$)	Annual Arithmetic Mean	0.030 ppm	0.053 ppm
Sulfur Dioxide (SO$_2$)	1-hour	0.25 ppm	None
	24-hour	0.04 ppm	0.14 ppm
	Annual Arithmetic Mean	None	0.030 ppm
Respirable Particulate Matter (PM$_{10}$)	24-hour	50 µg/m^3	150 µg/m^3
	Annual Arithmetic Mean	20 µg/m^3	None
Fine Particulate Matter (PM$_{2.5}$)	24-hour	None	35 µg/m^3
	Annual Arithmetic Mean	12 µg/m^3	15.0 µg/m^3
Sulfates	24-hour	25 µg/m^3	None
Lead	30-day	1.5 µg/m^3	None
	Quarter	None	1.5 µg/m^3
Visibility Reducing Particles	8 hour	Extinction coefficient of 0.23 per kilometer- visibility of ten miles or more (0.07-30 miles for	None

Pollutant	Averaging Time	State Standard	Federal Standard
		Lake Tahoe,	
Sulfates	*24 hour*	*25 µg/m³*	*None*
Hydrogen Sulfide	*1 hour*	*0.03 ppm*	*None*
Vinyl Chloride	*24 hour*	*0.01 ppm*	*None*

In order to gauge the significance of the air quality impacts generated by the project, those impacts, together with existing background air quality levels, must be compared to the applicable Federal and State Ambient Air Quality Standards.

The project would generate air pollutants from construction activities (e.g., fugitive dust and equipment exhaust) and in the long-term from project operation and area sources (e.g., vehicle emissions, landscape activities, etc.).

The pollutants that would be generated by the project include Particular Matter (both PM10 and PM 2.5), Carbon Monoxide (CO), and precursors of ozone (oxides of nitrogen [NOx] and Volatile Organic Compounds [VOC]), all of which are Non-Attainment criteria pollutants in the Air Pollution Control District.

Based on the air quality analysis prepared for the project, air pollution emissions are projected to be _below both the Federal and State Ambient Air Quality Standards._

Air Pollution Control District

Table 2 below identifies the Air Pollution Control District's Significance Thresholds.

Table 2. Air Quality Significance Thresholds

Mass Daily Thresholds/Lbs. Per Day		
Pollutant	**Construction**	**Operation**
Oxides of Nitrogen (NOx)	100	65
Volatile Organic Compounds (VOC)	85	65
Respirable Particulate Matter (PM10)	170	170
Fine Particulate Matter (PM2.5)	60	60
Sulfur Dioxide (SO2)	170	170
Carbon Monoxide (CO)	575	575
Lead	2	2

Construction Impacts

Impacts from short-term construction are a result of site grading and construction of the buildings, the parking areas, and related improvements. Construction related emissions were modeled using the California Air Resources Board approved URBEMIS 2007 Version 9.2.4 (URBEMIS) computer program as recommended by the District.

Table 3 below shows the construction related air pollution emissions based on the air quality analysis prepared for the project.

Table 3. Construction Emissions

Maximum Daily Emissions	Emissions (pounds per day)					
	VOC	**NOx**	**CO**	**SO2**	**PM10**	**PM 2.5**
Project	7.62	84.97	37.01	0.06	14.01	5.72
Threshold	85	100	575	170	170	60
Exceeds Threshold?	NO	NO	NO	NO	NO	NO
Source: Project Air Quality Report						

As shown in Table 3, air pollution emissions generated during all phases of construction are projected to be less than the District's Construction Emission Thresholds. No mitigation is required.

<u>Long-Term Operations Impacts</u>

Impacts from long-term operations are primarily a result of additional vehicle trips generated by the project and to some extent the use of natural gas for space and water heating devices and equipment used for maintenance of the project.

Table 4 below shows the operational related air pollution emissions based on the air quality analysis prepared for the project.

Table 4. Operational Emissions

Maximum Daily Emissions	Emissions (pounds per day)					
	VOC	NOx	CO	SO2	PM10	PM 2.5
Summer	10.81	7.70	65.67	0.05	8.45	1.65
Winter	11.12	9.09	62.18	0.04	8.45	1.65
Threshold	65	65	575	170	170	60
Exceeds Threshold?	NO	NO	NO	NO	NO	NO
Source: Project Air Quality Report						

As shown in Table 4, the project will not exceed the District's Operational Emission Thresholds. No mitigation is required.

In summary, based on the above analysis, project air pollution emissions are less than significant because they do not exceed Federal or State Ambient Air Quality Standards or Emission Thresholds of the District and thus would not violate or contribute substantially to an existing or projected air quality violation.

The response takes into account both parts of the question by:

(1) Determining that the project does not violate Federal and State Ambient Air Quality Standards and the applicable Air Quality Management District air pollution standards/thresholds, and

(2) Determining that the project will not violate or contribute substantially to an existing or projected air quality violation.

The following example does not answer the question comprehensively:

The project is a 35 unit apartment complex. Greater air quality impacts could be seen from increased vehicular trips and increased heating uses. Implementation of the mitigation measures adopted in the City's General Plan goals and policies will reduce the air emission impacts.

The response does not identify nor evaluate air pollutant emissions against the State and Federal Ambient Air Quality Standard or the air quality standards or significance thresholds of the applicable Air Quality Management District/Air Pollution Control District.

It also assumes that mitigation measures contained in a general plan are adequate to reduce impacts to a less than significant level. General plan level mitigation measures are typically not project specific so this assumption may be incorrect.

Finally, there is no conclusion made about whether or not a violation or substantial contribution is made to an existing or projected air quality violation.

4. Determining Significance

Following are some general factors to consider for determining significance:

- Are there any Thresholds of Significance that were formally adopted by the lead agency that are applicable to the project?

- Has the lead agency set a precedent in previously approved CEQA documents in responding to the question? If so, the Initial Study Checklist preparer should be aware of

how other CEQA documents have responded to the question.

- A project is considered to have a significant impact if its air pollution emissions are forecast to exceed Federal and State Ambient Air Quality Standards and/or the standards or significance thresholds established by the applicable Air Quality Control District/Air Quality Management District in which the project site is located.

III. AIR QUALITY (Cont.)

(c) Result in a cumulatively considerable net increase of any criteria pollutant for which the project region is non-attainment under an applicable federal or state ambient air quality standard (including releasing emissions which exceed quantitative thresholds for ozone precursors)?

1. Determining the Scope of the Question

In order to determine the scope of the question, it is separated into the following parts:

Criteria Pollutant for Which the Project Region is Non-Attainment Under an Applicable Federal or State Ambient Air Quality Standard

The U.S. Environmental Protection Agency and the California Air Resources Board have identified Federal and/or State Ambient Air Quality Standards for Criteria Pollutants.

These Criteria Pollutants are:

> Ozone (O3)
> Respirable Particulate Matter (PM10)
> Fine Particulate Matter (PM2.5)
> Carbon Monoxide (CO)
> Nitrogen Dioxide (NO2)
> Sulfur Dioxide (SO2)
> Lead
> Sulfates*
> Hydrogen Sulfide*
> Visibility Reducing Particles*
> Vinyl Chloride*

Not a Federal Criteria Pollutant.

Author's Note: *The California Air Resources Board has identified Lead and Vinyl Chloride as "toxic air contaminants" with no threshold level of exposure for adverse health effects determined. These actions allow for the implementation of control measures at levels below the ambient concentrations specified for these pollutants.*

The Federal and/or State Ambient Air Quality Standards are health and welfare-based standards for outdoor air which identify the maximum acceptable average concentrations of air pollutants during a specified period of time according to the California Air Resources Board. (See Table 1 on Pages 65-66 for an example).

The California Air Resources Board defines a Non-Attainment Area as *"A geographic area identified by the U.S. Environmental Protection Agency and/or California Air Resources Board as not meeting either National Ambient Air Quality Standards or California Ambient Air Quality Standards for a given pollutant."* (Ref. *Glossary of Air Pollution Terms*, California Air Resources Board Website).

In summary, this question deals with criteria pollutants in an area that is determined to be in Non-Attainment because it exceeds the Federal and State Ambient Air Quality Standards

Including Releasing Emissions Which Exceed Quantitative Thresholds for Ozone Precursors

Ozone forms when two key pollutants, Nitrogen Oxides (NO_2) and Volatile Organic Compounds react in the atmosphere in the presence of sunlight. These pollutants are precursors to ozone formation, meaning they must be present in the air for ozone to form. Therefore, they are called "ozone precursors."

In the context of this question ozone precursors are to be analyzed as a criteria pollutant as described in the section above because they may form into Ozone which is a criteria pollutant.

Result in a Cumulatively Considerable Net Increase

If an area is in Non-Attainment for a criteria pollutant, then the background concentration of that pollutant has historically been over the Federal and/or State Ambient Air Quality Standard. With respect to air quality, no individual project would by itself result in Non-Attainment of the Federal or State Ambient Air Quality Standard.

However, a project's air pollution emissions although individually limited, may be cumulatively considerable when taken in combination with past, present, and future development projects. [Ref. *CEQA Guidelines* Section 15355(b)].

The determination of whether or not a project's air pollutant emissions would be considered cumulatively considerable may require an analysis using air quality computer modeling. The Initial Study Checklist preparer is encouraged to consult with the webpage resources listed below to find information about cumulatively considerable impacts for criteria pollutants.

2. Where to Find the Factual Data to Answer the Question

- The Air Quality Control District or the Air Quality Management District in which the project site is located. A list of District's can be found at:

  www.arb.ca.gov/capcoa/roster.htm or enter "california local air district directory" in an Internet search engine.

- The Urban Emissions Model" (URBEMIS) is a modeling tool used to estimate air quality impacts from land use projects. Many Air Quality Control District/Air Quality Management District's recommend using URBEMIS. The most recently updated version of the model (URBEMIS, Version 9.2.4), can be downloaded from the following sites:

  www.aqmd.gov/ceqa/urbemis.html and **www.urbemis.com** or enter "urbemis 2007" in an Internet search engine.

- ICF Jones and Stokes (now ICF International) has prepared an excellent guide called *Software User's Guide: URBEMIS 2007 for Windows* that can help in using URBEMIS. The guide can be located at:

  www.urbemis.com/support/manual.ht ml or enter "urbemis users manual" in an Internet search engine.

- The *California Emissions Estimator Model* (CalEEMod) was developed by Environ in collaboration with the South Coast Air Quality Management District and other California Air Quality Districts and can be used to calculate the criteria pollutant and greenhouse gas emissions associated with land-use development projects throughout California.

  The model quantifies direct emissions from construction and operation (including vehicle use), as well as indirect emissions, such as GHG emissions from energy production, solid waste handling, vegetation planting and/or removal, and water conveyance.

  Information about the CalEEMod Software is available from the following website:

  www.caleemod.com/

- The *Air Quality and Land Use Handbook: A Community Health Perspective* adopted by the California Air Resources Board, has some tools to assist in conducting assessments of cumulative emissions. The handbook's webpage is located at:

  www.arb.ca.gov/ch/landuse.htm   or enter "air quality land use handbook" in an Internet search engine.

- It is recommended that the California Environmental Resources Evaluation System website be consulted to see if there is any

information related to this question. The website is located at:

ceres.ca.gov or enter "ceres evaluation" in an Internet search engine.

3. Example Answers

The following example answers the question comprehensively:

The air emission pollutants that would be generated by the project include Particular Matter (both PM10 and PM 2.5), Carbon Monoxide (CO), and precursors of ozone (oxides of nitrogen [NOx] and Volatile Organic Compounds [VOC]), all of which are considered to be Non-Attainment criteria pollutants in the air basin.

Based on the air quality report prepared for the project, air emission impacts are not projected to exceed Federal or State Ambient Air Quality Standards and thus would not result in a cumulatively considerable net increase of any criteria pollutant for which the region is Non-Attainment under an applicable Federal or State Ambient Air Quality Standard (including releasing emissions which exceed quantitative thresholds for ozone).

The response describes the reason why the project would not contribute to a cumulatively considerable net increase in any criteria pollutants for which the project region is in Non-Attainment.

The following example does not answer the question comprehensively:

The project is a convenience market and gas station which is consistent with the City's existing General Plan and Zoning designations. The projected air pollutant emissions of criteria pollutants as a result of the project are expected to be below emissions thresholds established for the region. Likewise, no net increase in criteria pollutants for future cumulative (nonattainment status) conditions is anticipated. Therefore, cumulative impacts are less than significant. No mitigation is required.

This response provides no factual data to support the conclusion (i.e. air quality report, use of a screening table, or computer model). It assumes that consistency with the general plan and zoning designations will result in air emissions that are not cumulatively considerable. Although consistency with a general plan and zoning may be a criterion that is used in an analysis of cumulative impacts, it should not be the sole criteria.

4. Determining Significance

Following are some general factors to consider for determining significance:

- Are there any Thresholds of Significance that were formally adopted by the lead agency that are applicable to the project?

- Has the lead agency set a precedent in previously approved CEQA documents in responding to the question? If so, the Initial Study Checklist preparer should be aware of how other CEQA documents have responded to the question.

- An impact may be significant if a project's air pollution emissions resulted in a net increase of any criteria pollutant for which the project region is Non-Attainment under an applicable National or State Ambient Air Quality Standard (including releasing emissions which exceed quantitative thresholds for ozone precursors).

- Any new development that results in an increase in air pollutant emissions above those assumed in an air quality plan would contribute to cumulative air quality impacts and may be significant.

III. AIR QUALITY (Cont.)

(d) Expose sensitive receptors to substantial pollutant concentrations?

1. Determining the Scope of the Question

In order to determine the scope of the question, it is separated into the following parts:

Sensitive Receptors

The California Air Pollution Control Officers Association has an excellent definition of sensitive receptors which is contained in their publication titled *Health Risk Assessments for Proposed Land Use Projects.* The definition is as follows:

"Receptors include sensitive receptors and worker receptors. Sensitive receptors refer to those segments of the population most susceptible to poor air quality (i.e., children, the elderly, and those with pre-existing serious health problems affected by air quality). Land uses where sensitive individuals are most likely to spend time include schools and schoolyards, parks and playgrounds, daycare centers, nursing homes, hospitals, and residential communities (these sensitive land uses may also be referred to as sensitive receptors). Worker receptors refer to employees and locations where people work."

Substantial Pollution Concentrations

In the context of the question, a substantial pollution concentration would be one that exceeded established air pollution thresholds and would consequently have an adverse impact on sensitive receptors. Various methodologies are used to determine what constitutes a "substantial pollution concentration" depending on the Air Pollution Control District/Air Quality Management District in which the project is located in.

Although the methodology may vary, each of them have the common goal of evaluating high concentrations of Carbon Monoxide, Fine Particulate Matter or Toxic Air Contaminants that may impact sensitive receptors.

2. Where to Find the Factual Data to Answer the Question

- Consult the staff of the applicable Air Quality Control District or the Air Quality Management District or their website in which the project site is located to find out what methodology is used for determining if sensitive receptors will be significantly impacted by a project. A list of Districts can be found at:

  www.arb.ca.gov/capcoa/roster.htm or enter "california local air district directory" in an Internet search engine.

- The California Air Resources Board published the *Air Quality and Land Use Handbook: A Community Health Perspective* in 2005. The Handbook provides information and guidance on siting sensitive receptors in relation to sources of toxic air contaminates.

The Handbook is available online at
www.arb.ca.gov/ch/landuse.htm or
enter "california air quality landuse
handbook" in an Internet search engine.

- *The Community Health Air Pollution
  Information System* is a user friendly,
  Internet-based system for displaying
  information on emissions from sources of air
  pollution in an easy to use mapping format.

  The system contains information on air
  pollution emissions from selected large
  facilities and small businesses that emit
  criteria and toxic air pollutants. The
  webpage is located at:

  **www.arb.ca.gov/ch/chapis1/chapis1.ht
  m** or enter "chapis emission maps" in an
  Internet search engine.

- *The Hot Spots Analysis and Reporting
  Program* is a software database package that
  evaluates emissions from one or more
  facilities to determine the overall health risk
  posed by the facility(-ies) on the surrounding
  community.

  Proper use of software package ensures that
  the risk assessment meets the latest risk
  assessment guidelines published by the
  State Office of Environmental Health Hazard
  Assessment. *The Hot Spots Analysis and
  Reporting Program* is designed with air
  quality professionals in mind and is available
  from the Air Resources Board. The webpage
  is located at:

www.arb.ca.gov/toxics/harp/harp.htm
or enter "arb harp" in an Internet
search engine.

- The California Air Pollution Control Officers
Association has an excellent publication titled
*Health Risk Assessments for Proposed Land
Use Projects* which deals with this issue. The
document can be found at:

**www.capcoa.org/wpcontent/uploads/d
ownloads/2010/05CAPCOA_HRA_LU_G
uidelines_8-6-09.pdf** or enter "capcoa" in
an Internet search engine and click on the
link to the publication.

- The California Air Pollution Control Officers
Association has general information on the
effects of air pollution on human health. The
webpage is located at:

www.capcoa.org/health-effects/

However, as useful as the above resources may be,
it is suggested that an air quality report prepared
by a qualified individual or firm be prepared for
large or complex projects if sensitive receptors are
located in the vicinity of a project or if a project is
proposed to be located in close proximity to a
facility that would generate air pollution emissions
that could affect sensitive receptors.

3. Example Answers

***The following example answers the question
comprehensively:***

Example 1

The project is a 54 unit apartment complex. The following table summarizes the land uses in the vicinity of the project that could potentially generate air pollution emissions that could adversely impact sensitive receptors.

Source Category	Distance from Project Site	Recommended Separation Distance
Freeways and High Traffic Roads	1,300 feet	500 feet
Distribution Center	5,500 feet	1,000 feet
Gasoline Dispensing Facility	1,200 feet	300 feet

As shown on the table above, the project is not located within the recommend separation distances for siting new sensitive land uses based on the California Air Resources Board publication titled <u>Air Quality and Land Use Handbook: A Community Health Perspective, 2005</u>. Therefore, the project is not anticipated to be exposed to air pollution emissions that would adversely impact sensitive receptors.

The response describes the land uses that could potentially cause adverse impacts to sensitive receptors and indicated that because of the separation distances from these land uses the project will not be significantly impacted.

Author's Note*: Although this methodology is acceptable in some cases for evaluating impacts, it is* not as comprehensive as a methodology that considers factors other than distance, such as construction impacts (e.g. number and type of construction equipment used, the hours of operation, and the distance from equipment to the nearest off-site receptors).This is of particular concern if a project is large and constructed in phases that overlap. It is suggested that the Initial Study Checklist preparer use a methodology that is recommended by the applicable Air Quality Pollution Control District/Air Quality Management District if available.

Example 2

The Project is a 47 unit condominium complex on 4.62 acres located in the South Coast Air Quality Management District. To the north, south, and west of the project site is multiple-family housing. These uses are considered sensitive receptors. In addition, the project itself is considered a sensitive receptor because it is a residential use.

Construction Localized Significance Threshold Analysis

The South Coast Air Quality Management District's Localized Significance Threshold document entitled *Final Methodology to Calculate PM $_{2.5}$ and PM $_{2.5}$ Significance Thresholds* includes lookup tables that can be used for projects less than 5 acres in size to determine the maximum allowable daily emissions that would satisfy the localized significance criteria. The allowable emission rate depends on the (1) Source Receptor Area in which the project is located, (2), the size of the project site, and (3) the distance between the project site and the nearest sensitive receptor (e.g. residences, schools, hospitals).

For purposes of this analysis the following parameters were used:

- _Source Receptor Area: 33 (Southwest San Bernardino Valley)._

- _Site Size: 4.62 acres._

- _Nearest Sensitive Receptors: Residential uses less than 25 meters to the north, west, and south of the site._

Based on the analysis, the project's construction emissions are not projected to exceed the Localized Significance Threshold Construction Emission Thresholds as shown in Table 1 below. Therefore, sensitive receptors will not be adversely impacted.

Table 1. Localized Significance Thresholds Emissions

Maximum Daily Emissions	Pollutant Emissions (pounds per day)			
	PM10	**PM 2.5**	**NO2**	**CO**
Project	9.89	2.07	28.0	13.56
Localized Significance Threshold	14.73	8.49	450	1755
Exceeds Threshold?	NO	NO	NO	NO

Carbon Monoxide Analysis (CO Hotspot)

In addition to the Localized Significance Threshold analysis conducted above, a CO Hotspot Analysis was conducted for the project and is included in the air quality report prepared for the project.

Carbon Monoxide is the most notable source of emissions concentration at intersections because of *motor vehicle idling. The CO Hotspot Analysis evaluated nearby intersections where CO Hot Spots have the potential to occur. The analysis concluded that no intersection would exceed the Federal or State 1-hour and 8-hour standards based on estimated future conditions. Therefore, no significant CO Hotspot impacts would occur to sensitive receptors in the vicinity of the project.*

The response describes the project site and it surroundings to determine if any sensitive receptors will be impacted. It then identifies potential impacts and discusses why those impacts will be less than significant based on a methodology recommended by the applicable Air Quality Management District (in this case the South Coast Air Quality Management District).

Author's Note: *This example is based on a methodology recommended by the South Coast Air Quality Management District. It is intended for illustrative purposes only and it is not implied that the South Coast Air Quality Management District has approved its technical accuracy. In addition, the Initial Study Checklist preparer should use the methodology recommended by the applicable Air Pollution Control District/Air Quality Management District in which the project is located.*

The following example does not answer the question comprehensively:

The project will not result in concentrations of carbon monoxide which exceed the Air Quality Management District thresholds. Therefore, sensitive receptors will not be subject to substantial pollutant concentrations as a result of the project. No mitigation is required.

This response only focuses on carbon monoxide emissions. It does not discuss other types of air pollution emissions that may affect sensitive receptors such as Particulate Matter (PM_{10} and $PM_{2.5}$).

4. Determining Significance

Following are some general factors to consider for determining significance:

- Are there any Thresholds of Significance that were formally adopted by the lead agency that are applicable to the project?

- Has the lead agency set a precedent in previously approved CEQA documents in responding to the question? If so, the Initial Study Checklist preparer should be aware of how other CEQA documents have responded to the question.

- An impact may be significant if a project's emissions expose sensitive receptors to substantial pollutant concentrations.

III. AIR QUALITY (Cont.)

(e) Create objectionable odors affecting a substantial number of people?

1. Determining the Scope of the Question

In order to determine the scope of the question, it is separated into the following parts:

Objectionable Odors

Examples of common land use types that typically create objectionable odors include, but are not limited to:

- ✓ Asphalt batch plant;

- ✓ Chemical manufacturing plants;

- ✓ Composting/green waste facilities;

- ✓ Food packaging plants;

- ✓ Painting/Coating operations;

- ✓ Petroleum refineries;

- ✓ Recycling facilities;

- ✓ Rendering plants;

- ✓ Sanitary landfills, and

- ✓ Wastewater treatment plants.

Other types of objectionable odors include, but are not limited to:

✓ Diesel exhaust from heavy equipment during construction;

✓ Diesel exhaust from trucks (such as from a truck terminal or truck stop);and

✓ Paints and architectural coatings applied during building construction.

<u>Substantial Number of People</u>

The number of people impacted by odors will vary depending on various factors, such as the type of odor generating use, its location relative to people, and the type of land use buffering between people and the source.

Therefore, there is no definitive number of people identified that would be considered "substantial" (e.g. if a project emits objectionable odors affecting 500 people or more that would be considered a significant impact).

2. Where to Find the Factual Data to Answer the Question

- The California Air Resources Board adopted the <u>Air Quality and Land Use Handbook: A Community Health Perspective</u> in 2005. The Land Use Handbook provides information and guidance on siting sensitive receptors in relation to sources of odors. The handbook can be located online at:

www.arb.ca.gov/ch/handbook.pdf or enter "air quality and land use planning handbook" in an Internet search engine.

- It is recommended that the California Environmental Resources Evaluation System website be consulted to see if there is any information related to this question. The website is located at:

ceres.ca.gov or enter "ceres evaluation" in an Internet search engine.

3. Example Answers

The following example answers the question comprehensively:

The project is located in the Imperial County Air Pollution Control District. The project is a 7,000 square foot office building. During construction, there is the potential for the generation of objectionable odors in the form of diesel exhaust and volatile organic compounds (from architectural coatings and paint) in the immediate vicinity of the site. However, these emissions will rapidly dissipate and be diluted by the atmosphere downwind of the site.

Further criteria for the evaluation of odor impacts are found in Table 3 of the Imperial County Air Pollution Control District's CEQA Air Quality Handbook.

Based on Table 3 of the Handbook, if the project is located within one mile of a wastewater treatment plant, sanitary landfill, composting station, feedlot, asphalt batching plant, painting/coating operations (including auto body shops), or rendering plant, odor impacts may be significant. The project site is not located within one mile of any of the odor generating land uses described above, therefore, the project will not subject a substantial number of people to objectionable odors.

This response identifies potential sources of odors and explains why they will not result in significant impacts. It cites data from the applicable Air Quality Pollution Control District/Air Quality Management District to support its conclusions.

Author's Note: *This example is based on a methodology recommended by the Imperial County Air Pollution Control District. It is intended for illustrative purposes only and it is not implied that the Imperial County Air Pollution Control District has approved its technical accuracy. In addition, the Initial Study Checklist preparer should use the methodology recommended by the applicable Air Pollution Control District/Air Quality Management District in which the project is located.*

The following example does not answer the question comprehensively:

Less than significant air quality impacts would result during both the construction phase and ultimate build out of the proposed 108 single-family residences. There are no known objectionable odors associated with this type of use that could affect the nearby working/living populations. Therefore, no mitigation measures are required.

This response does not describe the potential odors associated with construction, such as diesel exhaust from grading and the application of architectural coatings and paints applied during construction of the houses. It also does not describe the location of the project site in relation to potential stationary sources of odors such as a landfill, wastewater treatment plant etc.

4. Determining Significance

Following are some general factors to consider for determining significance:

- Are there any Thresholds of Significance that were formally adopted by the lead agency that are applicable to the project?

- Has the lead agency set a precedent in previously approved CEQA documents in responding to the question? If so, the Initial Study Checklist preparer should be aware of how other CEQA documents have responded to the question.

- An impact may be significant if objectionable odors generated by the construction or operation of the project would adversely impact people in the vicinity of the project.

- If a project is located in the vicinity of the following uses or activities odor impacts may be significant:

    ✓ Asphalt batch plant;

    ✓ Chemical manufacturing plants;

✓ Composting/green waste facilities;

✓ Food packaging plants;

✓ Painting/Coating operations;

✓ Petroleum refineries;

✓ Recycling facilities;

✓ Rendering plants;

✓ Sanitary landfills;

✓ Wastewater treatment plants;

✓ Diesel exhaust from heavy equipment during construction;

✓ Diesel exhaust from trucks (such as from a truck terminal or truck stop);and

✓ Paints and architectural coatings applied during building construction.

Chapter IV

Biological Resources

Introduction

Biological Resources deals with a project's impacts on sensitive plant and animal species and the natural habitat that supports them. Adverse impacts from a project can occur either directly, through activities that destroy the species itself, or indirectly by degrading the habitat that supports the species so that it no longer can survive.

In order to determine the scope of the questions posed in this Chapter, it is useful to understand the regulatory framework for biological resources. The regulatory framework identifies the federal, state, and local statutes, ordinances, or policies that govern the conservation and protection of biological resources and must be considered by the lead agency during the decision-making process for projects that have the potential to affect biological resources.

The following regulatory framework does not list every federal or state statute, but describes the most salient regulations in the context of the questions posed by Appendix G of the CEQA Guidelines.

Federal

Federal Endangered Species Act

The Federal Endangered Species Act is intended to provide a means to conserve the ecosystems upon which endangered and threatened species depend and provide programs for the conservation of those species, thus preventing extinction of plants and animals. The law is administered by the U.S. Fish and Wildlife Service and Commerce Department's National Oceanic and Atmospheric Administration Fisheries, depending on the species.

The Migratory Bird Treaty Act

The Migratory Bird Treaty Act makes it unlawful to pursue, capture, kill, or possess or attempt to do the same to any migratory bird or part, nest, or egg of any such bird listed in wildlife protection treaties between the United States, Great Britain, Mexico, Japan, and the countries of the former Soviet Union.

Section 404 of the Federal Clean Water Act

Section 404 of the Federal Clean Water Act, which is administered by the U.S. Army Corps of Engineers, regulates the discharge of dredge and fill material into waters of the United States. Waters of the United States include surface waters, rivers, lakes, estuaries, coastal waters, and wetlands.

State

California Endangered Species Act

The California Endangered Species Act protects all native species of plants and animals. The Act generally parallels the main provisions of the Federal Endangered Species Act and is administered by the California Department of Fish and Game.

Native Plant Protection Act

The Native Plant Protection Act includes measures to preserve, protect, and enhance rare and endangered native plants. The Act is administered by the California Department of Fish and Game.

Section 1600 of the State Fish and Game Code

All diversions, obstructions, or changes to the natural flow or bed, channel, or bank of any river, stream, or lake in California are subject to the regulatory authority of the California Department of Fish and Game.

Under the Code, a stream is defined as a body of water that flows at least periodically, or intermittently, through a bed or channel having banks and supporting fish or other aquatic life. Included are watercourses with surface or subsurface flows that support or have supported riparian vegetation.

The California Department of Fish and Game also has jurisdiction within altered or artificial waterways based on the value of those waterways to fish and wildlife, and also has jurisdiction over dry washes that carry water for a short period of time during storm events (also called "ephemeral waters").

<u>Natural Community Conservation Planning Program</u>

This program was initiated in 1991 and is managed by the California Department of Fish and Game, is designed to conserve multiple species and their habitats, while also providing for the compatible use of private land. Through local planning, the Natural Community Conservation Planning Program planning process protects wildlife and habitat before the landscape becomes so fragmented or degraded by development that listings are required under the Federal and or California Endangered Species Act.

Local

Local agencies (such as a city, county, or conservation district) may have regulations that apply to a project in addition to Federal and/or State regulations. These regulations typically implement Federal and/or State regulations at the local level but often times they have regulations that protect certain species that are important to a community.

IV. BIOLOGICAL RESOURCES

Would the project:

(a) Have a substantial adverse effect, either directly or through habitat modifications, on any species identified as a candidate, sensitive, or special status species in local or regional plans, policies, or regulations, or by the California Department of Fish and Game or U.S. Fish and Wildlife Service?

Author's Note: *This question uses the term "species." In practice, the term "species" typically refers to a "plant or animal species." Therefore, throughout this Chapter the term "species" means a plant or animal species.*

1. Determining the Scope of the Question

In order to determine the scope of the question, it is separated into the following parts:

Substantial Adverse Direct Effect

A direct effect would be the taking of a protected species (i.e. basically hunt, pursue, catch, capture, or kill).

Substantial Adverse Effect Through Habitat Modifications

Habitat modifications are actions that result in destruction or adverse modification of critical habitat. An example of habitat modification is grading land that destroys the habitat that supports a protected species.

Candidate, Sensitive, and Special Status Species

The terms "candidate", "sensitive", or "special status" are used to identify a species of plant or animal that is regulated in local or regional plans, policies, or regulations, or by the California Department of Fish and Game or U.S. Fish and Wildlife Service

"Candidate" species is defined as follows:

- ✓ *"Candidate Species"* (California). Candidate species means a native species or subspecies of a bird, mammal, fish, amphibian, reptile, or plant that has formally noticed as being under review by the Department of Fish and Game for addition to either the list of endangered species or the list of threatened species, or a species for which a notice of proposed regulation to add the species to either list has been published.

- ✓ "Candidate Species" (Federal). Candidate species are plants and animals for which the U.S. Fish and Wildlife Service has sufficient information on their biological status and threats to propose them as endangered or threatened under the Endangered Species Act but for which development of a proposed listing regulation is precluded by other higher priority listing activities.

The terms "sensitive" and "special status" species are not formally defined by either the California Department of Fish and Game or the U.S. Fish and Wildlife Service. However, in the context of the question, these terms are commonly defined as follows:

✓ *"Sensitive Species"* is any species of plant or animal experiencing general or localized population decline. "Endangered" and "Threatened" species would generally fall under this category.

✓ *"Special Status Species"* is a universal term used in the scientific community for species that are considered sufficiently rare that they require special consideration and/or protection and should be, or have been, listed as rare, threatened or endangered by the Federal and/or State governments.

Author's Note: *The definitions for "sensitive" and "special status" species described above were derived from biological assessments the author has used to prepare Initial Study Checklists.*

There are several other terms that are commonly used in biological assessments. These terms, in alphabetical order, include but are not limited to:

✓ *"Endangered"*

✓ *"Fully Protected"*

✓ *"Listed Species"*

✓ *"Proposed"*

✓ *"Rare"*

✓ *"Special"*

✓ *"Species of Concern"*

✓ *"Species of Special Concern"*

✓ *"Threatened"*

In addition to above described terms, CEQA Guidelines Section 15380 contains definitions for "endangered", "rare" or "threatened" species.

As shown above, there are numerous terms that describe the status of plant and animal species. In the opinion of the author, all of the above terms (as well as others) should be used to answer the question in an appropriate context as long as the term is intended to identify a plant or animal species whose population is considered to be in decline.

A qualified biologist should determine what terms should be used to address plant and animal species under this question.

2. Where to Find the Factual Data to Answer the Question

Federal

- Information on endangered species can be found on the U.S. Fish and Wildlife Service website located at:

    www.fws.gov/endangered/ or enter "us endangered species program" in an Internet search engine.

State

- Information on endangered species can be found on the California Department of Fish and Game website located at:

www.dfg.ca.gov/habcon/ or enter "dfg habitat conservation" in an Internet search engine.

- The California Natural Diversity Database is a program that inventories the status and locations of rare plants and animals in California. California Natural Diversity Database staff work with partners to maintain current lists of rare species as well as maintain a database of GIS-mapped locations for these species. The website is located at:

www.dfg.ca.gov/biogeodata/cnddb/ or enter "cnddb" in an Internet search engine.

- It is recommended that the California Environmental Resources Evaluation System website be consulted to see if there is any information related to this question. The website is located at:

ceres.ca.gov or enter "ceres evaluation" in an Internet search engine.

Local

- Information on local or regional plans, policies, or regulations can be obtained from the local agency in which the project is located.

As informative as the above resources are, they are not a replacement for a Preliminary Biological Assessment prepared by a qualified biologist.

If a project site contains vacant land that is not paved, a Preliminary Biological Assessment should be prepared by a qualified biologist. _Even if the land has been cleared or grubbed or otherwise disturbed, it still may contain suitable habitat for a candidate, sensitive, or special status plant or animal species._

Appendix B contains a suggested format for a Preliminary Biological Assessment.

3. Example Answers

The following examples answer the question comprehensively:

Example 1

Based on the Preliminary Biological Assessment prepared for the project, there are several sensitive plant and animal species identified by the California Natural Diversity Data Base as having potential to occur in the vicinity of the project.

However, the potential to find such species on the project site or in the area immediately surrounding the project site is very low due to the lack of natural vegetation, the heavy disturbance of the natural environment, and the lack of undisturbed habitat.

Therefore, there will not be a substantial adverse effect on candidate, sensitive, or special status species. No further study will be necessary

This response identifies the site conditions and why candidate, sensitive, or special status plant or animal species will not be impacted. As a source of information, it cites the California Natural Diversity Data Base and the Preliminary Biological Assessment prepared for the project.

Example 2

One species covered by the Western Riverside Multiple Species Habitat Conservation Plan ("Plan") occurs within the site, the Burrowing Owl. Additionally, the site supports approximately 17 acres of suitable habitat for the Burrowing Owl.

The project will result in the permanent loss of 17 acres of suitable Burrowing Owl foraging and dispersing habitat. One (1) Burrowing Owl territory is considered to be permanently impacted by the project and it occurs within a designated Criteria Cell of the Plan.

Therefore, impacts to one Burrowing Owl territory and to 17 acres of suitable habitat is potentially significant.

The following Mitigation Measures are recommended to reduce impacts to less than significant.

MM BR-1a: Prior to any ground-disturbing activity occurring on the project site, a preconstruction survey will be conducted to determine if any Burrowing Owls are present in the disturbance limits. The California Burrowing Owl Consortium (1993) recommends that no disturbance occur within 50 meters (approximately 160 feet) of occupied burrows during the nonbreeding season of September 1 through January 31 or within 75 meters (approximately 250 feet) during the breeding season of February 1 through August 31.

Avoidance also requires that a minimum of 6.5 acres (a radius of 300 feet) of foraging habitat be maintained contiguous with occupied burrow sites for each pair of breeding Burrowing Owl (with or without dependent young) or single unpaired resident bird.

MM BR-1b: The following passive relocation measures will be followed:

1. Passive relocation will occur September 1-January 31, which is outside of the breeding season for Burrowing Owl; and

2. The owls occupying the project site will be banded using a U.S. Fish and Wildlife Service metal band and colored band.

3. The existing burrows on the project site will be systematically collapsed, using the California Burrowing Owl Consortium Burrowing Owl Protocol and Mitigation Guidelines. This will ensure that no owls reside inside burrows to be collapsed. Burrowing Owls will be excluded from burrows in the immediate impact zone by installing one-way doors in burrow entrances. The one way doors will be left in place 48 hours to insure owls have left the burrow before excavation.

After 48 hours, existing burrows will be systematically collapsed. Burrows will be excavated using hand tools and refilled to prevent reoccupation. The project area will be monitored daily for one week to confirm the Burrowing Owls have vacated the project site before recommending commencement of grading. Artificial burrows will be constructed at the mitigation area in accordance with the measures described in the Determination of Biologically Equivalent or Superior Preservation required by the Western Riverside County Multiple Species Habitat Conservation Plan.

MM BR-1c: In order to compensate for the loss of occupied Burrowing Owl habitat, an offsite conservation area has been identified that provides suitable habitat. The conservation area is located in an undevelopable triangular parcel that is approximately 1000 feet to the west of the project site. The parcel is bound by the Stuart Aqueduct to the west and a future water pipeline to the east and currently provides high quality foraging and dispersing habitat.

Because it abuts the easement associated with the Stuart Aqueduct, this parcel will remain connected to similar habitat and therefore provides conservation value to the Burrowing Owl. It is also located in Criteria Cell 4007 of the Western Riverside County Multiple Species Habitat Conservation Plan. Due to the close proximity of the conservation area to the project site, it is considered onsite mitigation under the California Burrowing Owl Consortium (1993).

The California Burrowing Owl Consortium (1993) recommends that on-site mitigation include a minimum of 6.5 acres of conservation land, which has been achieved with the proposed conservation area.

This conservation area contributes to the Burrowing Owl objectives listed in Table 9-2 of the Western Riverside County Multiple Habitat Conservation

Plan. Specifically, the conservation area provides suitable primary grassland habitat for the Burrowing Owl and therefore meets Objective 1. It will remain connected to similar habitat to the north via the Stuart Aqueduct where proposed Noncontiguous Habitat Block 7 will occur.

The mitigation area will be managed and monitored in accordance with the measures described in the approved Determination of Biologically Equivalent or Superior Preservation.

This response is an example of how extensive mitigation measures may be for a species. Mitigation measures will vary from species to species. This response addresses all parts of the question by:

1) Identifying that the Burrowing Owl is a species that is covered by a habitat conservation plan.

2) By discussing direct impacts on the Burrowing owl and through habitat modification.

3) By describing why adverse impacts will be mitigated to less than significant.

The following example does not answer the question comprehensively:

The proposed project would not result in any direct effect on any candidate, sensitive, or special status species or modification to any habitat of such species. As such, impacts on any candidate, sensitive, or listed species are not anticipated as a result of project implementation.

This response does not provide any factual data to support the conclusion. It merely repeats the question in the negative.

4. Determining Significance

Following are some general factors to consider for determining significance:

- Are there any Thresholds of Significance that were formally adopted by the lead agency that are applicable to the project?

- Has the lead agency set a precedent in previously approved CEQA documents in responding to the question? If so, the Initial Study Checklist preparer should be aware of how other CEQA documents have responded to the question.

- Any project that would adversely impact a candidate, sensitive, special status species (or other classification of species as determined by a qualified biologist) either directly (e.g. catch, capture, or kill) or through adverse habitat modification (e.g. grading of land) may have a significant impact.

IV. BIOLOGICAL RESOURCES (cont.)

(b) Have a substantial adverse effect on any riparian habitat or other sensitive natural community identified in local or regional plans, policies, regulations or by the California Department of Fish and Game or US Fish and Wildlife Service?

1. Determining the Scope of the Question

In order to determine the scope of the question, it is separated into the following parts:

Riparian Habitat

Generally, a riparian habitat is characterized by vegetated areas along bodies of freshwater including streams, lakes and rivers. Common vegetation found in a riparian habitat includes forests, woodlands, shrublands, meadows and grasslands.

Sensitive Natural Community

Sensitive Natural Communities are ranked by their rarity by the California Natural Diversity Data Base which is part of the Department of Fish and Game. Threat to a Sensitive Natural Community is an important facet of their classification.

Sensitive Natural Communities generally are classified as:

- ✓ Dunes (e.g. coastal and desert);

- ✓ Scrub and Chaparral;

✓ Bog and Marsh;

✓ Riparian and Bottomland Habitat (e.g. riparian forest, willow riparian forest, California Sycamore, Alder);

✓ Broad Leafed Upland Tree dominated (e.g. oak woodlands, coastal live oak);

✓ Coniferous Upland Forest & Woodland (e.g. cypress, scrub, woodlands, and forests); and

✓ Alpine Habitats (e.g. boulder and rock fields).

***

A qualified biologist should establish the regulatory framework appropriate for riparian habitat or a sensitive natural community if such resources are associated with a project so the question will be answered in an appropriate context.

When in doubt whether riparian habitat or a sensitive natural community exists, a Preliminary Biological Assessment (See Appendix B) should be prepared by a qualified biologist to determine the presence of absence of these resources.

Substantial Adverse Effect

Activities that could adversely affect riparian habitat and sensitive natural communities include but are not limited to:

✓ The dredging, filling or erosion into these areas;
✓ The construction of roads;

✓ Urban development that causes fragmentation of these areas; or

✓ Increasing or decreasing the water supply to the area by off-site development or diverting the flow of water to the area.

2. Where to Find the Factual Data to Answer the Question

- Information on Natural Communities can be found on the California Department of Fish and Game website located at:

  www.dfg.ca.gov/biogeodata/vegcamp/ natural_communities.asp or enter "cdfg biological information natural communities" in an Internet search engine.

- The *Protocols for Surveying and Evaluating Impacts to Special Status Native Plant Populations and Natural Communities* published by the California Department of Fish and Game may help Initial Study Checklist preparers review environmental documents, determine when a botanical survey is needed, how field surveys may be conducted, what information to include in a survey report, and what qualifications to consider for surveyors. The document can be located at:

  www.dfg.ca.gov/biogeodata/cnddb/pdf s/Protocols_for_Surveying_and_Evaluat ing_Impacts.pdf or enter "dfg protocols for surveying natural communities" in an Internet search engine.

- It is recommended that the California Environmental Resources Evaluation System website be consulted to see if there is any information related to this question. The website is located at:

  ceres.ca.gov or enter "ceres evaluation" in an Internet search engine.

  However, as informative as the above resources are, they are not a replacement for a biological assessment prepared by a qualified biologist. If a project site contains any features that may be considered riparian habitat or a natural community, a Preliminary Biological Assessment (See Appendix B) should be prepared by a qualified biologist.

3. Example Answers

The following examples answer the question comprehensively:

Example 1

Based on the Preliminary Biological Assessment prepared for the project, the following was determined:

Riparian Habitat:

There are no year-round streams on the site. There are two ephemeral drainages and two ephemeral ditches on the site, however, there is no presence of typical riparian plants such as willow, cottonwood, wild rose, or box elder within these drainage areas.

Sensitive Natural Communities:

Oak woodlands exist on the western portion of the site. Oak woodlands are a sensitive natural community. However, the area containing the oak woodlands is designated as Open Space Lot "A" on the tentative tract map for the project and thus will not be disturbed by development.

This response states that no riparian habitat exists on the site. In addition, although a sensitive natural community (i.e. oak woodlands) is present on the site it will not be impacted because it will be left undisturbed within an open space lot.

Example 2

Based on the Biological Assessment, prepared for the project, construction of an access road through of the site would impact approximately 0.17 acre of Southern Coast Live Oak Riparian Forest habitat.

Permits for impacts to this habitat are required from U.S. Army Corps of Engineers, the California Department of Fish and Game, and from the California Regional Water Quality Control Board.

Mitigation Measure BIO-1 is recommended to mitigate impacts to less than significant levels:

BIO-1: Prior to the issuance of a grading permit, the project proponent shall provide evidence that permits have been obtained from the U.S. Army Corps of Engineers, the California Department of

Fish and Game, and the Santa Ana Regional Water Quality Control Board as required.

The U.S. Army Corps of Engineers and the California Department of Fish and Game permits shall contain verification to the City that the loss of Southern Live Oak Riparian Forest has been mitigated through acquisition of off-site credits at a maximum ratio of 3:1 in a mitigation area for similar vegetation established by the City, if available, or at another mitigation area acceptable to the City and the U.S. Army Corps of Engineers and the California Department of Fish and Game.

The response is based on a Biological Assessment and in this case, mitigation was recommended for the loss of Southern Live Oak Riparian Forest, which is a riparian habitat/sensitive natural community.

The following example does not answer the question comprehensively:

The project site is not a known natural habitat for endangered, threatened or rare species; therefore, no impacts are identified as a result of this project.

This response does not describe the site features in the context of a riparian habitat /sensitive natural community and the reason why the project will not impact these resources.

4. Determining Significance

Following are some general factors to consider for determining significance:

- Are there any Thresholds of Significance that were formally adopted by the lead agency that are applicable to the project?

- Has the lead agency set a precedent in previously approved CEQA documents in responding to the question? If so, the Initial Study Checklist preparer should be aware of how other CEQA documents have responded to the question.

- Activities that could adversely affect riparian habitat and sensitive natural communities include but is not limited to:

  ✓ The dredging, filling or erosion into these areas;

  ✓ The construction of roads;

  ✓ Urban development that causes fragmentation of these areas; or

  ✓ Increasing or decreasing the water supply to the area by off-site development or diverting the flow of water to the area.

IV. BIOLOGICAL RESOURCES (cont.)

1. Determining the Scope of the Question

(c) Have a substantial adverse effect on federally protected wetlands as defined by Section 404 of the Clean Water Act (including, but not limited to, marsh, vernal pool, coastal, etc.) through direct removal, filling, hydrological interruption, or other means?

In order to determine the scope of the question, it is separated into the following parts:

Wetlands as Defined by Section 404 of the Clean Water Act

Section 404 of the Clean Water Act defines wetlands as *"those areas that are inundated or saturated by surface or groundwater at a frequency and duration sufficient to support, and that under normal circumstances do support, a prevalence of vegetation typically adapted for life in saturated soil conditions. Wetlands generally include swamps, marshes, bogs and similar areas."* [Ref. EPA Regulations listed at 40 CFR 230.3(t)].

Although the strict interpretation of this question deals with "federally protected wetlands", in practice, wetlands under the jurisdiction the California Department of Fish and Game are typically also are addressed in responding to this question.

Because of the changing and complex nature of the regulations affecting wetlands as a result of the Rapanos Supreme Court Decision, a "jurisdictional evaluation or delineation" should be prepared by a qualified biologist if there are any types of features present that may constitute a "wetland" (i.e. rivers, lakes, streams, creeks, drainages and other waters that have a bed and bank and support plant and animal species).

The Rapanos Supreme Court Decision involved four Michigan wetlands lying near ditches or man-made drains that eventually empty into traditional navigable waters. The United States brought civil enforcement proceedings against the Rapanos petitioners, who had backfilled three of the areas without a permit. The District Court found federal jurisdiction over the wetlands because they were adjacent to "waters of the United States" and held petitioners liable for Clean Water Act violations.

2. Where to Find the Factual Data to Answer the Question

- The U.S. Environmental Protection Agency has an excellent website that provides information on wetlands. It is located at:

    www.epa.gov/owow/wetlands/or enter "wetlands us epa" in an Internet search engine.

- The U.S. Fish and Wildlife Service, National Wetlands Inventory webpage contains a mapping system for wetlands. It is located at:

    www.fws.gov/wetlands/Data/Mapper. html or enter "usfws wetlands inventory" in an Internet search engine.

- The California Environmental Resources Evaluation System Land Use Planning Information Network (LUPIN) has an excellent website on California Wetlands. The website can be located at:

  http://ceres.ca.gov/wetlands/or enter "ceres california wetlands" in an Internet search engine.

- It is recommended that the California Environmental Resources Evaluation System website be consulted to see if there is any information related to this question. The website is located at:

  ceres.ca.gov or enter "ceres evaluation" in an Internet search engine.

As informative as the above websites are, they are not a replacement for a jurisdictional evaluation or delineation prepared by a qualified biologist. If there are any features of a wetland present, no matter how small they may seem, a Preliminary Biological Assessment should be prepared. (See Appendix B).

3. Example Answers

The following example answers the question comprehensively:

Based on the Jurisdictional Delineation prepared for the project, one drainage feature, flowing generally along the northern perimeter of the property, possesses characteristics that lend itself to

California Department Fish and Game jurisdiction (i.e. supporting wetland/riparian vegetation).

This feature collects mainly urban runoff from the larger developed watershed above it, and conveys it as surface sheet flow over an abandoned asphalt driveway onto Norton Road, where it flows into the City's drainage system.

The drainage feature does not lend itself to U.S. Army Corps of Engineers jurisdiction under Section 404 of the Clean Water Act as it does not have a definable bed and bank, an Ordinary High Water Mark, nor soils deeper than one to two inches to assess hydric characteristics.

Based on the above Jurisdictional Delineation it was determined that 0.72 acres of wetlands under jurisdiction of the California Department of Fish and Game would be impacted.

Mitigation Measure BIO-1 is intended to mitigate for the loss of the 0.72 acres of wetlands by requiring that permits be obtained from the California Department of Fish and Game and that the possible loss of wetlands be mitigated at a ratio of 3:1 either through acquisition of off-site credits at a maximum ratio of 3:1 in a mitigation area for similar resources established by the City, if available, or at another mitigation area acceptable to the California Department of Fish and Game.

This response includes a discussion of the factors that were used to determine if wetlands are present on the site and what agency has jurisdiction over them. It also recommends mitigation for the loss of wetlands.

The following example does not answer the question comprehensively:

Based on a review of the project site, there are no streams or waterways within the site or its vicinity. The nearest waterway is the Socorro River, which is located 5 miles west of the project site. Therefore, the proposed project will have no impact.

This response is making the conclusion that only streams or waterways qualify as wetlands when in fact wetlands can include marshes, swamps, bogs, or fens or drainage courses located on a site.

4. Determining Significance

Following are some general factors to consider for determining significance:

- Are there any Thresholds of Significance that were formally adopted by the lead agency that are applicable to the project?

- Has the lead agency set a precedent in previously approved CEQA documents in responding to the question? If so, the Initial Study Checklist preparer should be aware of how other CEQA documents have responded to the question.

- If a project site contains any areas that are saturated with water and contain plant and/or animal communities, they may be considered jurisdictional wetlands (i.e. under the jurisdiction of the California Department

124

of Fish and Game and/or the U.S. Army Corps of Engineers).

If the project will disturb these areas in any way, either directly or indirectly, then a Preliminary Biological Assessment as described in Appendix B should be conducted which would determine if they are jurisdictional wetlands requiring a formal delineation study and the need to obtain state or federal regulatory approvals prior to initiation of construction. Disturbance of such areas may have a significant impact.

Activities that could adversely affect wetlands include but are not limited to:

- ✓ Dredging, filling or erosion into wetlands;

- ✓ The construction of roads, urban development that causes fragmentation of wetland areas; or

- ✓ The construction of concrete drainage channels in wetlands.

IV. BIOLOGICAL RESOURCES (cont.)

(d) Interfere substantially with the movement of any native resident or migratory fish or wildlife species or with established native resident or migratory wildlife corridors, or impede the use of native wildlife nursery sites?

1. Determining the Scope of the Question

In order to determine the scope of the question, it is separated into the following parts:

<u>Interference with the Movement of Native Resident Migratory Fish or Wildlife Species</u>

Wildlife corridors link together areas of suitable habitat that are otherwise separated by rugged terrain, changes in vegetation, or human development. Corridors effectively act as links between different populations of a species.

Interference with the movement of native resident migratory fish or wildlife species occurs through the fragmentation of open space areas caused by urbanization.

Urbanization creates isolated "islands" of wildlife habitat. In the absence of habitat linkages that allow movement to adjoining open space areas, various studies have concluded that some wildlife species, especially the larger and more mobile mammals, will not likely persist over time in fragmented or isolated habitat areas because they prohibit the infusion of new individuals.

Impede the Use of Wildlife Nursery Sites

Wildlife nursery sites are areas that provide valuable spawning and nursery habitat for fish and wildlife.

Wildlife nursery sites occur in a variety of settings, such as trees, wetlands, rivers, lakes, forests, woodlands and grasslands to name a few.

The use of a nursery site would be impeded if the use of the nursery site was interfered with directly or indirectly by a project's development or activities.

2. Where to Find the Factual Data to Answer the Question

- The local agency's general plan may identify habitat linkages and other identified key habitats in a conservation and open space element or similar element.

- Regional conservation plans may identify wildlife linkages or habitat areas that sustain wildlife.

- The California Department of Fish and Game Biogeographic Data Branch has a webpage that identifies vegetation mapping, rare species tracking, and species range mapping that can assist in identifying wildlife movement corridors and nursery sites. The webpage is located at:

www.dfg.ca.gov/biogeodata/ or enter "dfg biogeographic data branch" in an Internet search engine.

As informative as the above webpages are, they are not a replacement for assessment prepared by a qualified biologist if there are any features that could support the movement of fish or wildlife or their nesting sites. A Preliminary Biological Assessment should be prepared. (See Appendix B).

- In 2007 the State Legislature required the Department of Fish and Game to identify high priority areas for vegetation mapping and to map known wildlife corridors in the state.

  A report was prepared titled: *Legislative Analyst's Office Supplemental Report of the 2007 Budget Act 2007-08 Fiscal Year*. This report contains an excellent overview on wildlife corridors. It can be found at:

  www.dfg.ca.gov/biogeodata/vegcamp/ pdfs/WCB_veg- Mapping_LAO_Supplemental_Report_20 07.pdf or enter "legislative analyst's office supplemental report item 3640-301-6051" in an Internet search engine.

- It is recommended that the California Environmental Resources Evaluation System website be consulted to see if there is any information related to this question. The website is located at:

ceres.ca.gov or enter "ceres evaluation" in an Internet search engine.

3. Example Answers

The following examples answers the question comprehensively:

Example 1

Based on the Preliminary Biological Assessment prepared for the project site, there are some sensitive wildlife species as having potential to occur in the project vicinity. However, the potential to find such species in or around the project area is very low due to the lack of natural vegetation on-site, the heavy disturbance of the natural environment, and the lack of undisturbed habitat in the project vicinity.

In addition, the project site is surrounded by existing development to the north, east, and west and by Tringali Avenue along its southern boundary. Consequently, the site does not serve as a wildlife movement corridor or wildlife nursery site.

This response describes how wildlife movement could occur and why the site does not support the features that support wildlife movement.

Example 2

The site contains shrubs and trees along the western perimeter of the site that could be used for nesting migratory birds. These trees and shrubs will not be removed due to development. Nesting migratory birds are protected under the Federal Migratory Bird Treaty Act and the California Fish and Game Code. This is considered a potentially significant impact. Mitigation Measure BIO-1 is recommended to mitigate impacts to less than significant:

BIO-1: If active nests are located during pre-construction surveys, in accordance with California Department of Fish and Game guidelines, clearing and construction activities within three-hundred (300) feet of the nest (five-hundred feet [500] for raptors) be postponed or halted until the nest is vacated and juveniles have fledged and there is no evidence of a second attempt at nesting, as determined by a City approved biologist.

Limits of construction to avoid an active nest shall be established in the field with flagging, fencing, or other appropriate barriers and construction personnel shall be instructed on the sensitivity of the nest areas. The biologist shall serve as a construction monitor during those periods when construction activities will occur near active nest areas to ensure that no inadvertent impacts on these nests will occur.

The results of the survey, and any avoidance measures taken, shall be submitted to the California Department of Fish and Game within thirty (30) days of completion of the pre-construction surveys and/or construction monitoring to document compliance with applicable state and federal laws pertaining to the protection of native birds.

This response provides a description of the biological conditions on the site and explains that a wildlife nursery site (i.e. trees for nesting migratory birds) could be significantly impacted but with implementation of a mitigation measure for nesting birds impacts will be less than significant.

The following example does not answer the question comprehensively:

The project will not interfere substantially with the movement of any native resident or migratory fish or wildlife species or with established native resident or migratory wildlife corridors, or impede the use of native wildlife nursery sites.

This response merely restates the question in the negative and does not provide any details as to the site conditions or its surroundings which justify the conclusions.

4. Determining Significance

Following are some general factors to consider for determining significance:

- Are there any Thresholds of Significance that were formally adopted by the lead agency that are applicable to the project?

- Has the lead agency set a precedent in previously approved CEQA documents in responding to the question? If so, the Initial Study Checklist preparer should be aware of how other CEQA documents have responded to the question.

- Actions that may impede wildlife movement can include the dredging, filling or erosion into streams and waterways, the construction of roads, urban development that causes fragmentation of natural areas, and the construction of concrete drainage channels. Any of these or similar actions may have a significant impact.

IV. BIOLOGICAL RESOURCES (cont.)

(e) Conflict with any local policies or ordinances protecting biological resources, such as a tree preservation policy or ordinance?

1. Determining the Scope of the Question

This question is often narrowly interpreted to apply only to tree preservation, but in fact many jurisdictions have policies and ordinances that address other biological resources. For example, some local agency general plans contain policies specific to wetland habitats or for certain sensitive plant or animal species.

2. Where to Find the Factual Data to Answer the Question

- A review of all local policies and ordinances, typically found in the general plan and zoning code should be conducted to see if there are other biological resources other than trees regulated at the local level.

- It is recommended that the California Environmental Resources Evaluation System website be consulted to see if there is any information related to this question. The website is located at:

  ceres.ca.gov or enter "ceres evaluation" in an Internet search engine.

3. Example Answers

The following example answers the question comprehensively:

The project will not affect any protected biological resources because it is a developed site that is only proposing the addition of a new retail store on an existing building pad that contains a foundation. There is no vegetation on the area to be developed. However, the proposed project may require the removal of three (3) trees adjacent to the building pad.

The City has regulations governing the removal of trees greater than 24 inches in diameter and at least 15 feet in height. Based on an assessment by the City's Landscape Architect, the trees do not meet the diameter and height requirements necessary for protection. Therefore, the proposed project would not conflict with any local policies or ordinance protecting biological resources.

This response addresses all biological resources and not exclusively trees. It also discusses why the project will not be in conflict with local ordinance and policies protecting biological resources.

The following example does not answer the question comprehensively:

The City does not have an ordinance to cover all trees, but deals with the issue on an individual project basis. In this case, the mature trees on site will be retained, and smaller trees will be removed or relocated as necessary to implement the Landscaping and Lighting Plan. Therefore, there will *be no impact regarding local biological policies and ordinances.*

This response only focuses on trees and does not discuss if the jurisdiction has other biological resources that may be protected by a policy or ordinance. It also does not describe the physical setting as it relates to biological resources other than trees.

4. Determining Significance

Following are some general factors to consider for determining significance:

- Are there any Thresholds of Significance that were formally adopted by the lead agency that are applicable to the project?

- Has the lead agency set a precedent in previously approved CEQA documents in responding to the question? If so, the Initial Study Checklist preparer should be aware of how other CEQA documents have responded to the question.

- If a project is in conflict with any local policies or ordinances protecting biological resources (including trees) then it may have a significant impact.

IV. BIOLOGICAL RESOURCES (cont.)

(f) Conflict with the provisions of an adopted Habitat Conservation Plan, Natural Community Conservation Plan, or other approved local, regional, or state habitat conservation plan?

1. Determining the Scope of the Question

In order to determine the scope of the question, it is separated into the following parts:

Habitat Conservation Plan

Habitat Conservation Plans are planning documents required as part of an application for an incidental take permit. These Plans are administered by the U.S. Fish and Wildlife Service under authority of the Federal Endangered Species Act.

According to the U.S. Fish and Wildlife website, _"individual homeowners, counties, states, and corporations have developed what have come to be known as Habitat Conservation Plans. Some are as small as a fraction of an acre, while others are larger than a million acres. Landowners are preparing Habitat Conservation Plans in connection with building golf courses, harvesting timber, managing ranches, operating nurseries, producing gas and oil, and constructing businesses and utilities."_

Natural Communities Conservation Plan

According to California Fish and Game Code Section 2805(g), a _"Natural Community Conservation Plan"_ *or "plan" means the plan prepared pursuant to a planning agreement entered into in accordance with subdivision (a) of Section 2810. The plan shall identify and provide for those measures necessary to conserve and manage natural biological diversity within the plan area while allowing compatible and appropriate economic development, growth, and other human uses."*

Natural Community Conservation Plans are considered to be a Habitat Conservation Plan as described above because the U.S. Fish and Wildlife Service must issue a permit if the Plan activities will result in the "incidental take" of a listed wildlife species.

Other Approved Local, Regional, or State Habitat Conservation Plan

Plans under this category are considered to be a Habitat Conservation Plan as described above if the U.S. Fish and Wildlife Service must issue a permit because the Plan would result in the "incidental take" of a federally listed species.

In addition, if the California Department of Fish and Game must issue a permit because the Plan would result in the "incidental take" of a state listed species, the Plan would be considered a Habitat Conservation Plan as well.

Author's Note: *if a response to the question addresses Habitat Conservation Plans and Natural Community Conservation Plans, it will cover plans that are described as "Other Approved Local, Regional, or State Habitat Conservation Plans" as well.*

2. Where to Find the Factual Data to Answer the Question

Habitat Conservation Plan

- The U.S. Fish and Wildlife Service website has a listing of Habitat Conservation Plans for California. The website is located at:

  http://ecos.fws.gov/conserv_plans/ser vlet/gov.doi.hcp.servlets.PlanSelect or enter "usfws conservation plans and agreements" in an Internet search engine. Click on the link for "Region 8, California and Nevada" to view a list of Plans.

Natural Community Conservation Plan

- The California Department of Fish and Game website has information about the Natural Community Conservation Planning Program. The website is located at:

  www.dfg.ca.gov/habcon/nccp/ or enter "california natural community conservation planning" in an Internet search engine. Click on the link "Summary Table" to view a list of Plans.

Other Approved Local, Regional, or State Habitat Conservation Plan

- Use the websites described above to determine if the project site is located within a local, regional, or state conservation plan.

- It is recommended that the California Environmental Resources Evaluation System website be consulted to see if there is any information related to this question. The website is located at:

  ceres.ca.gov or enter "ceres evaluation" in an Internet search engine.

3. Example Answers

The following examples answer the question comprehensively:

Example 1

The project site is within the adopted Western Riverside County Multiple Species Habitat Conservation Plan and extends into a designated Criteria Cell. The project has the potential to result in significant impacts to conservation areas of the Plan. The project must demonstrate conformance with the Plan to the satisfaction of the City prior to issuance of grading permits. Conformance with the Plan includes, but is not limited to the following:

✓ *Completion of the Habitat Evaluation and Acquisition Negotiation Process;*

✓ *Compliance with the Riparian/Riverine Areas and Vernal Pools Guidelines;*

✓ *Compliance with the Protection of Narrow Endemic Plant Species Guidelines;*

✓ *Completion of a Determination of Biological Equivalent or Superior Preservation for the burrowing owl;*

✓ Conformance with the Urban/Wildlands Interface Guidelines; and

✓ Payment of the Multiple Species Habitat Conservation Plan Local Development Mitigation Fee.

There are no other habitat conservation plans applicable to the project site.

With completion of the above, impacts to Habitat Conservation Plans would be less than significant.

This response identifies that the project is within a Habitat Conservation Plan and discusses how compliance with the Plan is achieved.

Author's Note: This example is based on a project located within the Western Riverside County Multiple Habitat Conservation Plan. It is intended for illustrative purposes only and it is not implied that the Western Riverside County Regional Conservation Authority has approved its technical accuracy.

Example 2

According to the California Department of Fish and Game's Natural Community Conservation Planning Program website accessed on July 6, 2009, the project site is not located within an adopted or proposed Natural Community Conservation Plan.

According to the U.S. Fish and Wildlife Service Habitat Conservation Plan website accessed on July 6, 2009, the project site is not located within an adopted or proposed Habitat Conservation Plan.

In addition, based on the above research, the project site is not identified as being located within a local, regional or state habitat conservation plan.

The response demonstrates that the project site is not located in either an adopted or proposed Habitat Conservation Plan, Natural Community Conservation Plan, a local, regional or state habitat conservation plan.

The following example does not answer the question comprehensively:

The proposed project would not conflict with any local policies, ordinances, or conservation plans that require the conservation of biological resources.

This response merely restates the question in the negative and does not provide any details which justify the conclusion.

4. Determining Significance

Following are some general factors to consider for determining significance:

- Are there any Thresholds of Significance that were formally adopted by the lead agency that are applicable to the project?

- Has the lead agency set a precedent in previously approved CEQA documents in responding to the question? If so, the Initial Study Checklist preparer should be aware of how other CEQA documents have responded to the question.

- If a project is located within a Habitat Conservation Plan, Natural Community Conservation Plan, or local, regional, or state conservation plan it must be consistent with the provisions of such plan or it may have a significant impact.

Chapter V

Cultural Resources

Introduction

Cultural Resources deals with how a project may impact historical resources, archaeological resources, paleontological resources, and human remains discovered outside of a formal cemetery.

In order to determine the scope of the questions posed in this Chapter, it is useful to understand the regulatory framework for Cultural Resources. The following regulatory framework does not list every federal or state statute, but describes the most salient regulations in the context of the questions posed by Appendix G of the CEQA Guidelines.

Historical Resources

Federal

National Historic Preservation Act of 1966 (as amended), Section 106 (Act)

The National Historic Preservation Act established the National Register of Historic Places, State Historic Preservation Offices and programs, and the Advisory Council on Historic Preservation. The Act establishes a national policy of historic preservation to protect, rehabilitate, restore, and reuse districts, sites, buildings, structures, and objects significant in American architecture, history, archaeology, and culture.

The Act applies to all properties on or eligible for inclusion in the National Register of Historic Places. Evaluation of a cultural resource consists of determining whether it is significant (i.e., if it meets one or more of the criteria for listing in the National Register of Historic Places). Section 106 requires consultation to mitigate damage to historic properties, including Native American traditional cultural places.

State

California Environmental Quality Act (CEQA)

CEQA requires public agencies to identify the environmental impacts of proposed discretionary activities or projects, determine if the impacts will be significant, and identify alternatives and mitigation measures that will substantially reduce or eliminate significant impacts to the environment.

Historical resources are considered part of the environment and a project that may cause a substantial adverse effect on the significance of a historical resource is a project that may have a significant effect on the environment. Resources listed in, or determined eligible for listing on the California Register are resources that must be given consideration in the CEQA process.

California Register of Historical Resources

In 1992, Assembly Bill 2881 was signed into law establishing the California Register of Historical Resources (California Register). The California Register is an authoritative guide in California used by state and local agencies, private groups, and citizens to identify the state's historical resources and to indicate what properties are to be protected, to the extent prudent and feasible, from substantial adverse change. The criteria for eligibility for the California Register are based upon the National Register of Historic Places criteria. Certain resources are determined by the statute to be included in the California Register, including properties formally determined eligible for, or listed in, the National Register of Historic Places, State Landmarks, and State Points of Interest.

Local

Local jurisdictions can regulate historic resources protection through the adoption of regulations that are codified at the local level.

Archaeological Resources

California Environmental Quality Act (CEQA)

CEQA Guidelines Section 15064.5 (a) (3) states:

"Any object, building, structure, site, area, place, record, or manuscript which a lead agency determines to be historically significant or significant in the architectural, engineering, scientific, economic, agricultural, educational, social, political, military, or cultural annals of California may be considered to be an historical resource, provided the lead agency's determination is supported by substantial evidence in light of the whole record.

Generally, a resource shall be considered by the lead agency to be 'historically significant' if the resource meets the criteria for listing on the

California Register of Historical Resources (Pub. Res. Code, § 5024.1, Title 14 CCR, Section 4852)."

Thus, an archaeological resource can also be considered a "historic resource." If an archeological site is an historical resource (i.e., listed or eligible for listing in the California Register) potential adverse impacts to it must be considered, just as for any other historical resource [PRC Sections 21084.1 and 21083.2(l)].

California Register of Historical Resources

As noted above, the California Register of Historical Resources ("California Register") is an authoritative guide in California used by state and local agencies, private groups, and citizens to identify the state's historical resources and to indicate what properties are to be protected, to the extent prudent and feasible, from substantial adverse change including archaeological resources.

California Public Resources Code Section 5097.9– 5097.991

These regulations provide protection to Native American historical and cultural resources, and sacred sites and identifies the powers and duties of the Native American Heritage Commission. It also requires notification of discoveries of Native American human remains and provides for treatment and disposition of human remains and associated grave goods.

California Coastal Act

The California Coastal Act, in part, authorizes the California Coastal Commission to review permit applications for development within the coastal zone and, where necessary, to require reasonable mitigation measures to offset effects of that development. Permits for development are issued with "special conditions" to ensure implementation of these mitigation measures.

Section 30244 of the Act, *"Archaeological or Paleontological Resources,"* states:

"*Where development would adversely impact archaeological or paleontological resources as identified by the State Historic Preservation Officer, reasonable mitigation measures shall be required.*"

Local

Local jurisdictions can regulate archaeological resource protection through the adoption of regulations that are codified at the local level. These regulations generally provide additional guidance on assessment and treatment measures for archeological resources subject to CEQA.

Paleontological Resources

Federal

There are various federal regulations that address paleontological resources. They generally become applicable to specific projects if the project involves federal land or requires a federal agency license, permit, approval, or funding. If these factors are involved, then compliance with the National Environmental Policy Act (NEPA) would be required.

State

California Environmental Quality Act (CEQA)

CEQA applies to Paleontological Resources because such resources are identified as an environmental resource and fall under the overall protection of environmental resources afforded by CEQA.

California Public Resources Code Section 5097.5

Public Resources Code 5097.5 prohibits the excavation upon, removal, or destruction, of a vertebrate paleontological site, including fossilized footprints, situated on public lands, except with the express permission of the public agency having jurisdiction over the lands.

California Coastal Act

The California Coastal Act, in part, authorizes the California Coastal Commission to review permit applications for development within the coastal zone and, where necessary, to require reasonable mitigation measures to offset effects of that development. Permits for development are issued with "special conditions" to ensure implementation of these mitigation measures.

Section 30244 of the Act, *"Archaeological or Paleontological Resources,"* states:

"Where development would adversely impact archaeological or paleontological resources as identified by the State Historic Preservation Officer, reasonable mitigation measures shall be required."

Local

Local jurisdictions can protect paleontological resources through the adoption of regulations that are codified at the local level. These regulations generally provide additional guidance on assessment and treatment measures for paleontological resources subject to CEQA.

Human Remains

For purposes of the CEQA Initial Study Checklist, human remains (which are usually associated with archaeological sites) are regulated by Health and Safety Code Section 7050.5 (c) which states:

"If the coroner determines that the remains are not subject to his or her authority and if the coroner recognizes the human remains to be those of a Native American, or has reason to believe that the are those of a Native American, he or she shall contact, by telephone within 24 hours, the Native American Heritage Commission."

V. CULTURAL RESOURCES

Would the project:

(a) Cause a substantial adverse change in the significance of a historical resource as defined in § 15064.5?

1. Determining the Scope of the Question

In order to determine the scope of the question, it is separated into the following parts:

Historical Resource

CEQA has several mechanisms for defining a historical resource:

- ✓ Resources that are listed in or eligible for listing in the California Register of Historical Resources are presumed to be archaeologically, historically, or culturally significant. [Ref. CEQA Guidelines Section 15064.5 (a) (1)].

- ✓ Resources that are listed in a local register or deemed significant in a historical resource survey as provided under Section 5020.1(k) are presumed to be significant unless the preponderance of evidence indicates they are not. [Ref. CEQA Guidelines Section 15064.5 (a) (2)].

- ✓ Resources that are not listed in the California Register but meet the criteria for listing [Ref. CEQA Guidelines Section 15064.5 (a) (3)].

The criteria are as follows:

A) Is associated with events that have made a significant contribution to the broad patterns of California's history and cultural heritage;

B) Is associated with the lives of persons important in our past;

C) Embodies the distinctive characteristics of a type, period, region, or method of construction, or represents the work of an important creative individual, or possesses high artistic values; or

D) Has yielded, or may be likely to yield, information important in prehistory or history.

✓ A resource does not need to have been identified previously either through listing or survey to be considered significant under CEQA. In addition to assessing whether historical resources potentially impacted by a proposed project are listed or have been identified in a survey process, lead agencies have a responsibility to evaluate them against the California Register criteria prior to making a finding as to a proposed project's impacts to historical resources [Ref. CEQA Guidelines Section 15064.5(3)].

The types of cultural resources eligible for nomination to the California Register, and thus considered historically or archaeologically significant by CEQA include: buildings, sites, structures, objects, and historic districts. When considering what constitutes a historical resource, be aware that it has a broad meaning and include such things as:

- ✓ A building or structure;

- ✓ A fence;

- ✓ A drainage canal;

- ✓ A railroad track;

- ✓ A wall;

- ✓ A tree;

- ✓ A parcel of land; or

- ✓ A setting.

The examples are not all inclusive but are intended to make the Initial Study Checklist preparer aware that many things can be considered a historical resource (including archaeological resources).

Substantial Adverse Change

According to CEQA Guidelines Section 15064.5 (b), a substantial adverse change is defined as follows:

> *(1) Substantial adverse change in the significance of an historical resource means physical demolition, destruction, relocation, or alteration of the resource or its immediate surroundings such that the significance of an historical resource would be materially impaired.*
>
> *(2) The significance of an historical resource is materially impaired when a project:*

(A) Demolishes or materially alters in an adverse manner those physical characteristics of an historical resource that convey its historical significance and that justify its inclusion in, or eligibility for, inclusion in the California Register of Historical Resources; or

(B) Demolishes or materially alters in an adverse manner those physical characteristics that account for its inclusion in a local register of historical resources pursuant to section 5020.1(k) of the Public Resources Code or its identification in an historical resources survey meeting the requirements of section 5024.1(g) of the Public Resources Code, unless the public agency reviewing the effects of the project establishes by a preponderance of evidence that the resource is not historically or culturally significant; or

(C) Demolishes or materially alters in an adverse manner those physical characteristics of a historical resource that convey its historical significance and that justify its eligibility for inclusion in the California Register of Historical Resources as determined by a lead agency for purposes of CEQA.

2. Where to Find the Factual Data to Answer the Question

- National Register of Historic Places

The National Park Service website has a listing of properties that are listed in the National Register of Historic Places. The website can be located at:

www.nationalregisterofhistoricplaces.com/or enter "national register of historic places listings" in an Internet search engine.

- California Register and General Records Search

  The California Historic Research Information System maintains the statewide Historical Resources Inventory database which provides current archaeological and historical resource information for the entire State of California.

  As a standard practice, a records search should be requested from the applicable Regional Information Center in the county in which the project is located.

  A Regional Information Center Roster can be located at:

  www.parks.ca.gov/pages/1068/files/ic%20roster.pdf or enter "california ic roster" in an Internet search engine and click on the "IC Roster" link.

- Local agency regulatory documents such as general plans, specific plans, and zoning ordinances.

- Documents, such as project EIRs, City or County surveys, cultural resources reports in the project vicinity etc.

- A Phase 1 Cultural Resources Assessment prepared by a qualified professional.

- A good resource to consult with respect to cultural resources is the *California State Law and Historic Preservation Statutes, Regulations & Administrative Policies Regarding the Preservation and Protection of Cultural and Historical Resources*. The document can be located at:

  www.parks.ca.gov/pages/1069/files/1 0%20comb.pdf or enter "california historic preservation statutes" in an Internet search engine.

- It is recommended that the California Environmental Resources Evaluation System website be consulted to see if there is any information related to this question. The website is located at:

  ceres.ca.gov or enter "ceres evaluation" in an Internet search engine.

3. Example Answers

The following answers the question comprehensively:

As part of the Phase I Cultural Resources Assessment for the project, the project area was surveyed to identify potentially significant cultural resources. Based on the survey, historical resources found that are considered to be significant are the ranch buildings and the renovated barns. Both of these historic resources are located in Planning Area 1, but are not within _the areas that will be developed by the project. Therefore, implementation of the project would not affect historical resources and no mitigation measures would be required._

This response is based on a survey that was done for historical resources as part of a Phase I Cultural Resources Assessment and discusses the project location with respect to the location of the historical resources on the site.

The following does not answer the question comprehensively:

There are no historical resources listed for the project site. The existing building was built in 1973 and does not meet the requisite criteria for consideration of listing under the National Register and is therefore not considered an historic resource. No impacts would result.

This response is very narrow in its scope. It does not state what list was referenced to make the determination that there are no historical resources within the project site nor does it address the range of resources that could be considered as historical resources other than buildings.

It also concludes that if the existing building does not meet the eligibility requirements for listing on the National Register it is not considered a historic resource, when in fact that is not the only criteria under CEQA used to determine historical significance. (See discussion on Pages 147-148).

4. Determining Significance

Following are some general factors to consider for determining significance:

- Are there any Thresholds of Significance that were formally adopted by the lead agency that are applicable to the project?

- Has the lead agency set a precedent in previously approved CEQA documents in responding to the question? If so, the Initial Study Checklist preparer should be aware of how other CEQA documents have responded to the question.

- If a project will cause a substantial adverse change in the significance of an historical resource such as physical demolition, destruction, relocation, or alteration of the resource or its immediate surroundings such that the significance of an historical resource would be materially impaired, then it will have a significant impact.

V. CULTURAL RESOURCES (cont.)

(b) Cause a substantial adverse change in the significance of an archaeological resource pursuant to § 15064.5?

1. Determining the Scope of the Question

In order to determine the scope of the question, it is separated into the following parts:

Archaeological Resource

CEQA Guidelines Section 21083.2 (g) states:

"unique archaeological resource" means an archaeological artifact, object, or site about which it can be clearly demonstrated that, without merely adding to the current body of knowledge, there is a high probability that it meets any of the following criteria:

(1) Contains information needed to answer important scientific research questions and that there is a demonstrable public interest in that information.

(2) Has a special and particular quality such as being the oldest of its type or the best available example of its type.

(3) Is directly associated with a scientifically recognized important prehistoric or historic event or person."

Archaeological resources are typically found in sites that previously contained villages, hunting, gathering and fishing areas, religious and ceremonial locations, trails and rock art sites. In addition, there are more modern archaeological sites such as gold mines and mills, lime kilns, iron and brass foundries, logging railroads, lumber mills, shipyards and airplane factories.

Public Resources Code Section 21083.2 (h) states:

"nonunique archaeological resource" means an archaeological artifact, object, or site which does not meet the criteria in subdivision (g). A nonunique archaeological resource need be given no further consideration, other than the simple recording of its existence by the lead agency if it so elects."

TIP: *A qualified professional should be consulted to determine the difference between unique and nonunique archaeological resources.*

Substantial Adverse Change

According to Public Resources Code Section 21083.2(b), if it can be demonstrated that a project will cause damage to a unique archaeological resource, the lead agency may require reasonable efforts to be made to permit any or all of these resources to be preserved in place or left in an undisturbed state.

Damage to an archaeological resource generally involves: excavation upon, removal, or destruction.

If these activities occur then impacts may be significant.

2. *Where to Find the Factual Data to Answer the Question*

- The California Historic Research Information System (CHRIS) maintains the statewide Historical Resources Inventory database which provides current archaeological and historical resource information for the entire state of California.

  As a standard practice, a records search should be requested from the applicable Regional Information Center in the county in which the project is located.

  A Regional Information Center Roster can be located at:

  www.parks.ca.gov/pages/1068/files/ic%20roster.pdf or enter "california ic roster" in an Internet search engine and click on the "IC Roster" link.

- If the records search indicates the potential for archaeological resources to be present, then a Cultural Resources Assessment should be prepared by a qualified professional. At this level of review, these are typically called "Phase 1 Cultural Resource Assessments."

  The specific contents of a Phase 1 Cultural Resource Assessment may vary depending on the circumstances. The qualified professional will recommend what is needed based on the circumstances of the property and its surroundings.

TIP: SB 18 (2004) requires cities and counties to contact, and consult with, California Native American tribes prior to amending or adopting a general plan or specific plan, or designating land as open space. Does the project involve any of these actions? If so, see the OPR website at:www.opr.ca.gov/.

- It is recommended that the California Environmental Resources Evaluation System website be consulted to see if there is any information related to this question. The website is located at:

  ceres.ca.gov or enter "ceres evaluation" in an Internet search engine.

3. Example Answers

The following answers the question comprehensively:

Example 1

As part of this Initial Study, a records search was requested from the Eastern Information Center at the University of California, Riverside. The record search found no record of archaeological resources on the project site or within a quarter-mile radius of the project site. In addition, the project site is covered in asphalt and is bordered on all sides by City streets. Because the entirety of the project has been built upon, and has been built upon _repeatedly, there little probability that archaeological resources will be encountered during project construction._

This response states that a records search was conducted to determine if previously recorded archaeological sites were located on the site and the immediate surrounding area. In addition, the response describes the site conditions which supports the conclusion that there is little probability that archaeological resources are present on the site.

Example 2

Archaeological resources were not observed within the project boundaries during the field survey. However, the subject property is located within CA-RIR-04/H, an extensive archaeological site possessing both prehistoric (i.e. Native American) and historic-era elements.

Several cultural resources studies have been conducted on land surrounding the subject property, but each excluded the subject property because the subject property was occupied and was not included in any development plan.

Each of the studies revealed significant surface and subsurface cultural deposits, including two cremations within 35 meters of the subject property. Based on the results of previous cultural resources studies, there is a high probability that a subsurface cultural deposit exists within the project boundaries.

In order to minimize impacts to unknown archaeological resources, the following mitigation measure is applied to the project:

CR-1. Monitoring by a qualified archaeologist shall be required during all earthmoving, grading, grubbing, trenching or other earth-disturbing activities on the project site. A City-approved Project Archaeologist must create a mitigation-monitoring plan prior to earthmoving in the project area. A pre-grade meeting associated with the details of that plan must occur between the monitoring archaeologist, the City representative, and the grading contractor before issuance of a grading permit.

The plan must discuss contingency plans associated with Native American tribal representation if any prehistoric artifacts are found during earthmoving. These may be considered sacred items by Native American tribes. The mitigation-monitoring plan document must contain a description of how and where artifacts will be curated if found during monitoring.

The response indicates that based on a field survey and previous records searches that the potential for archaeological resources is considered a high probability. Appropriate mitigation is also identified.

The following does not answer the question comprehensively:

The project site is located in an urbanized area. There are no known archaeological resources on the project site. No impacts would result from project activities.

This response provides no factual data to support how the conclusion that was reached.

4. Determining Significance

Following are some general factors to consider for determining significance.

- Are there any Thresholds of Significance that were formally adopted by the lead agency that are applicable to the project?

- Has the lead agency set a precedent in previously approved CEQA documents in responding to the question? If so, the Initial Study Checklist preparer should be aware of how other CEQA documents have responded to the question.

- Any actions that would not preserve unique archaeological resources in place or leave them in an undisturbed state would be considered to damage the resource and thus result in a significant adverse effect. Mitigation is required for such a situation.

V. CULTURAL RESOURCES (cont.)

(d) Directly or indirectly destroy a unique paleontological resource or site or unique geologic feature?

1. Determining the Scope of the Question

Paleontology primarily involves the study of animal and plant life in past geologic time. It is a natural science closely associated with geology and biology. Paleontological resources are fossilized remains of ancient environments, including fossilized bone, shell, and plant parts and impressions of plant, insect, or animal parts preserved in geologic rock formations where they were originally buried.

Paleontological resources are different than archaeological resources in that archaeological resources involve human artifacts (e.g. objects that have been made by humans) and human remains while paleontology typically involves fossilized remains of plants and animals.

Question V(d) uses the term "unique" in referring to a paleontological resource or site and a geologic feature. The determination of what is "unique" is best left to a qualified professional.

The key to this question is understanding under what conditions a paleontological resource may be present so that the proper analysis can be done. The potential for paleontological resources to be present is primarily based on the geologic conditions of an area. A formation or rock unit has paleontological sensitivity if it previously has produced, or has characteristics conducive to the preservation of paleontological resources.

Most cities and counties have maps identifying areas that may yield paleontological resources within their planning area.

2. Where to Find the Factual Data to Answer the Question

- One of the best sources of information can be found at the local level either in the general plan, general plan EIR, or local maps.

  A Geographic Information System maintained by a city or county may also identify the areas which have the potential to yield paleontological resources.

  If a city does not have information, check with the county. Many counties have a Geographic Information System that contains environmental information (including paleontological sensitivity maps) that covers the area within a city.

- The California Historic Research Information System maintains the statewide Historical Resources Inventory database which provides current archaeological and historical resource information for the entire state of California.

  As a standard practice, a records search should be requested from the applicable Regional Information Center in the county in which the project is located. Although the

California Historic Research Information System primarily consists of historic and archaeological resources, reports that have been submitted often times includes information of paleontological resources.

A Regional Information Center Roster can be located at:

www.parks.ca.gov/pages/1068/files/ic%20roster.pdf or enter "california ic roster" in an Internet search engine and click on the "IC Roster" link.

- It is recommended that the California Environmental Resources Evaluation System website be consulted to see if there is any information related to this question. The website is located at:

  ceres.ca.gov or enter "ceres evaluation" in an Internet search engine.

3. Example Answers

The following answers the question comprehensively:

The Natural History Museum of Los Angeles County maintains a database of vertebrate fossil finds throughout Southern California. The museum was contacted, and a search of their database was requested. According to their research, the very northern portion of the project area includes surficial deposits composed of older Quaternary Alluvium, while the majority of the project area has surficial deposits composed of younger Quaternary Alluvium. These younger Quaternary Alluvium deposits typically do not contain significant vertebrate fossils, at least in the uppermost layers, but they are likely underlain, possibly at relatively shallow depths, by deposits of older Quaternary Alluvium.

The museum has indicated that fossils have been recovered from these deposits of older Quaternary Alluvium relatively near the project site. As the project would require ground-disturbing activities, it is possible that older Quaternary deposits could be disturbed. Undiscovered paleontological resources may be impacted by required ground disturbing activities. Mitigation Measure CUL-1 requires that during earth disturbing activities be monitored by a qualified paleontologist.

This response indicates that an accepted paleontological resource database was consulted to determine if the project site was located in an area that had the potential to yield paleontological resources. It then goes on to describe the geologic conditions as they pertain to paleontological resources and concludes that there is a high probability to encounter resources during earth disturbing activities. Mitigation is then recommended.

The following does not answer the question comprehensively:

The project site does not contain any unique geologic features, therefore, the project is not anticipated to directly or indirectly destroy a unique paleontological resource or site or unique geologic feature.

This response does not provide the factual data (i.e. research or description of geologic conditions) necessary to support the conclusion.

4. Determining Significance

Following are some general factors to consider for determining significance:

- Are there any Thresholds of Significance that were formally adopted by the lead agency that are applicable to the project?

- Has the lead agency set a precedent in previously approved CEQA documents in responding to the question? If so, the Initial Study Checklist preparer should be aware of how other CEQA documents have responded to the question.

- Public Resources Code 5097.5 prohibits the excavation upon, removal, or destruction, of a vertebrate paleontological site, including fossilized footprints, situated on public lands, except with the express permission of the public agency having jurisdiction over the lands.

- Any project activities which would not preserve unique paleontological resources in place or leave in an undisturbed state may have a significant adverse effect.

V. CULTURAL RESOURCES (Cont.)

(e) Disturb any human remains, including those interred outside of formal cemeteries?

1. Determining the Scope of the Question

The question deals with the discovery of human remains primarily associated with archaeological sites. Disturbance of human remains inside a formal cemetery is addressed in other statutes and is not a CEQA issue per se.

If based on a records search from the applicable California Historic Research Information System Regional Information Center or a cultural resources assessment, it is determined that the site may have the potential for archaeological resources, then the potential for discovering human remains during earth disturbing activities is very possible

California State Health and Safety Code Section 7050.5 dictates that in the event of an accidental discovery or recognition of any human remains during ground-disturbing activities, no further disturbance shall occur until the County Coroner has made the necessary findings as to origin and disposition pursuant to CEQA regulations and Public Resources Code Section 5097.98 (a).

Thus, compliance with California State Health and Safety Code Section7050.5 is typically all that is required.

2. Where to Find the Factual Data to Answer the Question

- Because this issue is closely associated with archeological sites, the most pertinent source of information would be the records search from the California Historic Research Information System and any cultural resource assessment conducted for the project.

  The California Historic Research Information System maintains the statewide Historical Resources Inventory database which provides current archaeological and historical resource information for the entire state of California.

  As a standard practice, a records search should be requested from the applicable Regional Information Center in the county in which the project is located.

  A Regional Information Center Roster can be located at:

  www.parks.ca.gov/pages/1068/files/ic %20roster.pdf or enter "california ic roster" in an Internet search engine and click on the "IC Roster" link.

- It is recommended that the California Environmental Resources Evaluation System website be consulted to see if there is any information related to this question. The website is located at:

ceres.ca.gov or enter "ceres evaluation" in an Internet search engine.

3. Example Answers

The following answers the question comprehensively:

Previous cultural resources investigations revealed two cremations within 35 meters of the project area's southern boundary, another within 150 meters, and a fourth within 200 meters, all of which are in a generally linear alignment with the subject property. Based on the distance and patterning, there is a high probability that at least one cremation will be discovered during earthmoving activities.

In the event of an accidental discovery or recognition of any human remains, California State Health and Safety Code Section 7050.5 dictates that no further disturbances shall occur until the County Corner has made the necessary findings as to origin and disposition pursuant to CEQA regulations and Public Resources Code Section 5097.98. With adherence to State Health and Safety Code Section 7050.5 which stipulates the process to be followed when human remains are encountered, no mitigation measures are necessary.

This response explains that human remains may be encountered because of the proximity of cremations found within a known archaeological site. It then states the applicable provisions of law if human remains are encountered.

The following does not answer the question comprehensively:

The project is not located on or within the vicinity of a formal cemetery. As such, it is anticipated that the project will not disturb any human remains.

This response limits its analysis to human remains that may be found within a formal cemetery. The appropriate context for the question is for human remains that may be found outside of a formal cemetery (e.g. an archaeological site).

4. Determining Significance

Following are some general factors to consider for determining significance.

- Are there any Thresholds of Significance that were formally adopted by the lead agency that are applicable to the project?

- Has the lead agency set a precedent in previously approved CEQA documents in responding to the question? If so, the Initial Study Checklist preparer should be aware of how other CEQA documents have responded to the question.

- Because the disturbance of human remains is typically associated with archaeological sites, the determination of significance should conducted by a qualified professional consistent with the provisions of State Health and Safety Code Section 7050.5 which stipulates the process to be followed when human remains are encountered.

Chapter VI

Geology and Soils

Introduction

This chapter deals with a variety of issues related to geology and soils such as:

- ✓ Earthquakes and the secondary effects of earthquakes including strong seismic ground shaking, seismic related ground failure (e.g. liquefaction and landslides);

- ✓ Soil erosion and loss of topsoil;

- ✓ Geologic conditions not related to earthquakes that could result in landslides, lateral spreading, subsidence, and liquefaction;

- ✓ Expansive soils; and

- ✓ Soil suitability for septic systems or alternative waste water disposal systems.

VI. GEOLOGY and SOILS

Would the project:

(a) Expose people or structures to potential substantial adverse effects, including the risk of loss, injury, or death involving:

i) Rupture of a known earthquake fault, as delineated on the most recent Alquist-Priolo Earthquake Fault Zoning Map issued by the State Geologist for the area or based on other substantial evidence of a known fault? Refer to Division of Mines and Geology Special Publication 42.

ii) Strong seismic ground shaking?

iii) Seismic-related ground failure, including liquefaction?

iv) Landslides?

1. Determining the Scope of the Question

This question is divided into four (4) subparts. They all pertain to an earthquake but represent different events that can happen during an earthquake.

i) <u>Rupture of a Alquist-Priolo Earthquake Fault or Other Know Fault</u>

The Alquist-Priolo Earthquake Fault Zoning Act requires the preparation of maps that delineate Earthquake Fault Zones. A rupture of an earthquake fault is a break in the ground along an earthquake fault line during an earthquake. This rupture causes movement in masses of rock and resulting shock waves.

The question deals with the rupture of a known fault identified by the Alquist-Priolo Earthquake Fault Zoning Act and its potential impact on people or structures.

Whenever structures for human occupancy are proposed in the vicinity of a fault certain restrictions are applied including, but not limited to, building and structure setbacks from the fault and special requirements for building foundation construction.

Recommendations to mitigate impacts from fault rupture are required to be indentified in a geologic report and approved by the local agency and filed with the State Geologist.

ii) Strong Seismic Ground Shaking

Seismic ground shaking is caused by the movement in masses of rock and resulting shock waves from an earthquake. The intensity of the ground shaking is influenced by the proximity of the site to an earthquake fault, the intensity of the earthquake, and the underlying soil composition. Seismic ground shaking is calculated considering earthquake magnitudes and rates.

iii) Seismic-related Ground Failure, Including Liquefaction

The term "ground failure" is a general reference to landslides, liquefaction, lateral spreads, and any other consequence of shaking that affects the stability of the ground.

Liquefaction occurs when loosely packed, water-logged sediments at or near the ground surface lose their strength in response to strong ground shaking. Liquefaction occurring beneath buildings and other structures can cause major damage during earthquakes.

iv) Landslides

A landslide is a movement of earth materials down a slope. The proximity of a project site to slope areas that have sufficient height, slope ratio, and underlying geologic conditions that can result in landslides is the key factor in determining risk.

2. Where to Find the Factual Data to Answer the Question

- Alquist-Priolo Earthquake Fault Zones

  The question makes reference to Division of Mines and Geology Special Publication 42 which is titled: *Fault-Rupture Hazard Zones in California, Alquist-Priolo Earthquake Fault Zoning Act with Index to Earthquake Fault Zone Maps.*

  The most recent publication is the Interim 2007 edition. It is available from the California Department of Conservation website located at:

  ftp://ftp.consrv.ca.gov/pub/dmg/pubs /sp/Sp42.pdf or enter "dmg special publication 42" in an Internet search engine.

Alquist-Priolo Earthquake Fault Zone Maps and related information are available from the California Department of Conservation website located at:

www.consrv.ca.gov/cgs/rghm/ap/Page s/index.aspx or enter "alquist-priolo fault maps" in an Internet search engine.

- Strong Seismic Ground Shaking

  Probabilistic Seismic Hazard Maps can be found on the California Department of Conservation website located at:

  www.conservation.ca.gov/cgs/rghm/ps ha/Pages/index.aspx or enter "seismic hazard shaking maps of california" in an Internet search engine.

  Author's Note: *These maps are not intended for site-specific hazard analysis, but only provide a regional perspective of earthquake hazard in California.*

  Overall information on seismic shaking hazards can be found under the California Department of Conservation Seismic Hazard Zonation Program Data Access Page located at:

  http://gmw.consrv.ca.gov/shmp/MapP rocessor.asp?Action=SHMP&Location=A ll&Version=8&Browser=IE&Platform=W in or enter "seismic hazard zonation program data access page" in an Internet search engine.

- Seismic-related Ground Failure, Including Liquefaction

    The California Department of Conservation website has maps that are intended to assist cities and counties in fulfilling their responsibilities for protecting the public from ground failure caused by earthquakes.

    Maps showing liquefaction and landslide hazard areas for Northern California can be found at:

    http://gmw.consrv.ca.gov/shmp/html/ pdf_maps_no.html or enter "seismic hazards zonation program" in an Internet search engine and click on the "Quickview/Download PDF Maps" link.

    Maps showing liquefaction and landslide hazard areas for Southern California can be found at:

    http://gmw.consrv.ca.gov/shmp/html/ pdf_maps_so.html or enter "seismic hazards zonation program" in an Internet search engine and click on the "Quickview/Download PDF Maps" link.

- Landslides

    The California Department of Conservation has a program called the Seismic Hazard Zonation Program. The program prepares maps that identify existing landslides and designates landslide zones of require preparation of site-specific studies and reports that recommend measures to mitigate impacts from landslides. Information on the program can be found at the California Department of Conservation website located at:

www.conservation.ca.gov/cgs/shzp/Pages/Index.aspx or enter "seismic hazard zonation program" in an Internet search engine.

However informative the above information is, please note that *California Geological Survey Special Publication 117* states:

"The fact that a site lies outside a zone of required investigation does not necessarily mean that the site is free from seismic or other geologic hazards, regardless of the information shown on the Seismic Hazard Zone Maps.

The zones do not always include landslide or lateral spread run-out areas. Project sites that are outside of any zone may be affected by ground failure runout from adjacent or nearby sites. Finally, neither the information on the Seismic Hazard Zone Maps, nor in any technical reports that describe how the maps were prepared nor what data were used is sufficient to serve as a substitute for the required site-investigation reports called for in the Act."

Special Publication 117 can be found at:

www.conservation.ca.gov/smgb/Guidel ines/Documents/SP117-091508.pdf or enter "California Geological Survey Special Publication 117" in an Internet search engine.

- An excellent source of information for all of the above topics is the California Department of Conservation website located at:

   www.conservation.ca.gov/ and click on the "Geology" link and then click on the "California Geological Survey" link.

TIP: A geologic report is the best source of information, particularly if it is formatted to address CEQA issues. Appendix C contains a sample format for a geologic report that will answer the questions posed by this section.

- It is recommended that the California Environmental Resources Evaluation System website be consulted to see if there is any information related to this question. The website is located at:

   Ceres.ca.gov or enter "ceres evaluation" in an Internet search engine.

3. Example Answers

The following example answers the question comprehensively:

i) Alquist-Priolo Zone: Based on the "Fault Rupture Hazard Zones in California, Special Publication 42, Interim Revision 2007", published by the State of California Conservation Department and the geologic report prepared for the project, the site is not located within an identified Alquist-Priolo Earthquake Hazard Zone. Therefore, impacts are considered less than significant. No mitigation measures are required.

ii) Seismic Ground Shaking: Seismic ground shaking is influenced by the proximity of the site to an earthquake fault, the intensity of the seismic event, and the underlying soil composition. The geologic report prepared for the project indicates that the estimated peak horizontal ground acceleration at the site location has a 2-in-100 probability of exceedance in 50 years of 3.2g which is considered a lower hazard level.

Given that the site is not located on an earthquake fault and the general soil composition in the area, the risk from ground shaking is less than significant. No mitigation measures are required.

iii) Seismic Ground Failure (Liquefaction): According to the geologic report prepared for the project, the soil conditions at the site are not considered to be susceptible to liquefaction. Impacts from liquefaction are less than significant. No mitigation measures are required.

iv) Landslide: According to the geologic report prepared for the project and the California Geological Survey Seismic Hazard Zonation Program, the site is not located within a designated area where previous occurrence of landslide _movement, or local topographic, geological, geotechnical and subsurface water conditions indicate a potential for landslides. Impacts from landslides are less than significant._

In addition, the site is relatively flat and is not in the vicinity of slopes that would be susceptible to landslides (e.g. slope areas that have sufficient height, slope ratio, and underlying geologic conditions that can result in landslides).No mitigation measures are required.

The response addresses all the issues associated with a fault rupture. It also relies on factual data from a project specific geologic report as well as information from the California Geological Survey.

The following example does not answer the question comprehensively:

The site is not located within a designated Special Studies Seismic Hazard Zone and is relatively level, with minor grade differences throughout the site for drainage purposes.

This response provides little factual data to support the conclusion and does not specifically address the issues of seismic ground shaking and liquefaction.

4. Determining Significance

Following are some general factors to consider in determining significance:

- Are there any Thresholds of Significance that were formally adopted by the lead agency that are applicable to the project?

- Has the lead agency set a precedent in previously approved CEQA documents in responding to the question? If so, the Initial Study Checklist preparer should be aware of how other CEQA documents have responded to the question.

- The significance of impacts pertaining to an Alquist-Priolo Earthquake Fault Zone is directly related to whether or not a site is located within a known earthquake fault zone. If a site is located within an earthquake fault zone that impacts are potentially significant and certain regulatory measures will apply based on the proposed land use. Some typical examples of regulatory measures are building and structure setbacks from the earthquake fault zone and the construction of special building foundations.

- The impacts pertaining to Strong Seismic Ground Shaking and Seismic Related Ground Failure are directly related the sites proximity to an earthquake fault, the intensity of the earthquake, and the underlying soil composition.

- The determination for significance is typically dependent upon technical data found in a geologic report prepared by a qualified professional. In some cases, the maps provided by the California Department of Conservation, or maps contained in the local agency's General Plan or other planning documents can be used.

- The impacts pertaining to landslides are directly related to the project site's proximity to slopes that are capable of producing landslides.

VI. GEOLOGY and SOILS (cont.)

(b) Result in substantial soil erosion or the loss of topsoil?

1. *Understanding the Context of the Question*

In order to determine the scope of the question, it is separated into the following parts:

Soil Erosion

Although soil erosion is a naturally occurring process on land, it can be exacerbated as the result of a project's activities. The following are some common examples of project activities that can result in soil erosion:

- ✓ Altering the natural land form by clearing, grubbing, grading, or removing vegetation (e.g. tree roots help in holding the soil together, and therefore depletion of vegetation cover is bound to make soil vulnerable to erosion by running water).

  These activities leave the soil in a condition that makes it susceptible to erosion by water (e.g. heavy rainfall) or wind.

- ✓ Creating impervious surfaces that cause increased surface runoff which in turn can result in downstream soil erosion.

Soil erosion may be a slow process that continues over extended periods of time or it may occur at faster rates (i.e. during heavy rains or winds).

Some of the impacts to the environment caused by soil erosion include:

- ✓ Soil quality, structure, stability and texture can be affected by the loss of soil. The breakdown of aggregates and the removal of smaller particles or entire layers of soil or organic matter can weaken the structure and even change the texture. Textural changes can in turn affect the water-holding capacity of the soil, making it more susceptible to an extreme condition such as drought.

- ✓ Sediment which reaches streams or watercourses can accelerate bank erosion, clog drainage ditches and stream channels, deposit silt in reservoirs, cover fish spawning grounds and reduce downstream water quality.

- ✓ Pesticides and fertilizers, frequently transported along with the eroding soil can contaminate or pollute downstream water sources.

Loss of Topsoil

The loss of topsoil is mostly associated with negative impacts on agricultural production. Issues pertaining to agricultural production are addressed in Chapter II, *Agricultural and Forestry Resources*.

In the context of this question, the loss of topsoil is associated with soil erosion. The damage from topsoil loss results in a breakdown in general growth capacity, a loss of nutrients and less water retention. Enough topsoil damage can create completely barren soil incapable of supporting vegetation. Without vegetation the loss of more top soil and underlying soils goes on unabated. The soil itself ends up as silt that plugs storm drains and natural drainage systems, leading to flooding, loss of wildlife habitat and poor water quality. Loss of vegetation also impacts air purification and contributes to climate change.

2. Where to Find the Factual Data to Answer the Question

The data to answer this question should be available from the following sources:

- Project plans;

- Grading plans; and

- Stormwater Pollution Prevention Plan (if one is required) per the National Pollution Discharge Elimination System.

  The Stormwater Pollution Prevention Plan will include information on site conditions such as soils, slopes, vegetation, current drainage patterns, and the amount of impervious surfaces. It will identify measures to control erosion and sediment control through Best Management Practices. Not all projects require the preparation of a Stormwater Pollution Prevention Plan. In this case, the project plans, grading plans (if any), and field investigation should provide the information needed to address the question.

- It is recommended that the California Environmental Resources Evaluation System website be consulted to see if there is any information related to this question. The website is located at:

  ceres.ca.gov or enter "ceres evaluation" in an Internet search engine.

3. Example Answers

The following example answers the question comprehensively:

The site is currently vacant with vegetation consisting primarily of scattered eucalyptus trees and ruderal plant species. Development of the site will remove the existing vegetation. In the short term, construction activity associated with project development may result in wind and water driven soil erosion and loss of topsoil due to grading activities if soil is stockpiled or exposed.

The applicant will be required to adhere to conditions under the National Pollutant Discharge Elimination System Permit issued by the Regional Water Quality Control Board and prepare and submit a Storm Water Pollution Prevention Plan to be administered throughout project construction.

The Storm Water Pollution Prevention Plan will incorporate Best Management Practices to ensure that potential water quality impacts during construction from soil erosion would be reduced to less than significant levels.

In the long-term, previously undisturbed soil will be replaced with structures, pavement and new landscaping as part of the project. These improvements will not contribute to the conditions that result in on-site soil erosion.

Based on the hydrology report prepared for the project, off-site runoff will not contribute to factors that will impact soil erosion and loss of topsoil to other properties. Therefore, impacts would be less than significant. No mitigation measures are required.

This response describes the existing site conditions and how the development of the site would contribute to soil erosion and the loss of topsoil during the construction phase. It also explains how soil erosion and the loss of topsoil would not be significant because of implementation of a Storm Water Pollution Prevention Plan.

It also explains that under the post development conditions off-site runoff will not contribute to factors that will cause soil erosion and loss of topsoil to other properties.

The following example does not answer the question comprehensively:

Development will require minimal grading which will remove topsoil. Said grading shall occur in accordance with City standards. The City will require the Applicant to submit for review and approval grading and improvement plans. This process will ensure that any grading and/or construction activities are done in accordance with the applicable standards and regulations. Therefore, project impacts are less than significant.

This response does not focus enough detail on the factors that contribute to soil erosion and loss of topsoil.

4. Determining Significance

Following are some general factors to consider for determining significance:

- Are there any Thresholds of Significance that were formally adopted by the lead agency that are applicable to the project?

- Has the lead agency set a precedent in previously approved CEQA documents in responding to the question? If so, the Initial Study Checklist preparer should be aware of how other CEQA documents have responded to the question.

- Would soil erosion result in such things as depositing sediment which reaches streams or watercourses that accelerates stream bank erosion; clog drainage facilities; or contain pesticides and fertilizers that could contaminate or pollute downstream water sources? If so, the impacts may be significant.

- Would increased runoff from development of a site cause soil erosion or loss of topsoil on other sites? If so, the impacts may be significant.

- Would the loss of topsoil on a site result in the inability to support vegetation? If so, the impacts may be significant.

- During construction would the removal and grading of topsoil lead to potential erosion of the project site soils because disturbed soil would not have as much connectivity to the ground as undisturbed soil? If so, the impacts may be significant.

VI. GEOLOGY and SOILS (cont.)

(c) Be located on a geologic unit or soil that is unstable, or that would become unstable as a result of the project, and potentially result in on or off-site landslide, lateral spreading, subsidence, liquefaction or collapse?

1. Determining the Scope of the Question

This question is somewhat different than Question VI (a) on Page 172 although it deals with similar issues like landslides and liquefaction.

The landslide and liquefaction impacts that are discussed in Question VI (a) are related to earthquakes. In Question VI(c) they are related to the existing conditions of the underlying geological unit (i.e. a kind of rock such as sandstone, bedrock, shale etc.) and whether the geologic unit is unstable or will become unstable as a result of the development of the project site.

Many Initial Study Checklists combine Question VI (a) and Question VI(c) into one answer. However, if that is done, be sure to address all of the issues posed by Question VI (a) and Question Vi(c) in the context of both earthquakes **and** unstable geologic units.

In order to determine the scope of the question, it is separated into the following parts:

Landslide

A landslide is a movement of earth materials down a slope. Landslides that are not caused by an earthquake are typically caused by weak soil materials, weathered soil materials, excavation of a slope or the toe of the slope which compromises its structural integrity, and loss of vegetation that was stabilizing a slope.

Lateral Spreading

Lateral spreading is a term referring to landslides that commonly form on gentle slopes and that have rapid fluid-like flow horizontal movement. Most lateral spreading is caused by earthquakes but it is also caused by landslides.

Subsidence

Subsidence is the downward movement of the ground caused by the underlying soil conditions. Certain soils, such as clay soils are particularly vulnerable since they shrink and swell depending on their moisture content. Subsidence is an issue if buildings or structures sink which causes damage to the building or structure. Subsidence is usually remedied by excavating the soil the depth of the underlying bedrock and then recompacting the soil so that it is able to support buildings and structures.

Liquefaction or Collapse

Liquefaction, in the context of this question, occurs in saturated soils in which the space between individual particles is completely filled with water. This water exerts a pressure on the soil particles that influences how tightly the particles themselves are pressed together. The soils lose their strength beneath buildings and other structures.

Although liquefaction primarily occurs as a result of an earthquake, there are other factors that can cause liquefaction such as the static loading (i.e. a nonvarying load weight) applied by new buildings on a slope that exert additional forces on the soil beneath the foundations, blasting, and pile driving.

2. Where to Find the Factual Data to Answer the Question

- Liquefaction

  The California Department of Conservation website has maps that identify liquefaction and landslide hazard areas. For Northern California these maps can be found at:

  http://gmw.consrv.ca.gov/shmp/html/ pdf_maps_no.html or enter "seismic hazards zonation program" in an Internet search engine and click on the "Quickview/Download PDF Maps" link.

  Maps showing liquefaction and landslide hazard areas for Southern California can be found at:

  http://gmw.consrv.ca.gov/shmp/html/ pdf_maps_so.html or enter "seismic hazards zonation program" in an Internet search engine and click on the "Quickview/Download PDF Maps" link.

- Landslides

  The California Department of Conservation has a program called the Seismic Hazard

Zonation Program. The program prepares maps that identify existing landslides and designates landslide zones that require preparation of site-specific studies and reports that recommend measures to mitigate impacts from landslides. Information on the program can be found at the California Department of Conservation website located at:

www.conservation.ca.gov/cgs/shzp/Pages/Index.aspx or enter "seismic hazard zonation program" in an Internet search engine.

However informative the above information is, please note that *California Geological Survey Special Publication 117* states:

"The fact that a site lies outside a zone of required investigation does not necessarily mean that the site is free from seismic or other geologic hazards, regardless of the information shown on the Seismic Hazard Zone Maps.

The zones do not always include landslide or lateral spread run-out areas. Project sites that are outside of any zone may be affected by ground failure runout from adjacent or nearby sites. Finally, neither the information on the Seismic Hazard Zone Maps, nor in any technical reports that describe how the maps were prepared nor what data were used is sufficient to serve as a substitute for the required site-investigation reports called for in the Act."

Special Publication 117 can be found at:

www.conservation.ca.gov/smgb/Guidel ines/Documents/SP117-091508.pdf or enter *"California Geological Survey Special Publication 117"* in an Internet search engine.

- Lateral Spreading

  Because lateral spreading is associated with landslides, please refer to the information under Landslides above.

- An excellent source of information for all of the above topics is the California Department of Conservation website located at:

  www.conservation.ca.gov/ and click on the "Geology" link and then click on the "California Geological Survey" link.

- It is recommended that the California Environmental Resources Evaluation System website be consulted to see if there is any information related to this question. The website is located at:

  ceres.ca.gov or enter "ceres evaluation" in an Internet search engine.

3. Example Answers

The following example answers the question comprehensively:

The following analysis is based on the geologic report prepared for the project and hazard maps contained in the City's General Plan:

Liquefaction or Collapse: The soil conditions at the site are not considered to be susceptible to liquefaction. Impacts from liquefaction are less than significant. No mitigation measures are required.

Landslide: The site is not located within a designated area where previous occurrence of landslide movement, or local topographic, geological, geotechnical and subsurface water conditions indicate a potential for landslides.

In addition, the site is relatively flat and is not in the vicinity of slopes that would be susceptible to landslides (e.g. slope areas that have sufficient height, slope ratio, and underlying geologic conditions that can result in landslides). Impacts from landslides are less than significant. No mitigation measures are required.

Lateral Spreading: As discussed in the response to landslides (see above) the site is not located in an identified landslide hazard area, is relatively flat, and is not in the vicinity of slopes that would be susceptible to landslides (e.g. slope areas that have sufficient height, slope ratio, and underlying geologic conditions that can result in landslides). Impacts from lateral spreading are less than significant. No mitigation measures are required.

Subsidence: The soil conditions at the site are not considered to be susceptible to subsidence.

Impacts from subsidence are less than significant. No mitigation measures are required.

This response discusses the existing geological conditions of the site and whether site is unstable or will become unstable as a result of the development of the project.

The following example does not answer the question comprehensively:

Development of the site will result in some grading and soil compaction in order to obtain proper drainage. However, the site is not located within a designated Special Studies Seismic Hazard Zone or high liquefaction area and is relatively level.

As a standard City procedure, the project will require the preparation of precise grading plans, which will be reviewed and approved by the City Engineer before grading can commence. Furthermore, all new construction requires a Geotechnical Report and compliance with the Uniform Building Code's provisions relating to current seismic risk factors and their mitigation. A Geotechnical Report will be prepared for the site prior to grading plan check submittal.

This response is answered primarily in the context of earthquake caused landslides and liquefaction as it makes reference to a "Special Studies Seismic Hazard Zone." However, the appropriate context for this question should be with respect to the overall geological conditions of the site and not just earthquake induced events.

In addition, reference is made to a future geotechnical report that will be submitted prior to grading. A preliminary geotechnical report should be prepared as part of the technical studies required to prepare the Initial Study Checklist analysis and not after the fact.

4. Determining Significance

Following are some general factors to consider for determining significance:

- Are there any Thresholds of Significance that were formally adopted by the lead agency that are applicable to the project?

- Has the lead agency set a precedent in previously approved CEQA documents in responding to the question? If so, the Initial Study Checklist preparer should be aware of how other CEQA documents have responded to the question.

- The impacts pertaining to landslides and lateral spreading as a result of landsides are directly related to the presence or absence of slopes of sufficient height, mass, and ratio and their underlying soil composition. The sites proximity to such slopes is a key factor in determining risk.

- Impacts from liquefaction, collapse, and subsidence are based on a project's location relative to the soil and geologic conditions that underlay the site.

Areas susceptible to liquefaction, collapse, and subsidence are often times shown on maps or identified in a geological report.

If a map or geologic report indicates the site is susceptible to liquefaction, collapse, or subsidence, impacts may be significant and mitigation may be required.

VI. GEOLOGY and SOILS (cont.)

(d) Be located on expansive soil, as defined in Table 18-1-B of the Uniform Building Code (1994), creating substantial risks to life or property?

1. Determining the Scope of the Question

Expansive soils are soils that swell and contract depending on the amount of water that is present. This question makes specific reference to Table 18-1-B of the Uniform Building Code (1994) to define expansive soils.

The 2007 edition of the Uniform Building Code is the latest edition of the Uniform Building Code and it no longer contains Table 18-1-B.

Table 18-1-B has been superseded by Chapter 18A of the 2007 California Building Code which states in part:

"...in areas likely to have expansive soils, the building official shall require soil tests to determine where such soils do exist."

In practice, project developers routinely have soils tests prepared early in the development process. These soils tests can be used to determine if expansive soils are present.

2. Where to Find the Factual Data to Answer the Question

- A project specific geological report is always the best source of information.

- Geologic maps prepared for a general plan are also a good source of information.

- A Geographic Information System for the local agency at the city or county level may identify areas where expansive soils are present.

- The Natural Resources Conservation Agency has prepared manuscripts and soils maps for California counties that are available online at:

  http://soils.usda.gov/survey/Online_S urveys/California/ or enter "california online soil survey manuscripts" in an Internet search engine.

  Another source of maps provided by the Natural Resources Conservation Agency show soil classification. The Initial Study Checklist preparer will have to know what types of soils are considered to have expansive characteristics. (These are generally clay soils).

  The maps can be found at:

  http://websoilsurvey.ncrs.usda.gov/ap p/ or enter "nrca web soil survey" in an Internet search engine.

- It is recommended that the California Environmental Resources Evaluation System website be consulted to see if there is any information related to this question. The website is located at:

ceres.ca.gov or enter "ceres evaluation" in an Internet search engine.

3. Example Answers

The following example answers the question comprehensively:

The Preliminary Soil Investigation Report prepared for the project indicated that soils encountered at the site were generally dense, alternating layers of sands and silty sands with varying amounts of fine to coarse gravel.

The report indicated that expansive soils were not encountered so there is no evidence that expansive soils exist on the property. Therefore, no known or anticipated impacts will occur as result of implementation of the project.

This response is based on a preliminary soil investigation which is adequate to determine the presence or absence of expansive soils on the site.

The following example does not answer the question comprehensively:

The project will comply with Chapter 18 of the 2007 California Building Code so potential impacts from expansive soils will be minimal. Therefore, impacts will have a less than significant impact.

Chapter 18 of the 2007 California Building Code states in part: "*...in areas likely to have expansive soils, the building official shall require soil tests to determine where such soils do exist.*"

The response does not take address whether or not the site area is likely to have expansive soils as required by Chapter 18 the California Building Code. It merely states that it will comply with the California Building Code.

However, in order to comply, a soil test may be required and the results of the soil test should be discussed in the Initial Study Checklist and not after the fact.

4. Determining Significance

Following are some general factors to consider for determining significance:

- Are there any Thresholds of Significance that were formally adopted by the lead agency that are applicable to the project?

- Has the lead agency set a precedent in previously approved CEQA documents in responding to the question? If so, the Initial Study Checklist preparer should be aware of how other CEQA documents have responded to the question.

- What types of soils are on the project site based on local agency soils maps, geographic information system databases, maps prepared by the Natural Resources Conservation Agency or soils reports prepared for the project?

   Are these soils the type that has expansive characteristics (e.g. clay)? If so, impacts may be significant and mitigation may be required.

VI. GEOLOGY and SOILS (Cont.)

(e) Have soils incapable of adequately supporting the use of septic tanks or alternative waste water disposal systems where sewers are not available for the disposal of waste water?

1. Determining the Scope of the Question

A septic tank system and most alternative waste water disposal system need soils capable of supporting the system (i.e. permeable soils). A Percolation Test (i.e. a method of testing water absorption of the soil) is used to establish soil suitability for a septic system or an alternative wastewater disposal system design.

A typical septic system has four main components:

✓ A pipe from the building structure;

✓ A septic tank;

✓ A leach field; and

✓ The soil.

Microbes in the soil digest or remove most contaminants from wastewater before it eventually reaches groundwater. For effective wastewater treatment, prospective soils should be relatively permeable and should remain unsaturated to several feet below the septic system depth. In addition, the soil absorption system should be set well above water tables and bedrock.

Alternative systems (e.g. recirculating sand filters, peat-based systems, package aeration units) can be installed in areas where soils, bedrock, fluctuating ground water levels, or lot sizes limit the use of a conventional septic tank system. Alternative technologies typically are applied to the treatment train beyond the septic tank

2. Where to Find the Factual Data to Answer the Question

- AB 885, a law passed in 2000, requires the State Water Board to develop statewide regulations for septic systems. AB 885 can be found in the Water Code, Section 13290-13291.7.

  A local agency in practice may implement AB 885, or a portion thereof, as authorized by the State Water Resources Control Board or by a Regional Water Board through agreement, adopted resolution, or Memorandum of Understanding.

  Any Memorandum of Understanding, adopted resolution, or similar agreement must require compliance with the statewide regulations and the applicable Regional Water Board basin plan. Local agencies, (mostly counties) are required to develop plans to manage septic systems, especially in urbanizing areas.

  Contact the local agency (most likely the county health department) for septic tank system requirements.

- It is recommended that the California Environmental Resources Evaluation System website be consulted to see if there is any information related to this question. The website is located at:

  ceres.ca.gov or enter "ceres evaluation" in an Internet search engine.

3. Example Answers

The following example answers the question comprehensively:

The project proposes to use an on-site septic system to dispose of wastewater. A percolation testing report was prepared by DeSante Disposal Systems and approved by the County Health Department. The report concluded that soil conditions were particularly favorable to support the use of the system. Therefore, there are no impacts.

This response indicates that the capability of soils to support a septic system is adequate based on a percolation test approved by the County Health Department.

The following example does not answer the question comprehensively:

Septic systems would be required for the project. All septic systems must comply with the requirements of the County Health Department. Compliance with County standards will ensure impacts are less than significant.

This response does not answer the question directly. Although it states that the septic systems will have to meet county requirements, it does not discuss the suitability of the existing soils to support the septic tank system. This information should be known in advance of approving the project.

4. Determining Significance

Following are some general factors to consider for determining significance:

- Are there any Thresholds of Significance that were formally adopted by the lead agency that are applicable to the project?

- Has the lead agency set a precedent in previously approved CEQA documents in responding to the question? If so, the Initial Study Checklist preparer should be aware of how other CEQA documents have responded to the question.

- An impact may be significant if the underlying soils are not capable to adequately filter wastewater after it discharges from the septic tank or alternative wastewater disposal system. This could potentially violate a water quality standard or otherwise substantially degrade water quality in the area.

Chapter VII

Greenhouse Gas Emissions

Introduction

The Natural Resources Agency adopted amendments to the CEQA Guidelines on December 30, 2009 in order to implement the requirements of Senate Bill 97 pertaining to the effects of greenhouse gas emissions.

Two questions were added to Appendix G under a new heading called "Greenhouse Gas Emissions." The first question deals with the generation of greenhouse gas emissions and the second question deals with potential conflicts with plans, policies, or regulations whose purpose is to reduce greenhouse gas emissions.

How to evaluate greenhouse gas emissions in CEQA documents is continuing to evolve as ongoing methods to identify and reduce these emissions come forward. Greenhouse gas emission policy and analytical methods will continue to evolve rapidly, so the Initial Study Checklist preparer should be alert for any new information that becomes available.

In order to understand the questions posed in this Chapter, it is useful to understand the current regulatory framework for greenhouse gas emissions in California.

Assembly Bill 32 – The Global Warming Solutions Act

Assembly Bill 32 requires the California Air Resources Board to establish regulations designed to reduce California's greenhouse gas emissions to 1990 levels by 2020.

On December 11, 2008, the California Air Resources Board adopted its Scoping Plan, setting forth a framework for future regulatory action on how California will achieve this goal.

The California Air Resources Board must adopt rules and regulations to implement the greenhouse gas emissions reductions envisioned in the Scoping Plan by January 1, 2012.

Senate Bill 375-(Steinberg)

Senate Bill 375 requires the California Air Resources Board to develop greenhouse gas emission reduction targets for the automobile and light truck sector for each metropolitan planning organization.

A metropolitan planning organization is a federally-mandated and federally-funded transportation policy-making organization that is made up of representatives from local government and governmental transportation authorities.

Some examples of metropolitan planning organizations in California include; Association of Bay Area Governments, Sacramento Area Council of Governments, Southern California Association of

Governments, and the San Diego Association of Governments just to name a few.

Once that target is set, each metropolitan planning organization must develop a sustainable communities strategy as part of its regional transportation plan that will set forth a development pattern that will achieve the reduction target approved by the California Air Resources Board.

The metropolitan planning organization's transportation planning activities must be consistent with the adopted sustainable communities strategy. A sustainable communities strategy does not supersede a local agency's land use authority.

Senate Bill 97-(Dutton)

Senate Bill 97 provides greater certainty to lead agencies in evaluating impacts from greenhouse gas emissions for a review of a project under CEQA. Pursuant to Senate Bill 97, the Office of Planning and Research adopted amendments to the State CEQA Guidelines to address analysis and mitigation of the potential effects of greenhouse gas emissions in CEQA documents. These amendments became effective on March 18, 2010.

VII. GREENHOUSE GAS EMISSIONS

Would the project:

(a) Generate greenhouse gas emissions, either directly or indirectly, that may have a significant impact on the environment?

1. Determining the Scope of the Question

According to the amended CEQA Guidelines Section 15364.5 greenhouse gas: "... *includes but is not limited to: carbon dioxide, methane, nitrous oxide, hydrofluorocarbons, perfluorocarbons and sulfur hexafluoride.*"

These gases are described below based on information from the Environmental Protection Agency:

Carbon Dioxide (CO_2): Carbon dioxide enters the atmosphere through the burning of fossil fuels (oil, natural gas, and coal), solid waste, trees and wood products, and also as a result of other chemical reactions (e.g., manufacturing of cement). Carbon dioxide is also removed from the atmosphere (or "sequestered") when it is absorbed by plants as part of the biological carbon cycle.

Methane (CH_4): Methane is emitted during the production and transport of coal, natural gas, and oil. Methane emissions also result from livestock and other agricultural practices and by the decay of organic waste in municipal solid waste landfills.

Nitrous Oxide (N_2O): Nitrous oxide is emitted during agricultural and industrial activities, as well as during combustion of fossil fuels and solid waste.

Hydrofluorocarbons, Perflurorcarbons and Sulfur Hexafluoride: These are referred to as "Fluorinated Gases: Hydrofluorocarbons, perfluorocarbons, and sulfur hexafluoride are synthetic, powerful greenhouse gases that are emitted from a variety of industrial processes.

These gases are typically emitted in smaller quantities, but because they are potent greenhouse gases, they are sometimes referred to as High Global Warming Potential gases.

***

Evaluating greenhouse gas emissions can be a complicated task that requires the expertise of persons well versed in the subject, especially for larger projects than contain a variety of land uses.

The Governor's Office of Planning and Research published a Technical Advisory titled: *CEQA AND CLIMATE CHANGE: Addressing Climate Change Through California Environmental Quality Act (CEQA) Review.*

The Technical Advisory recommends the following approach for a CEQA analysis:

- ***Identify Greenhouse Gas Emissions:*** Lead agencies should make a good-faith effort, based on available information, to calculate, model, or estimate the amount of CO_2 and other greenhouse gas emissions from a project

The amended CEQA Guidelines added Section 15064.4(a) to provide further guidance for identifying greenhouse gas emissions. In part, Section 15064.4(a) states:

"A lead agency shall have discretion to determine, in the context of a particular project, whether to:

(1) Use a model or methodology to quantify greenhouse gas emissions resulting from a project, and which model or methodology to use. The lead agency has discretion to select the model or methodology it considers most appropriate provided it supports its decision with substantial evidence. The lead agency should explain the limitations of the particular model or methodology selected for use; and/or

(2) Rely on a qualitative analysis or performance based standards."

As noted on Pages 215 and 216, there are several types of greenhouse gases that can be emitted by a project. CO_2 is the most common form of greenhouse gas emissions from a land development project. Although the other greenhouse gases have a higher global warming potential they are typically emitted in fewer quantities than CO_2.

Greenhouse gas emissions are emitted both directly and indirectly from a project. Direct emissions can be from construction and operation of a project. Indirect emissions can be from off-site waste disposal, wastewater treatment, and the energy needed to provide electricity to a project.

Therefore, the complexity of a greenhouse gas emission analysis increases with the size and scope of the project. Most often one or more computer modeling programs are needed to conduct a greenhouse gas emissions analysis for larger projects.

Update: *Subsequent to the publication of this book in July 2010, ENVIRON International Corporation announced that starting in February 2011 ,that the new California Emissions Estimator Model(CalEEMod) Software would be available for use free of charge to provide a uniform platform for conducting an air quality analysis by government agencies, land use planners, and environmental professionals. CalEEMod was developed by Environ in collaboration with the South Coast Air Quality Management District and other California Air Quality Districts and can be used to calculate the criteria pollutant and greenhouse gas emissions associated with land-use development projects throughout California.*

The model quantifies direct emissions from construction and operation (including vehicle use), as well as indirect emissions, such as GHG emissions from energy production, solid waste handling, vegetation planting and/or removal, and water conveyance.

Information about the CalEEMod Software is available from the following website:

www.caleemod.com/

It is not the purpose of this book to provide a detailed methodology to conduct a greenhouse gas emission analysis.

However, the author recommends that the CEQA Initial Study Checklist preparer read the publication titled: *CEQA and Climate Change, Evaluating and Addressing Greenhouse Gas Emissions from Projects Subject to the California Environmental Quality Act, June 2008* published by the California Air Pollution Control Officers Association. It is an excellent resource on various methods used to evaluate greenhouse gas emissions.

The publication can be found on the California Air Pollution Control Officers Association website. (See Section 2 below).

- ***Determine Significance****:* As with any environmental impact, lead agencies must determine what constitutes a significant impact. In the absence of regulatory standards for greenhouse gas emissions or other scientific data to clearly define what constitutes a "significant impact" for greenhouse gas emissions, individual lead agencies may undertake a project by-project analysis, consistent with available guidance and current CEQA practice.

  The amended CEQA Guidelines added Section 15064.4(b) to provide further guidance for determining the significance from greenhouse gas emissions.

  Section 15064.4(b) states:

  "A lead agency should consider the following factors, among others, when assessing the significance of impacts from greenhouse gas emissions on the environment:

(1) The extent to which the project may increase or reduce greenhouse gas emissions as compared to the existing environmental setting;

(2) Whether the project emissions exceed a threshold of significance that the lead agency determines applies to the project.

(3) The extent to which the project complies with regulations or requirements adopted to implement a statewide, regional, or local plan for the reduction or mitigation of greenhouse gas emissions. Such requirements must be adopted by the relevant public agency through a public review process and must reduce or mitigate the project's incremental contribution of greenhouse gas emissions. If there is substantial evidence that the possible effects of a particular project are still cumulatively considerable notwithstanding compliance with the adopted regulations or requirements, an EIR must be prepared for the project.

As noted above, it is not the purpose of this book to provide a detailed methodology to conduct a greenhouse gas emission analysis. However, an accepted practice to determine significance is to compare the projects greenhouse gas emissions against the identified greenhouse gas emissions statewide. (See pages 225-227 for an example).

- ***Mitigate Impacts****:* Mitigation measures will vary with the type of project being contemplated, but may include alternative project designs or locations that conserve energy and water, measures that reduce vehicle miles traveled by fossil-fueled vehicles, measures that contribute to established regional or programmatic mitigation strategies, and measures that sequester carbon to offset the emissions from the project.

The amended CEQA Guidelines added Section 15126.4(c) to provide further guidance for mitigating impacts from greenhouse gas emissions.

Section 15126.4 (c) states:

> *"Consistent with section 15126.4(a), lead agencies shall consider feasible means, supported by substantial evidence and subject to monitoring or reporting, of mitigating the significant effects of greenhouse gas emissions. Measures to mitigate the significant effects of greenhouse gas emissions may include, among others:*
>
> *(1) Measures in an existing plan or mitigation program for the reduction of emissions that are required as part of the lead agency's decision;*
>
> *(2) Reductions in emissions resulting from a project through implementation of project features, project design, or other measures, such as those described in Appendix F [of the CEQA Guidelines];*

(3) Off-site measures, including offsets that are not otherwise required, to mitigate a project's emissions;

(4) Measures that sequester greenhouse gases;

(5) In the case of the adoption of a plan, such as a general plan, long range development plan, or plans for the reduction of greenhouse gas emissions, mitigation may include the identification of specific measures that may be implemented on a project-by-project basis. Mitigation may also include the incorporation of specific measures or policies found in an adopted ordinance or regulation that reduces the cumulative effect of emissions."

***

In order to answer the question in an appropriate context, the above described methodology should be used (i.e. Identify Greenhouse Gas Emissions, Determine Significance, and Mitigate Impacts).

2. Where to Find the Factual Data to Answer the Question

- The best source of information would be from a technical report prepared consistent with CEQA Guidelines Sections 15064.4(a)-(b) and 15126.4(c) and guidance from Governor's Office of Planning and Research Technical Advisory on Climate Change referenced on Page 216.

The document can be found at:

www.opr.ca.gov/ceqa/pdfs/june08-ceqa.pdf or enter "opr technical advisory ceqa and climate change" in an Internet search engine.

- The Office of Planning and Research website also contains an abundance of information on greenhouse gases. The website is located at:

www.opr.ca.gov/. Click on the link "CEQA GUIDELINES AND GREENHOUSE GASES." or enter "opr ghg emissions" in an Internet search engine and follow the above links.

The Office of Planning and Research website also has links to other websites that deal with greenhouse gases in California.

- The Natural Resources Agency's *Final Statement of Reasons for Regulatory Action, Amendments to the State CEQA Guidelines Addressing Analysis and Mitigation of Greenhouse Gas Emissions Pursuant to SB97, December 2009* provides an excellent overview of greenhouse gas emissions as they pertain to CEQA. The document can be found at:

http://ceres.ca.gov/ceqa/docs/Final_Statement_of_Reasons.pdf or enter "final statement of reasons for regulatory action ghg" in an Internet search engine.

- *CEQA and Climate Change, Evaluating and Addressing Greenhouse Gas Emissions from Projects Subject to the California Environmental Quality Act, June 2008* published by the California Air Pollution Control Officers Association is an excellent resource on this topic.

The publication can be found at:

www.capcoa.org/or enter "capcoa" in an Internet search engine.

- The AB 32 Scoping Plan can be found at:

www.arb.ca.gov/cc/scopingplan/scopin gplan.htm or enter "ab 32 scoping plan" in an Internet search engine.

- The *California Emissions Estimator Model* (CalEEMod) was developed by Environ in collaboration with the South Coast Air Quality Management District and other California Air Quality Districts and can be used to calculate the criteria pollutant and greenhouse gas emissions associated with land-use development projects throughout California.

The model quantifies direct emissions from construction and operation (including vehicle use), as well as indirect emissions, such as GHG emissions from energy production, solid waste handling, vegetation planting and/or removal, and water conveyance.

Information about the CalEEMod Software is available from the following website:

www.caleemod.com/

- It is recommended that the California Environmental Resources Evaluation System website be consulted to see if there is any information related to this question. The website is located at:

  ceres.ca.gov or enter "ceres evaluation" in an Internet search engine.

3. Example Answers

The following example answers the question comprehensively:

The project consists of 65 condominium units located in the South Coast Air Quality Management District. The following analysis is based on a Climate Change Report prepared for the project.

Identify Greenhouse Gas Emissions

Construction Emissions:

The project would result in short-term emissions of greenhouse gases during construction. These emissions, primarily CO_2, CH_4, and N_2O, are the result of fuel combustion by construction equipment and motor vehicles. The other primary greenhouse gases (hydrofluorocarbons, perfluorocarbons, and sulfur hexafluoride) are typically associated with specific industrial sources and are not expected to be emitted by the project because it is a residential project.
Table 1 lists the estimated greenhouse gas emissions associated with construction of the project.

Table 1.Estimated Construction Emissions

Emission Source	Emissions (Metric Tons CO_2e/Year
Construction 2010	242.64
Construction 2011	200.32
TOTAL	442.96
Annualized Over Project Lifetime	14.77

Operational Emissions:

At full buildout, the project would result in direct annual emissions of greenhouse gases during project operation. These emissions, primarily CO_2, CH_4, and N_2O, are the result of fuel combustion from building heating systems and motor vehicles.

Direct emissions of CO_2 emitted from operation of the project are primarily due to natural gas consumption and mobile source emissions (e.g. motor vehicles).

The project would also result in indirect greenhouse emissions due to the electricity demands of the project. In addition to electrical demand, the project would also result in indirect greenhouse gas emissions due to wastewater treatment needs and solid waste handling.

Table 2 lists the estimated greenhouse gas emissions associated with operations of the project.

Table 2. Estimated Annual Operational Emissions

Operational Emissions Source	GHG Emissions (MTCO2e/year)*
Operational (Mobile) Sources	796.18
Area Sources	137.21
Electrical Consumption	73.06
Solid Waste Generation	4.74
Water Supply	19.11
Wastewater Generation	3.79
TOTAL	1,034.09
*MT = Metric Tons	

Determining Significance:

Table 3 compares the estimated greenhouse gas emissions of the project to the emissions for California.

Table 3. Comparison of Emissions

Emitting Entity	Emissions (MTCO2e/year)
Proposed Project	1,034.09 MT
California	483.87 MMT*
Percent of State Emissions	0.00022%
*MMT = Million Metric Tons	

As shown in Table 3, the project would contribute approximately 0.00022% to the annual state greenhouse gas inventory. It is generally the case that an individual project of this size is of insufficient magnitude by itself to influence climate change or result in a substantial contribution to the global greenhouse gas inventory.

In addition, while the South Coast Air Quality Management District has not formally adopted a significance threshold and has only drafted a threshold of 3,000 MTCO2e for residential projects, it could be used as an indicator of a project's significance under CEQA.

As shown in Table 2, the proposed project would result in greenhouse gas emissions equal to approximately one third of the 3,000 MTCO2e draft threshold.

Finally, the project incorporates greenhouse gas reduction measures and design features to reduce greenhouse gas emissions including but not limited to:

- ✓ *Use of a solar heating system for the swimming pool;*

- ✓ *Installation of energy efficient appliances in all units;*

- ✓ *Building complexes that are oriented to maximize advantage of sunlight;*

- ✓ *Use of "cool roofs" on all buildings; and*

- ✓ *Use of LED lighting for outdoor lighting in the parking areas and walkways.*

Based on the above analysis, the project's greenhouse gas emissions would be less than significant.

This response includes all of the components necessary to evaluate greenhouse gas emissions consistent with OPR's Technical Advisory on Climate Change and CEQA Guidelines Sections 15064.4 (a) and (b), and 15126.4(c).

The following example does not answer the question comprehensively:

The project consists of a neighborhood retail center totaling 19,820 square feet on a 1.6 acre site. Greenhouse gas emissions include Carbon Dioxide (CO_2), Methane (CH_4), and Nitrous Oxide (N_2O).

There are currently no adopted thresholds for determining the significance of greenhouse emissions in California. The most common form of greenhouse gas emissions from the project would be from CO_2 emissions as a result of vehicles traveling to and from the site.

Because of the small size of the project and the insignificant amount of CO_2 that would be generated in comparison to larger projects, impacts would be less than significant.

This response does not rely on any type of methodology consistent with the provisions of CEQA Guidelines Sections 15064(a)-(b) as described on Pages 216-220.

4. Determining Significance

Following are some general factors to consider for determining significance:

- Are there any Thresholds of Significance that were formally adopted by the lead agency that are applicable to the project?

- Has the lead agency set a precedent in previously approved CEQA documents in responding to the question? If so, the Initial

Study Checklist preparer should be aware of how other CEQA documents have responded to the question.

- Use Section 15064.4(a) and (b) to determine if impacts are significant. These sections state:

"(a) The determination of the significance of greenhouse gas emissions calls for a careful judgment by the lead agency consistent with the provisions in section 15064. A lead agency should make a good-faith effort, based to the extent possible on scientific and factual data, to describe, calculate or estimate the amount of greenhouse gas emissions resulting from a project.

(b) A lead agency should consider the following factors, among others, when assessing the significance of impacts from greenhouse gas emissions on the environment:

(1) The extent to which the project may increase or reduce greenhouse gas emissions as compared to the existing environmental setting;

(2) Whether the project emissions exceed a threshold of significance that the lead agency determines applies to the project; and

(3) The extent to which the project complies with regulations or requirements adopted to implement a statewide, regional, or local plan for the reduction or mitigation of

greenhouse gas emissions. Such requirements must be adopted by the relevant public agency through a public review process and must reduce or mitigate the project's incremental contribution of greenhouse gas emissions. If there is substantial evidence that the possible effects of a particular project are still cumulatively considerable notwithstanding compliance with the adopted regulations or requirements, an EIR must be prepared for the project."

As noted earlier, it is not the purpose of this book to provide a detailed methodology to conduct a greenhouse gas emission analysis. However, an accepted practice to determine significance is to compare the projects greenhouse gas emissions against the identified greenhouse gas emissions statewide. (See Table 3 on Page 227 for an example).

VII. GREENHOUSE GAS EMISSISONS (cont.)

Would the project:

(b) Conflict with an applicable plan, policy or regulation adopted for the purpose of reducing the emissions of greenhouse gases?

1. Determining the Scope of the Question

As described on Pages 213 and 214, the primary regulatory mechanisms in place at the State level to address greenhouse gas emissions are Assembly Bill 32 and Senate Bill 375.

In the opinion of the author, the requirements of Assembly Bill 32 and Senate Bill 375 would be considered an appropriate "applicable plan, policy, or regulation" in the context of this question.

Generally there are two primary criteria to consider when answering this question.

1. A project is consistent with a greenhouse gas emission plan, policy, or regulation if it will not result in an increase in the frequency or severity of greenhouse gas emissions or delay timely attainment of greenhouse emission reduction goals.

2. A project would be consistent if it is not in conflict with the recommended actions contained in a plan or the provisions of a policy or regulation to reduce greenhouse gas emissions.

In addition, because greenhouse gas emission plans, policies, and regulations are emerging at a fast pace, the Initial Study Checklist preparer should frequently check the status of the greenhouse gas emissions regulatory framework by visiting the California Air Resources Board website at **www.arb.ca.gov/** or the Governor's Office of Planning and Research website at **www.opr.ca.gov/**.

2. Where to Find the Factual Data to Answer the Question

- The AB 32 Scoping Plan can be found at the California Air Resources Board website located at **www.arb.ca.gov/**.

- In addition, the Office of Planning and Research website also contains an abundance of information on greenhouse gas emissions located at **www.opr.ca.gov/**. Click on the link "CEQA GUIDELINES AND GREENHOUSE GASES". There are also links to other websites that deal with greenhouse gas emissions in California.

- It is recommended that the California Environmental Resources Evaluation System website be consulted to see if there is any information related to this question. The website is located at:

  ceres.ca.gov or enter "ceres evaluation" in an Internet search engine.

3. Example Answers.

The following example answers the question comprehensively:

The project consists of 187 single-family detached units. For purposes of this analysis, the project was evaluated against the following applicable plans, policies, and regulations: 1) AB 32 Scoping Plan, and 2) the City's General Plan. At present, there are no other applicable local or regional plans policies or regulations pertaining to greenhouse gas emissions that apply to the project.

The AB 32 Scoping Plan

- The project is proposing to exceed the energy efficiency levels required by State Title 24 Building Energy Efficiency Standards. This action would implement an Emission Reduction Action for Energy Efficiency contained in the Scoping Plan.

- The project is proposing the use of low flush toilets and low flow plumbing fixtures. This action would implement an Emission Reduction Action for Water contained in the Scoping Plan.

City General Plan

- The project is proposing water efficient landscaping in all the parkways and medians which implements General Plan Policy GHG-1: "The City will encourage green building design which could include conserving non-renewable energy and materials, promoting water efficient landscaping and other methods to support environmental conservation and to assist in the concerns of global warming."

- *The project is oriented to maximize advantage from sunlight which implements General Plan Policy GHG-2: "Encourage the use of site planning techniques, building orientation and building designs that reduce energy use."*

- *The project is proposing the use of "cool roofs" which implements General Plan Policy GHG-3: "Encourage Green Building Construction."*

The response describes the applicable greenhouse gas emission plans, policies, and regulations at the state level and the local level and discusses how the project is consistent with these provisions.

The following example does not answer the question comprehensively:

The project would result in greenhouse gas emissions equal to approximately one third of the 3,000 MTCO2e draft threshold established by the South Coast Air Quality Management District. Therefore, it would not conflict with the District's proposed plan for reducing greenhouse gas emissions. Impacts would be less than significant.

This response addresses the question only in the context of meeting a greenhouse gas emission threshold when it should be discussing how the project is consistent with the applicable plans, policies, and regulations that are intended to reduce greenhouse gas emissions, such as mandated by Assembly Bill 32 or the lead agency's general plan.

4. Determining Significance

- In the opinion of the author, a project's impacts would be less than significant if:

  1. It is consistent with applicable greenhouse gas emission plans, policies, or regulations; and

  2. It will not result in an increase in the frequency or severity of greenhouse gas emissions or delay the timely attainment of greenhouse emission reduction goals.

Chapter VIII

Hazards and Hazardous Materials

Introduction

This section of the Initial Study Checklist contains 8 questions. Questions VIII a-d deal with hazardous materials and Questions VIII e-h deal with hazards related to airports, private airstrips, wildland fires and impacts to emergency response and evacuation plans.

In order to address these topics, this chapter is divided into two parts; *Hazardous Materials* and *Other Hazard Issues*.

Part 1: Hazardous Materials

There are numerous regulations that pertain to Hazardous Materials. It is helpful to know the general regulatory framework as it applies to Hazardous Materials to thoroughly address this issue in the Initial Study Checklist. The regulations relating to hazardous materials are found at the federal, state, and local level. The following provides a brief summary of the regulatory framework.

Federal Environmental Protection Agency: The Federal Environmental Protection Agency is the primary federal agency responsible for the implementation and enforcement of hazardous materials regulations. In most cases, enforcement of the federal laws and regulations is delegated to state and local environmental regulatory agencies.

237

California Environmental Protection Agency: The California Environmental Protection Agency has broad jurisdiction over hazardous materials management in the State. The California Environmental Protection Agency oversees five (5) boards, departments, and offices. The following diagram illustrates the five (5) boards, departments, and offices. The relationship is not hierarchical.

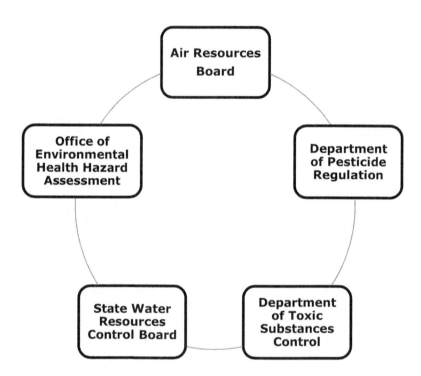

Each of these boards, departments, and offices has authority over various types of hazardous materials.

Although each of these regulatory agencies have control over different aspects of hazardous materials, in the context of Questions VIIIa-d, the most salient regulatory framework for hazardous materials is shown in the following diagram:

Department of Toxic Substances Control

The Unified Program

Certified Uniform Program Agency

The Department of Toxic Substances Control: The Department regulates hazardous waste cleans-up, existing contamination, and looks for ways to reduce the hazardous waste produced in California. The staff of the Department of Toxic Substances Control includes scientists, engineers, and specialized support staff who make sure that companies and individuals handle, transport, store, treat, dispose of, and clean-up hazardous wastes appropriately.

The Unified Program: This program consolidates, coordinates, and makes consistent the administrative requirements, permits, inspections, and enforcement activities of six environmental and emergency response programs identified below:

✓ *Hazardous Materials Release Response Plans and Inventories;*

✓ *California Accidental Release Prevention Program;*

✓ *Underground Storage Tank Program;*

✓ *Above Ground Petroleum Storage Act Program;*

✓ *Hazardous Waste Generator and Onsite Hazardous Waste Treatment Programs; and*

✓ *California Uniform Fire Code: Hazardous Material Management Plans and Hazardous Material Inventory Statements.*

Certified Unified Program Agency: A Certified Unified Program Agency addresses impacts from hazardous wastes to meet the requirements identified by the Unified Program. Most Certified Unified Program Agencies have been established as a function of a county environmental health department or a local fire department or fire district.

VIII. HAZARDS and HAZARDOUS MATERIALS (cont).

Would the project:

(a) Create a significant hazard to the public or the environment through the routine transport, use, or disposal of hazardous materials?

1. Determining the Scope of the Question

In order to determine the scope of the question, it is separated into the following parts:

Hazardous Materials

California Health and Safety Code Section 25501(o)) states:

"Hazardous Material means any material that, because of its quantity, concentration, or physical or chemical characteristics, poses a significant present or potential hazard to human health and safety or to the environment if released into the workplace or the environment. Hazardous materials include, but are not limited to, hazardous substances, hazardous waste, and any material which a handler or the administering regulatory agency has a reasonable basis for believing would be injurious to the health and safety of persons or harmful to the environment if released into the workplace or the environment."

A number of properties may cause a substance to be considered hazardous, including toxicity, ignitibility, corrosivity, or reactivity.

Routine Transport, Use, or Disposal

In the opinion of the author, the "routine transport, use, or disposal" of hazardous materials refers to facilities or activities that involve large quantities of hazardous materials, such as a "hazardous waste generator."

According to the U.S. Environmental Protection Agency, a hazardous waste generator includes, but is not limited to, the following:

- ✓ Chemical Manufacturers;

- ✓ Electronic manufacturers;

- ✓ Furniture/Wood Manufacturing and Refinishing;

- ✓ Laboratories;

- ✓ Laundries and Dry Cleaners;

- ✓ Metal Manufacturing;

- ✓ Motor Freight Terminals and Railroad Transportation;

- ✓ Other Manufacturing (textiles, plastics, leather);

- ✓ Pesticide End Users and Application Services;

- ✓ Printing and Allied Industries; or

- ✓ Vehicle Maintenance.

As the above list shows, the types of businesses and activities that are considered hazardous waste generators can vary widely.

2. Where to Find the Factual Data to Answer the Question

- The best source to consult is the local Certified Unified Program Agency which oversees hazardous materials at the local level. They work closely with local agencies through the project review process to evaluate the impacts from hazardous materials.

  Information about where to locate the Certified Unified Program Agency for a region can be found at:

  www.calepa.ca.gov/CUPA/Directory/def ault.aspx or enter "cupa directory search" in an Internet search engine.

- Additional information can be found at the following websites:

  U.S. Environmental Protection Agency website at **www.epa.gov/** or enter "us epa" in an Internet search engine.

  California Environmental Protection Agency website at **www.calepa.ca.gov/** or enter "cal epa" on an Internet search engine.

  Department of Toxic Substance Control website at **www.dtsc.ca.gov/** or enter "ca dtsc" in an Internet search engine.

- It is recommended that the California Environmental Resources Evaluation System website be consulted to see if there is any information related to this question. The website is located at:

  ceres.ca.gov or enter "ceres evaluation" in an Internet search engine.

3. Example Answers

The following example answers the question comprehensively:

The facility involves the dismantling and recycling of electronic devices such as TVs, fax machines, computer central processing units and computer peripherals such as monitors, keyboards and mice. The facility is estimated to handle approximately up to 700 pounds of hazardous materials per year such as lead, cadmium, copper, and chromium.

Based on Department of Toxic Substances Control regulations, the facility is required to notify the Department 30 days prior to starting operations and will have to submit to the Department an annual report on February 1.

The local Certified Uniform Program Agency has been consulted about the facility and the facility will be required to prepare a Hazardous Materials Business Plan. The Plan will be reviewed by the Agency to ensure the contents are current and adequate.

In addition, the Plan will contain measures for employee training to determine if they meet the requirements outlined in the Plan and measures for the review of hazardous waste disposal records to ensure documenting proper disposal methods and the amount of wastes generated by the facility.

As long as the facility is in operation, the Agency will conduct regular inspections and monitor activities to ensure that the routine transport, use, and disposal of hazardous materials will not pose a significant impact.

This response provides a description of the type of facility, the type and amount of hazardous wastes that will be generated at the facility, and how it will comply with Department of Toxic Substances Control and the Certified Unified Program Agency requirements.

The following example does not answer the question comprehensively:

The storage, handling and transport of hazardous materials by the project will be subject to State and Federal regulations. Compliance is mandatory, therefore impacts will be less than significant.

This response does not describe the project activities and simply defers management of hazardous materials to the mandatory requirements of State and Federal regulations.

Although it may be technically correct, it does not provide enough information about the nature and extent of hazardous materials related to the project so that the lead agency decision makers and the public can be fully informed,

246

4. Determining Significance

Following are some general factors to consider for determining significance:

- Are there any Thresholds of Significance that were formally adopted by the lead agency that are applicable to the project?

- Has the lead agency set a precedent in previously approved CEQA documents in responding to the question? If so, the Initial Study Checklist preparer should be aware of how other CEQA documents have responded to the question.

- Determining significance for this issue can be a complicated process because it is based on the type and amount of hazardous materials associated with the project and the nature of the project's operations.

  This requires expertise in hazardous materials and familiarity with the numerous federal, state, and local regulations. Any project which proposes the use of or generates hazardous materials should be submitted to the local Certified Unified Program Agency for review and consultation.

VIII. HAZARDS and HAZARDOUS MATERIALS (cont.)

Would the project:

(b) Create a significant hazard to the public or the environment through reasonably foreseeable upset and accident conditions involving the release of hazardous materials into the environment?

1. Determining the Scope of the Question

In order to determine the scope of the question, it is separated into the following parts:

Reasonably Foreseeable Upset

There are several ways in which hazardous materials can be released into the environment through a reasonably foreseeable upset. The following examples include, but are not limited to:

- ✓ Floods, earthquakes, or fires that would cause hazardous materials to be released into the environment from tank rupture, pipeline rupture, fumes, or carried by floodwaters.

- ✓ Through the release of naturally occurring asbestos.

  The following information is derived from the Office of Planning and Research publication titled: *CEQA AND ASBESTOS: Addressing Naturally Occurring Asbestos in CEQA Documents.*

248

Asbestos is classified as a known human carcinogen by the California Air Resources Board. All types of asbestos are hazardous and may cause lung disease and cancer.

Serpentinite is a rock composed of one or more serpentine group minerals and may contain chrysotile asbestos, especially near fault zones. Ultramafic rock, a rock closely related to serpentinite, may also contain asbestos minerals.

Asbestos can also be associated with other rock types in California, though much less frequently than with serpentinite and/or ultramafic rock.

Asbestos can be released from serpentinite and ultramafic rocks when the rock is broken or crushed. At the point of release, the asbestos fibers may become airborne, causing air quality and human health hazards. These rocks have been commonly used for unpaved gravel roads, landscaping, fill projects and other improvement projects in some localities.

Asbestos can also be released into the atmosphere due to vehicular traffic on unpaved roads, during grading for development projects, and at quarry operations. All of these activities may have the effect of releasing potentially harmful asbestos into the air.

During review of a project, the possibility of disturbing serpentinite or ultramafic rocks should be investigated.

Accident Conditions

There are several ways in which hazardous materials can be released into the environment through accident conditions. The following examples include, but are not limited to:

- ✓ Mistakes in chemical processing that could become volatile and explode causing release of hazardous materials into the environment.

- ✓ Accidents involving vehicles, such as trucks or trains, which are transporting hazardous materials to and from a facility.

- ✓ Through release associated with construction of a project. For example, construction equipment could accidentally release petroleum products in sufficient quantity to pose a hazard to people and the environment.

- ✓ Through demolition of older buildings that may contain lead paint or asbestos.

As the above examples show, there are various activities that could release hazardous materials into the environment through routine transport, use, disposal, or accidental release.

2. Where to Find the Factual Data to Answer the Question

- For hazardous materials, the best source to consult is the local Certified Unified Program Agency for the jurisdiction in which the lead agency is located. They work closely with lead agencies through the project review process to ascertain the impacts from hazardous materials.

  Information about where to locate the Certified Unified Program Agency for a region can be found at:

  www.calepa.ca.gov/CUPA/Directory/def ault.aspx or enter "cupa directory search" in an Internet search engine.

- For naturally occurring asbestos, the following sources provide good information:

  The Office of Planning and Research publication titled: *CEQA AND ASBESTOS: Addressing Naturally Occurring Asbestos in CEQA Documents* can be located at:

  www.opr.ca.gov/planning/publications /asbestos_advisory.pdf or enter "naturally occurring asbestos in ceqa documents" in an Internet search engine.

  The California Air Resources Board has state wide maps showing areas likely to contain naturally occurring asbestos. The website is located at:

www.arb.ca.gov/toxics/asbestos/genin fo.htm or enter "areas likely to contain naturally occurring asbestos California" in an Internet search engine.

- It is recommended that the California Environmental Resources Evaluation System website be consulted to see if there is any information related to this question. The website is located at:

ceres.ca.gov or enter "ceres evaluation" in an Internet search engine.

3. Example Answers

The following examples answer the question comprehensively:

Example 1

The project involves the recycling of components such as cathode ray tubes used for computer monitors, televisions, cash registers, and consumer electronic devices (including computers, computer peripherals, telephones, answering machines, radios, stereo equipment, tape player/recorders, phonographs, video cassette players/recorders, compact disc players/recorders, calculators, and some appliances). The hazardous materials associated with these components are typically heavy metals such as lead and mercury.

Because these hazardous materials are contained in individual electronic components, in the event of a foreseeable upset (e.g., fire, flood, earthquake, etc.) the hazardous materials would simply fall out of the component. It is unlikely that any upset would immediately and completely release hazardous materials into the air or onto the ground.

The response describes the type of facility and the nature of the hazardous materials. It then addresses the type of event that can cause a foreseeable upset (fire, flood, earthquake, etc.) and why the accidental release of hazardous materials would not cause a significant impact.

Example 2

The project consists of a 187 unit apartment complex. Upon occupancy of the project, site maintenance and landscaping will require ordinary types of hazardous materials such as pesticides and herbicides, but none of these will be used or stored on site in large quantities.

During construction there is a potential for accidental release of petroleum products in sufficient quantity to pose a hazard to people and the environment. Mitigation Measure HAZ-1 below is recommended to reduce impacts to less than significant:

> *HAZ-1: All spills or leakage of petroleum products during construction activities will be remediated in compliance with applicable state and local regulations regarding cleanup and disposal of the contaminant released. The contaminated waste will be collected and disposed of at an appropriately licensed disposal or treatment facility. This measure will be*

incorporated into the Storm Water Pollution Prevention Plan prepared for the project.

In addition, based on information from the project soils report, the site does not contain serpentines or ultramafic rocks, therefore, the potential for release of naturally occurring asbestos during construction activities is considered low to non-existent.

This response discusses the nature of the project and why its operation would not result in the release of hazardous materials. It identifies that there is a potential of hazardous materials to be released from construction equipment, but recommends mitigation to ensure that impacts are not significant.

It also discusses the potential for the release of naturally occurring asbestos during construction.

The following example does not answer the question comprehensively:

The project does not propose a land use that will have the potential for the release of hazardous materials into the environment. Therefore, there will be no impact.

This response does not supply enough factual data to support the conclusion. It does not describe the land use and it does not discuss the potential for construction or operational activities of the land use to release hazardous materials. In addition, it does not discuss potential impacts from naturally occurring asbestos.

4. Determining Significance

Following are some general factors to consider in determining significance:

- Are there any formally adopted Thresholds of Significance by the lead agency that are applicable to the project?

- Has the lead agency set a precedent in previously approved CEQA documents in responding to the question? If so, the Initial Study Checklist preparer should be aware of how other CEQA documents have responded to the question.

- Determining significance for this issue can be a complicated process if certain types of hazardous materials in large quantities are associated with the project.

  Any project which proposes the use of or generates hazardous materials in larger quantities should be submitted to the local Certified Unified Program Agency for review and consultation.

VIII. HAZARDS and HAZARDOUS MATERIALS (cont.)

Would the project:

(c) Emit hazardous emissions or handle hazardous or acutely hazardous materials, substances, or waste within one-quarter mile of an existing or proposed school?

1. Determining the Scope of the Question

This question introduces two additional terms pertaining to hazardous materials that are somewhat different than Questions VIII (a) and VIII (b). These terms are "hazardous emissions" and "acutely hazardous materials."

Hazardous emissions and acutely hazardous materials can have a greater impact than other types of hazardous materials, especially if they are present within one-quarter mile of a school.

In order to determine the scope of the question, it is separated into the following parts:

Hazardous Emissions

Hazardous emissions generally mean outdoor air toxics that are emitted during a manufacturing or operational process. Most outdoor air toxics originate from motor vehicles and stationary sources such as factories, refineries, power plants, dry cleaners, painting, and agricultural production.

The analysis required to evaluate outdoor air toxics emissions usually requires the expertise of air quality professionals.

256

Acutely Hazardous Materials

"Acutely hazardous materials" are generally materials that are toxic, reactive, flammable or explosive.

These types of materials are primarily regulated by the California Accidental Release Prevention Program under supervision of a local Certified Unified Program Agency.

***

In summary, hazardous emissions and acutely hazardous materials generally have a higher degree of toxicity than the hazardous materials discussed in Questions VII (a) and VIII (b). These types of hazardous materials are of particular concern if present within one-quarter mile of a school.

In the opinion of the author, although Question VII (c) deals specifically with hazardous emissions and acutely hazardous materials, **any** type of hazardous materials within one-quarter mile of a school should always be addressed in answering this question.

2. Where to Find the Factual Data to Answer the Question

- The best source of information for hazardous materials is the local Certified Unified Program Agency for the jurisdiction in which the lead agency is located. They work closely with lead agencies through the project review process to evaluate the impacts from hazardous materials.

- Information about where to locate the Certified Unified Program Agency for a region can be found at:

  www.calepa.ca.gov/CUPA/Directory/def ault.aspx or enter "cupa directory search" in an Internet search engine.

- The best source of information for hazardous emissions is the applicable Air Pollution Control District/Air Quality Management District. A list of districts can be found at:

  www.arb.ca.gov/capcoa/roster.htm or enter "california air districts" in an Internet search engine.

- A Phase I Environmental Site Assessment prepared for the project can also provide information.

- It is recommended that the California Environmental Resources Evaluation System website be consulted to see if there is any information related to this question. The website is located at:

  Ceres.ca.gov or enter "ceres evaluation" in an Internet search engine.

3. Example Answers

Author's Note: *The following answers are for projects that are located within one-quarter mile of a school. If the project is not located within one-quarter mile of a school then that fact should be noted and no further discussion is required.*

The following example answers the question comprehensively:

Madison Elementary School is located on Willow Drive which is less than one-quarter of a mile from the project site. The project is a gas station/convenience market that will have hazardous materials associated with its operation. The two potential hazards to the school are from underground storage tanks and toxic air contaminant emissions.

Underground Storage Tanks

Two (2) underground storage tanks for gasoline and diesel fuel are proposed; one (1) 20,000 gallon tank and one (1) 25,000 gallon tank.

The County Certified Unified Program Agency has extensive procedures in place regulating the design, installation, operation, and unplanned releases of hazardous substances related to the proposed underground storage tank system. The impact from the storage and use of gasoline and diesel fuel is considered potentially significant. The following mitigation measure is recommended:

HAZ-1: Prior to the installation of any underground storage tanks, the project applicant shall provide verification that all applicable applications and forms have been filed with and approved by the County Hazardous Material Division.

Toxic Air Emissions

A health risk assessment was conducted to address the potential for impacts associated with toxic air emissions from the gas station operations. Air dispersion modeling was conducted to determine the maximum acute (1-hour) and chronic (annual average) concentrations that could be expected downwind of the gas station.

Based on the emission estimates and the results of the air dispersion modeling, the maximum 1- hour and highest annual average concentrations of toxic air contaminants were estimated to be below the Air Quality Management District significance threshold.

Therefore no significant risks to the school are forecast.

This response addresses both hazardous materials impacts from underground storage tanks and toxic air emissions. It relies upon a review by the Certified Unified Program Agency and an air quality report to substantiate the conclusions.

The following example does not answer the question comprehensively:

The site is located less than one-quarter mile from Roscoe Elementary School. The potential storage, handling and transport of hazardous materials by future occupants of the project will be subject to State and Federal regulations. Compliance with these regulations is mandatory, so there will be no significant impacts.

This response does not describe the type and amount of acutely hazardous materials or if toxic air emissions may be involved. It correctly states that the regulation of such substances is subject to mandatory federal and state regulations but the lack of overall information in the response does not provide sufficient detail to inform decision makers or the public of the potential risks involved.

4. Determining Significance

Following are some general factors to consider for determining significance:

- Are there any Thresholds of Significance that were formally adopted by the lead agency that are applicable to the project?

- Has the lead agency set a precedent in previously approved CEQA documents in responding to the question? If so, the Initial Study Checklist preparer should be aware of how other CEQA documents have responded to the question.

- Determining significance for this issue can be a complicated process because it is based on the type and amount of hazardous materials associated with the project and the nature of the project's operations.

  This requires expertise in hazardous materials and familiarity with the numerous federal, state, and local regulations. Any project which proposes the use of or generates hazardous materials should be submitted to the local Certified Unified Program Agency for review and consultation.

VIII. HAZARDS and HAZARDOUS MATERIALS (cont.)

Would the project:

(d) Be located on a site which is included on a list of hazardous materials sites compiled pursuant to Government Code Section 65962.5 and, as a result, would it create a significant hazard to the public or the environment?

1. Determining the Scope of the Question

The list of hazardous materials sites is commonly known as the "Cortese List" in reference to the State Legislator who sponsored the legislation (Dominic Cortese).

According to the Department of Toxic Substances Control website: *"While Government Code Section 65962.5 makes reference to the preparation of a "list," many changes have occurred related to web-based information access since 1992 and this information is now largely available on the Internet sites of the responsible organizations.*

Those requesting a copy of the Cortese "list" are now referred directly to the appropriate information resources contained on the Internet web sites of the boards or departments that are referenced in the statute." (Ref. Government Code Section 65962.5).

Thus, there is **not one list** but **several lists** which make up the Cortese "list."

2. Where to Find the Factual Data to Answer the Question

As stated above, there is not one list but several lists which must be consulted to answer this question in an appropriate context. Following is a listing of these sources as identified by the Department of Toxic Substances Control:

- List of Hazardous Waste and Substances sites from Department of Toxic Substances Control EnviroStor database.

- List of Leaking Underground Storage Tank Sites by County and Fiscal Year from Water Board GeoTracker database.

- List of solid waste disposal sites identified by Water Board with waste constituents above hazardous waste levels outside the waste management unit.

- List of "active" Cease and Desist Orders and Cleanup and Abatement Orders from the Water Board.

- List of hazardous waste facilities subject to corrective action pursuant to Section 25187.5 of the Health and Safety Code, identified by Department of Toxic Substances Control.

  For more information on where to find these lists, consult the Cortese List website at:

www.calepa.ca.gov/SiteCleanup/Cortes eList/default.htm or enter "cortese list" in an Internet search engine.

- It is recommended that the California Environmental Resources Evaluation System website be consulted to see if there is any information related to this question. The website is located at:

  ceres.ca.gov or enter "ceres evaluation" in an Internet search engine.

3. Example Answers

The following example answers the question comprehensively:

Research of the California Environmental Protection Agency's website determined that the project site is not located on any of the lists which constitute the Cortese List.

This response properly cites the California Environmental Protection Agency's Cortese List as the source for determining if the project site is identified on the Cortese List.

The following example does not answer the question comprehensively:

The project site is currently vacant. The site does not contain any known hazardous material storage facilities. No impacts would occur.

This response does not indicate that information provided by the California Environmental Protection

Agency's Cortese List was consulted. Just because a site does not contain an active hazardous materials storage facility does not mean that there may be issues with hazardous materials from previous activities.

4. Determining Significance

- This question has only one criterion for determining significance: the presence or absence of a site of the Cortese List. If a project is identified as being on the Cortese List than impacts are considered potentially significant. If not, there are no impacts.

Part 2: Other Hazard Issues

VIII. HAZARDS and HAZARDOUS MATERIALS (cont.)

Would the project:

(e) For a project located within an airport land use plan or, where such a plan has not been adopted, within two miles of a public airport or public use airport, would the project result in a safety hazard for people residing or working in the project area?

1. Determining the Scope of the Question

In order to determine the scope of this question, it is useful to put the following terms in an appropriate context:

Public Airport or Public Use Airport

The question uses the terms "public airport" and "public use airport." It should be noted that there is no definition for a "public airport" in the California Code of Regulations.

However, there is a definition for a "public use airport" which is defined as follows by California Code of Regulations, Title 21, Section 3527(q):

"An airport that is open for aircraft operations to the general public and is listed in the current edition of the Airport/Facility Directory that is published by the National Ocean Service of the U.S. Department of Commerce."

In the opinion of the author, a "public airport" and a "public use airport" have the same meaning in the context of this question and will both be referred to as a "public use airport" in this Chapter.

In addition, it should also be noted that in California a "special use airport" can be covered by an Airport Compatibility Land Use Plan even though it is not considered a public use airport.

California Code of Regulations, Title 21, Section 3527(w) defines a Special-Use Airport as:

"An airport not open to the general public, access to which is controlled by the owner in support of commercial activities, public service operations and/or personal use."

The Kingdon Executive Airport located near Lodi in San Joaquin County is considered a special use airport and it is included in the San *Joaquin County Airport Land Use Compatibility Plan*.

Therefore, the author recommends that the response to this question should also address a special use airport.

Airport Land Use Plan

A key part of this question is whether or not the project is located within an airport land use plan. Thus, it is important to understand what is meant by the term "airport land use plan" in the context of the question.

The California Department of Transportation, Division of Aeronautics regulates public use airports. Impacts from a public use airport are addressed in plans called an "Airport Land Use Compatibility Plan." In the opinion of the author, an "airport land use plan" in the context of Question VIII(e) means an "Airport Land Use Compatibility Plan" and will be referred to as such in this Chapter.

An Airport Land Use Compatibility Plan is prepared at the local level and is administered by an Airport Land Use Commission.

An Airport Land Use Commission serves in an advisory capacity to a lead agency as it pertains to land uses that could be impacted by a public use airport.

Authors Note: *It should be noted that an Airport Land Use Compatibility Plan administered by an Airport Land Use Commission does not take precedence over a locally adopted Airport Land Use Compatibility Plan. For example, certain cities in San Bernardino and Kern Counties have jurisdiction (and not an Airport Land Use Commission) over land uses that could be impacted by a public use airport.*

An Airport Land Use Compatibility Plan's primary focus is on impacts aircraft may have on the land surrounding a public use airport. These plans differ from an "Airport Master Plan" in that the primary focus of the Airport Land Use Compatibility Plan is on the land **surrounding** a public use airport while an Airport Master Plan focuses on the land **within** a public use airport and its future operational activities.

This question is asking about an Airport Land Use Compatibility Plan and not an Airport Master Plan so it is important to distinguish the difference between the two types of plans in answering the question.

The Airport Land Use Compatibility Plan will contain a diagram(s) showing areas which are called "area of influence" or "airport referral area" or some similar term.

These areas contain various standards such as land use type, density, or height restrictions that serve to ensure compatibility between aircraft operations and to people and structures in the vicinity of a public use airport.

If the project site is located within the area of influence, referral area, or some similar area of a public use airport identified in an Airport Land Use Compatibility Plan, then a compatibility analysis must be conducted to determine potential impacts from the operation of the airport on the affected land.

Generally, a compatibility analysis would include the following components relating to aircraft hazards:

- ✓ Project consistency with the intensity and density limits in the airport land use compatibility plan;

- ✓ Project consistency with the local agency's building or structure height limits contained in a zoning code;

- ✓ Impact of the public use airport's existing and proposed operations on the project, specifically with regard to safety including an analysis of the project's location in relation to the *California Airport Land Use Planning Handbook* safety zone system;

✓ Potential project impact to existing and proposed public use airport operations and aircraft safety; and

✓ Compliance with land use restrictions as identified in the lead agency's general plan or zoning code.

The Initial Study Checklist preparer should refer to the applicable Airport Land Use Compatibility Plan for what should be included in a compatibility analysis for the particular public use airport.

Within Two Miles of a Public Airport or Public Use Airport

According to Question VIII (e), if a project is not located within the area covered by an Airport Land Use Compatibility Plan, then a two mile distance is used to evaluate impacts.

Often times this question is answered by some Initial Study Checklist preparers only in reference to a two mile distance to a public use airport.

The two mile distance criteria are **only** for circumstances where an Airport Land Use Compatibility Plan **has not been** adopted.

If an Airport Land Use Compatibility Plan has been adopted, the area covered by the Plan may encompass **more than two miles,** so the Initial

Study Checklist preparer should not restrict the analysis to a two mile distance.

2. *Where to Find the Factual Data to Answer the Question*

The following are excellent sources of information for this topic:

- A list of public use airports in California can be found at:

  www.dot.ca.gov/hq/planning/aeronaut /documents2/pubuse07.pdf or enter "california public use airports-2007 and military fields" in an Internet search engine.

- *The California Airport Land Use Planning Handbook, State of California Department of Transportation Division of Aeronautics* can be found at:

  www.dot.ca.gov/hq/planning/aeronaut /documents/aluhpComplete-7- 02rev.pdf or enter "california airport land use planning handbook" in an Internet search engine.

- Airport Land Use Commission Contacts by County can be found at:

  www.dot.ca.gov/ha/planning/aeronaut /documents2/ALUC3-2-09.pdf or enter "aluc contact list 3-2-09" in an Internet search engine.

- For specific guidance concerning airports in an area contact "Airport Land Use Compatibility Guidance" at:

  www.dot.ca.gov/hq/planning/landuse. html or enter "airport land use compatibility guidance" in an Internet search engine.

- It is recommended that the California Environmental Resources Evaluation System website be consulted to see if there is any information related to this question. The website is located at:

  ceres.ca.gov or enter "ceres evaluation" in an Internet search engine.

3. Example Answers

The following example answers the question comprehensively:

The project site is located approximately 3.2 miles from Powell Airport. According to the Comprehensive Land Use Plan for Powell Airport, the site is not located within the area of influence for the airport. Therefore, there will be no safety hazard for people residing or working in the project area from Powell Airport.

This response makes reference to the closest airport land use plan that could impact the project site and states that it is not within the area of influence of the Plan.

The following example does not answer the question comprehensively:

The site is not located within an Airport Land Use Compatibility Plan.

This response merely answers the question in the negative without providing any factual data to support the conclusion. In answering this question it is always better to identify the distance to the closest airport and discuss whether or not the project site is located within the area of influence of an Airport Land Use Compatibility Plan if there is one.

4. Determining Significance

Following are some general factors to consider for determining significance:

- Are there any Thresholds of Significance that were formally adopted by the lead agency that are applicable to the project?

- Has the lead agency set a precedent in previously approved CEQA documents in responding to the question? If so, the Initial Study Checklist preparer should be aware of how other CEQA documents have responded to the question.

- If the project site is not located within an airport land use plan area of influence as shown in the plan then there would be no impact.

- If the project site is located within an area covered by an airport land use compatibility plan or within two miles of a public use airport if a plan has not been adopted, potential impacts should be evaluated by conducting a compatibility analysis based on the standards contained in the plan.

VIII. HAZARDS and HAZARDOUS MATERIALS (cont.)

Would the project:

(f) For a project within the vicinity of a private airstrip, would the project result in a safety hazard for people residing or working in the project area?

1. Determining the Scope of the Question

This question refers to a "private airstrip" which is different than a public use airport which is regulated by the California Division of Aeronautics.

In the opinion of the author, the term "private airstrip" is more commonly referred to as a "personal use airport" which is defined by California Code of Regulations, Title 21, Section 3527(o) as:

"An airport limited to the noncommercial activities of an individual owner or family and occasional invited guests."

Therefore, a "private airstrip" is referred to as a "personal use airport" in this Chapter.

Unlike Question VIII (e), this question uses the phrase "in the vicinity of a private airstrip" as opposed to "within two miles of a public airport or public use airport".

Many times Initial Study Checklist preparers in responding to this question use the two mile distance to determine impacts when in fact the "vicinity" can be some other distance.

In the opinion of the author, it is best to evaluate impacts based on the same principles used in an airport compatibility analysis for a public use airport when evaluating impacts from a personal use airport as many of the same safety factors would apply. (See Pages 270 and 271).

2. Where to Find the Factual Data to Answer the Question

- Because personal use airports are exempted from the regulations applicable to public airports pursuant to California Code of Regulations Title 21, Section 3533, the best source of information is to check with the local agency planning department to see if a personal use airport has been permitted (typically through a conditional use permit).

- The California Division of Aeronautics maintains a document titled: "California Airport/Heliport/Master Records" which provides information on airports. This list may contain information on personal use airports.

  The website is located at:

  http://www.dot.ca.gov/hq/planning/a eronaut/ca.html or enter "california division of aeronautics" in an Internet search engine and click on the link "california airport/heliport/master records."

- It is recommended that the California Environmental Resources Evaluation System website be consulted to see if there is any

information related to this question. The website is located at:

ceres.ca.gov or enter "ceres evaluation" in an Internet search engine.

3. Example Answers

The following example answers the question comprehensively:

A review of county records and a review of the area surrounding the project site show that there are no personal use airports (i.e. private airstrips) operating in the vicinity (i.e. area that could be impacted by aircraft take offs and landings) of the project site. Therefore, there will be no impact.

The response is based on a review of county records, which would show if a conditional use permit or other land use entitlement was granted for a personal use airport. It also indicates that the "vicinity" of the project site was analyzed as opposed to a fixed 2 mile distance.

The following example does not answer the question comprehensively:

The project site is not located within two miles of a personal use airport (i.e. private airstrip). Therefore, there will be no impact.

The response uses the two mile distance instead of "within the vicinity" of a private airstrip (i.e. personal use airport) as posed by the question.

4. Determining Significance

Following are some general factors to consider for determining significance:

- Are there any Thresholds of Significance that were formally adopted by the lead agency that are applicable to the project?

- Has the lead agency set a precedent in previously approved CEQA documents in responding to the question? If so, the Initial Study Checklist preparer should be aware of how other CEQA documents have responded to the question.

- If the project site is not located within the vicinity of a personal use airport there would be no impact.

  When determining what geographic area is within the vicinity of a personal use airport, the Initial Study Checklist preparer should consider the relationship of a personal use airport to its surroundings with respect to aircraft takeoff and landing patterns.

- If the project site is located within the vicinity of a personal use airport then impacts should be evaluated by having an aviation professional familiar with Federal Aviation Regulations conduct a safety compatibility analysis.

VIII. HAZARDS and HAZARDOUS MATERIALS (cont.)

Would the project:

(g) Impair implementation of or physically interfere with an adopted emergency response plan or emergency evacuation plan?

1. Determining the Scope of the Question

In order to determine the scope of the question, it is separated into the following parts:

Emergency Response Plan

The Governor's Office of Emergency Services coordinates preparedness for and response to natural disasters such as earthquakes, fires and floods by activating the California Emergency Management System used by all California public safety agencies. An emergency response plan would be part of implementing the California Emergency Management System.

Emergency response plans can vary depending on the local jurisdiction but share the following primary components:

- ✓ Alert and warn citizens;

- ✓ Conduct evacuation;

- ✓ Provide short-term feeding and sheltering; and

- ✓ Conduct search and rescue operations.

In order for a project to "impair implementation of or physically interfere" with an emergency response plan it would have to prevent the above described functions from occurring.

Emergency Evacuation Plan

An "emergency evacuation plan" is a community wide plan that addresses how people are evacuated from an area during a disaster. It typically identifies evacuation routes in the event of a disaster.

Many general plans or other safety related documents identify designated emergency evacuation routes (i.e. roads and highways).

The Initial Study Checklist preparer should also evaluate how a project would impact the roadways adjacent to and in the immediate vicinity of the project site that are not officially designated as evacuation routes as these roadways can be used to connect to the designated emergency evacuation routes.

2. Where to Find the Factual Data to Answer the Question

- The local jurisdiction's Office of Emergency Services or fire department.

- The local jurisdictions General Plan Safety Element (or similar) and emergency planning documents.

- It is recommended that the California Environmental Resources Evaluation System website be consulted to see if there is any information related to this question. The website is located at:

ceres.ca.gov or enter "ceres evaluation" in an Internet search engine.

3. Example Answers

The following example answers the question comprehensively:

The project is a 12,500 square foot retail building located on Commerce Avenue which is an identified emergency evacuation route in the city. Emergency access to and in the vicinity of the project site could potentially be affected during construction activities.

During construction activities, the Public Works Department will require that vehicular access to Commerce Avenue remain open. Therefore, the project will not impair implementation of, or physically interfere with, an emergency evacuation or response plan.

This response discusses how the project could interfere with an emergency response or evacuation plan (i.e. the potential closing of a roadway that could be used to alert and warn citizens, conduct evacuation, provide access to short-term feeding and sheltering, and conduct search and rescue operations).

The following example does not answer the question comprehensively:

The project is required to comply with the adopted emergency response or emergency evacuation plan, and as such, will not conflict with said plans.

This response does not provide any details on how the project will not physically interfere with or prevent the implementation of an emergency evacuation or response plan.

4. Determining Significance

Following are some general factors to consider for determining significance:

- Are there any Thresholds of Significance that were formally adopted by the lead agency that are applicable to the project?

- Has the lead agency set a precedent in previously approved CEQA documents in responding to the question? If so, the Initial Study Checklist preparer should be aware of how other CEQA documents have responded to the question.

- Generally, the primary ways in which a project could impair implementation of an emergency evacuation or response plan would be through activities that would prevent:

  ✓ Alerting and warning citizens;

  ✓ Conducting evacuations;

✓ Providing short-term feeding and sheltering;

✓ Conducting search and rescue operations; or

✓ Using emergency evacuation routes.

VIII. HAZARDS and HAZARDOUS MATERIALS (cont.)

Would the project:

(h) Expose people or structures to a significant risk of loss, injury or death involving wildland fires, including where wildlands are adjacent to urbanized areas or where residences are intermixed with wildlands?

1. Determining the Scope of the Question

Government Code 51175 through 51189 directed the California Department of Forestry and Fire Protection to identify areas of Very High Fire Hazard Severity Zones within Local Responsibility Areas (i.e. counties and cities).

As a result, the California Department of Forestry and Fire Prevention maintains the Fire Hazard Severity Zones Maps.

These maps are often used in a local jurisdiction's general plan or as a planning tool to evaluate the potential for wildland fire risk. Any project within or adjacent to a mapped area must be evaluated for its exposure to a wildland fire.

2. Where to Find the Factual Data to Answer the Question

- The California Department of Forestry and Fire Prevention, Fire Hazard Severity Zones Maps identify wildland fire hazard areas. The webpage is located at:

**www.fire.ca.gov/fire_prevention/fire_p
revention_wildland_zones.php**

The webpage has links to county and city
level maps. The webpage can also be found
by an Internet search engine by entering
"california fire hazard severity zone maps."

- The local planning agency general plan,
building and safety department, or fire
department.

- The Office of Planning and Research
publication titled: *Fire Hazard* Planning is an
excellent source of information on wildland
fires. The document can be located at:

**http://www.opr.ca.gov/planning/publi
cations/Fire_Hazard_Planning-
Final_Report.pdf** or enter "fire hazard
planning california technical advice" in an
Internet search engine.

- Information of California Wildland Urban
Building Codes can be found at:

**www.fire.ca.gov/fire_prevention/fire_p
revention_wildland_codes.php** or enter
"california's wildland urban interface code
information" in an Internet search engine.

- It is recommended that the California
Environmental Resources Evaluation System
website be consulted to see if there is any
information related to this question. The
website is located at:

ceres.ca.gov or enter "ceres evaluation" in an Internet search engine.

3. Example Answers

The following examples answer the question comprehensively:

Example 1

The site is surrounded by urban development on all sides. According to the City Fire Hazard Overlay District Map dated May 11, 2010, the project site is not located in a Fire Hazard District. According to the California Department of Forestry and Fire Prevention, Fire Hazard Severity Zones Map, the project site is not located in a Very High Fire Hazard Severity Zone. Therefore, the project will not be exposed to risks from wildland fires.

This response describes the physical surroundings of the project site and why the project is not at risk from wildland fires. In addition, maps prepared by the city and the California Department of Forestry and Fire Prevention were consulted.

Example 2

Following is a sample answer for a project that is located in a high fire hazard area identified at the city level but not by the California Department of Forestry and Fire Prevention:

According to the City Fire Hazard Overlay District Map dated May 11, 2009, the project site is located in a Fire Hazard District. The surrounding area contains many undeveloped areas that are interspersed with clusters of residential dwellings. The project is required to comply with the standards contained in Municipal Code Section 32.54.730 as follows:

Construction Requirements:

1. Cantilevered or standard type decks shall be: (a) constructed with a minimum of at least one and one-half-inch wood decking; (b) protected on the underside with materials approved for one-hour fire resistive construction; and/or (c) be of noncombustible materials, as defined in the California Building Code.

2. A minimum of two three-quarter-inch faucets with hose connections, each served by a three-quarter-inch waterline and installed prior to any pressure-reducing device, shall be available per structure. One such faucet shall be on the rear of the structure.

3. All fences adjacent to fuel modification areas or wildland areas shall be constructed of noncombustible materials as defined in the California Building Code. All other fences, including those on the interior of such development project, are not subject to this requirement.

4. All exterior doors made of wood or wood portions shall be solid core wood.

5. All exterior window frame material shall be metallic.

Fuel Modification Requirements:

A one-hundred (100) foot wide fuel modification zone is required along the west and east boundaries of the project site. Any highly flammable native brush will be cleared and replaced with mostly low growing groundcover possessing potentially high moisture content in the fuel modification zone. These are mandatory requirements that will be included in the project's conditions of approval.

This response describes the surrounding environment and the types of conditions that will be imposed on the project to reduce impacts from wildland fires.

The following example does not answer the question comprehensively:

The project site not located in an area subject to wildfires.

This response provides no factual date to support the conclusion because it doesn't make reference to official fire hazard maps nor does it describe the site and its surroundings with respect to wildland fire hazards.

4. Determining Significance

Following are some general factors to consider for determining significance:

- Are there any Thresholds of Significance that were formally adopted by the lead agency that are applicable to the project?

- Has the lead agency set a precedent in previously approved CEQA documents in responding to the question? If so, the Initial Study Checklist preparer should be aware of how other CEQA documents have responded to the question.

- If a project is located in an area shown on a map used by the lead agency to identify wildland fire hazard areas then impacts are potentially significant.

  Mitigation measures such as establishing a fuel modification zone (e.g.. a strip of land where combustible native or ornamental vegetation has been modified and/or partially or totally replaced with drought-tolerant, low-fuel-volume plants) adjacent to the fire hazard area or applying building codes intended to address construction for areas that interface with wildland fire hazard area may be required.

Chapter IX

Hydrology and Water Quality

Introduction

This Chapter deals with hydrology (i.e. drainage and flooding) and water quality. In order to determine the scope of the questions posed in this Chapter, it is useful to know some background information pertaining to hydrology and water quality.

Hydrology

Hydrology deals with both surface drainage and flooding.

Surface Drainage

Surface water runoff is first handled at the local level by either a city or county through a storm drain system (i.e. gutters, culverts, storm drain pipes etc.). As surface water is collected it feeds into a larger system (i.e. large diameter pipes, channels, etc.) that are typically the responsibility of a county flood control district or similar entity.

Flooding

Flooding deals with flood risks as they pertain to flood hazard areas or zones, failure of a levee or dam, and inundation caused by seiche, tsunami, or mudflows. Flood effects can be local, impacting a neighborhood or community, or very large, affecting entire river basins.

In order to determine risk from certain types of floods, The National Flood Insurance Program, operated by the Federal Emergency Management Agency, prepares Flood Insurance Rate Maps to identify potential flooding problems.

Water Quality

The Porter-Cologne Water Quality Control Act is the principal law governing water quality regulation in California. This statute established the State Water Regional Control Board and nine (9) Regional Water Quality Control Boards which are charged with implementing its provisions.

According to the State Water Resources Board: *"The Water Boards regulate wastewater discharges to both surface water (rivers, ocean, etc.) and to groundwater (via land). The Water Boards also regulate storm water discharges from construction, industrial, and municipal activities; discharges from irrigated agriculture; dredge and fill activities; the alteration of any federal water body under the 401 certification program; and several other activities with practices that could degrade water quality."*

The following diagram shows the relationship for regulatory authority for water quality in California.

At the local level, operators of storm water drainage systems are required to obtain a National Pollutant Discharge Elimination System permit for municipal stormwater discharges involving medium (serving between 100,000 and 250,000 people) and large (serving 250,000 people) municipalities. Most of these permits are issued to a group of co-permittees encompassing an entire metropolitan area.

These permits require storm drain system operators to effectively prohibit non-stormwater discharges to the system and to implement controls to reduce the discharge of pollutants to the maximum extent practicable.

***

The series of questions in this section are intended to address how surface runoff is collected so that flooding does not occur and that water quality is not impacted by pollutants. In addition, questions are posed about flooding caused by dam and levee failure and sesiche, tsunami, and mudflow.

293

The Office of Planning and Research has an excellent Technical Advisory on hydrology and water quality titled: *CEQA and Low Impact Development Stormwater Design: Preserving Stormwater Quality and Stream Integrity Through California Environmental Quality Act (CEQA) Review.* The document can be found at:

www.opr.ca.gov/ceqa/pdfs/Technical_Advisory_LID.pdf or enter "ceqa low impact development storm water design" in an Internet search engine.

IX. HYDROLOGY and WATER QUALITY

Would the project:

(a) Violate any water quality standards or waste discharge requirements?

1. Determining the Scope of the Question

In order to determine the scope of the question, it is separated into the following parts:

Water Quality Standards

Water Quality Standards can be summarized as follows:

✓ State-adopted and U.S. Environmental Protection Agency approved ambient standards for water bodies. The standards prescribe the use of the water body and establish the water quality criteria that must be met.

✓ The limits or levels of water quality elements or biological characteristics established to reasonably protect the beneficial uses of water or the prevent problems within a specific area. Water quality objectives may be numeric or narrative.

✓ Levels of water quality determined by the U.S. Environmental Protection Agency and expected to render a body of water suitable for its designated use. Criteria are based on specific levels of pollutants that would make the water harmful if used for drinking, swimming, farming, fish production, or industrial processes.

The State Water Resources Control Board in conjunction with the nine (9) Regional Water Quality Control Boards is responsible for implementing water quality standards.

Waste Discharge Requirements

Water Code Section 13050((d) states:

"Waste includes sewage and any and all other waste substances, liquid, solid, gaseous, or radioactive, associated with human habitation, or of human or animal origin, or from any producing, manufacturing, or processing operation, including waste placed within containers of whatever nature prior to, and for purposes of, disposal."

Water Code Section 13260 requires that persons discharging or proposing to discharge waste that could affect the quality of the waters of the State, other than into a community sewer system, shall file a Report of Waste Discharge containing information which may be required by the appropriate Regional Water Quality Control Board.

According to the State Water Quality Control Board, Typical activities that affect water quality include, but are not limited to, the following:

- ✓ Discharge of process wastewater not discharging to a sewer (e.g. factories, cooling water);

✓ Confined animal facilities (e.g. dairies, feedlots);
✓ Waste containments (e.g. landfills, waste ponds);

✓ Construction sites;

✓ Boatyards and shipyards;

✓ Discharges of pumped groundwater and cleanups (e.g. underground tank cleanups, dewatering, spills);

✓ Material handling areas draining to storm drains;

✓ Sewage treatment facilities;

✓ Filling of wetlands;

✓ Dredging, filling, and disposal of dredge wastes;

✓ Commercial activities not discharging to a sewer (e.g. factory waste water, storm drain); and

✓ Waste discharges to land.

Therefore, a project should be evaluated for *any* activities, including the above, which have the potential to violate any water quality standards or waste discharge requirements.

2. Where to Find the Factual Data to Answer the Question.

- Project plans.

- National Pollution Discharge Elimination System website at:

  http://cfpub.epa.gov/npdes/npdesreg. cfm?program_id=45 or enter "npdes" in an Internet search engine.

- State Water Regional Quality Control Board website at:

  www.swrcb.ca.gov/ or enter "state water regional quality control board" in an Internet search engine.

- It is recommended that the California Environmental Resources Evaluation System website be consulted to see if there is any information related to this question. The website is located at:

  ceres.ca.gov or enter "ceres evaluation" in an Internet search engine.

3. Example Answers

The following example answers the question comprehensively:

According to the Preliminary Water Quality Management Plan and the Hydrology Report prepared for the project, all new catch basins will contain fossil filters and underground infiltrator chambers will be used in the on-site detention basin.

The drainage will be treated and will then flow through 24-inch storm drains into the storm drain system in Bell Road. The on-site storm drain system will be conditioned to comply with the National Pollutant Discharge Elimination System standards to ensure that pollutants are not discharged into the storm drain system.

The National Pollution Discharge Elimination System requires Best Management Practice for Site Design, Source Control, and Treatment of Pollutants.

The Water Quality Management Plan for the project identifies Site Design Best Management Practices to include: conservation of natural areas; construct streets, sidewalks, and parking lot aisles to the minimum width necessary; and minimize the use of impervious surfaces in the landscape design.

Source Control Best Management Practices include: street sweeping; roof runoff controls; and water efficient irrigation systems for landscaping.

Treatment Control Best Management Practices include: biofilters for trash and debris, bacteria and viruses, and oils and grease.

Prior to the issuance of building permits, a final Water Quality Control Management Plan will be submitted by the applicant and approved by the City's Engineering Division, and strict adherence to the program will be required. No additional requirements are necessary besides adherence to these mandatory National Pollution Discharge Elimination System and City standards.

This response describes how surface runoff will be collected and treated before entering the storm drain system and how through compliance with the National Pollution Discharge Elimination System, water quality standards will be met.

The following example does not answer the question comprehensively:

The project is a 23,500 square feet addition to an existing building for professional office use. Construction activities could result in some physical, chemical, and biological water quality impacts from runoff. Additional runoff will be similar to the existing discharges. Existing runoff has not violated any water quality standards or waste discharge requirements in the past. Therefore, impacts would be less than significant.

This answer does not describe how the additional surface runoff will be collected and treated or where it will be discharged to. No mention of National Pollution Discharge Elimination System requirements is made.

4. Determining Significance

Following are some general factors to consider for determining significance:

- Are there any Thresholds of Significance that were formally adopted by the lead agency that are applicable to the project?

- Has the lead agency set a precedent in previously approved CEQA documents in responding to the question? If so, the Initial Study Checklist preparer should be aware of how other CEQA documents have responded to the question.

- A significant impact may occur if the project was not in compliance with any regulations of the State Regional Water Control Board, Regional Water Quality Control Board, or any local requirements pertaining to water quality.

IX. HYDROLOGY and WATER QUALITY (cont.)

Would the project:

(b) Substantially deplete groundwater supplies or interfere substantially with groundwater recharge such that there would be a net deficit in aquifer volume or a lowering of the local groundwater table level (e.g., the production rate of preexisting nearby wells would drop to a level which would not support existing land uses or planned uses for which permits have been granted)?

1. Determining the Scope of the Question

In order determine the scope of the question, it is useful to know the following terms:

Groundwater

Water Code Section 1005.1 defines "groundwater" as: *"...water beneath the surface of the ground, whether or not flowing through known and definite channels."*

Many communities use groundwater as the main source for their water supply system. In more rural areas many individual residences use groundwater extracted by wells for their water supply.

Many water purveyors use a combination of groundwater and water purchased from other sources (e.g. Metropolitan Water District in Southern California) to provide water to the community.

Aquifer

An aquifer is an underground bed or layer of permeable rock, sediment, or soil that yields water. Groundwater is extracted by wells from the underlying aquifer either by an individual for their own use or by a water purveyor to provide water to the community.

Groundwater Recharge

Groundwater recharge occurs naturally by rain, snowmelt, rivers, lakes, and streams. Water purveyors also reintroduce water to the ground with techniques such as specialized reservoirs to restore groundwater to previous levels or to keep groundwater levels stable.

***

In order to put this question in an appropriate context, the question is separated into the following parts:

Substantially Depleting Groundwater Supplies

According to the California Department of Water Resources, There are three basic methods available for managing groundwater resources in California:

(1) Management by local agencies under authority granted in the California Water Code or other applicable State statutes;

(2) Local government groundwater ordinances or joint powers agreements; and

(3) Court adjudications where the amount of water that can be extracted has been defined by a court.

Therefore, in the opinion of the author, depletion of groundwater supplies is ultimately determined by the local water purveyor and is part of the project review process.

If the project is dependent upon individual wells, then the local water agency should be contacted to see if there is a groundwater management plan or ordinances in place that addresses the supply of water from wells and if the project is contributing to the depletion of groundwater supplies in the immediate area.

Interfere Substantially with Groundwater Recharge

In general, groundwater recharge occurs as surface water is absorbed into the soil and filters down into the underground water table. This occurs in areas that do not have impervious surfaces.

Water purveyors have formal recharge programs where water is delivered to earthen basins called spreading or recharge basins where the water can soak into the ground and ultimately becomes part of the groundwater system.

In the author's opinion, in order to interfere with groundwater recharge a project would have to:

- ✓ Create impervious surfaces over an area that is identified as a having suitable soils and characteristics for aquifer recharge with an intensity and type of development that would interfere with the aquifer recharge process.

✓ Directly interfere with an area used for aquifer recharge by a local water agency by contributing to soil contamination through downstream surface runoff into the recharge area.

2. Where to Find the Factual Data to Answer the Question

- Consult with the local water agency through the project review process.

- The Water Education Foundation has a webpage titled: "Where Does My Water Come From" that provides general information on water supply. The webpage is located at:

  www.ater-ed.org/watersources/or enter "where does my water come from" in an Internet search engine.

- The issue of future water supply reliability is discussed in the California Department of Water Resources' update to the State Water Plan, which can be viewed at:

  www.waterplan.water.ca.gov or enter "california state water plan" in an Internet search engine.

- Visit this U.S. EPA web site to learn more about the surface water resources in your region. The webpage is located at:

  http://cfpub.epa.gov/surf/locate/index .cfm or enter "us epa surf your watershed" in an Internet search engine.

- It is recommended that the California Environmental Resources Evaluation System website be consulted to see if there is any information related to this question. The website is located at:

  ceres.ca.gov or enter "ceres evaluation" in an Internet search engine.

3. Example Answers

The following example answers the question comprehensively:

The project will connect to the City's water supply system via an 8 inch pipe in Charles Street. The City's water supply is provided from various sources including the Leonard Valley Groundwater Basin.

The City's Water Master Plan evaluated the City's existing and planned water sources, and water distribution systems with their respect to their ability to meet a project's water demands.

The City's Water Master Plan considered the City's General Plan Land Use Plan in determining future water demand. The evaluation of water demands includes a comprehensive assessment of historical demands and a projection of future demands based on forecasted development of the remaining developable lands within the City's water service area.

Projections were done in 5-year increments, as estimated from the status and timing of currently approved development as well as probable future development within the context of the City's General Plan. The existing demands are based on actual observed water use, with future demands estimated from reasonable demand coefficients applied to various categories of land use.

The General Plan Land Use designation for the property is High Density Residential with a density of up to 25 dwelling units per acre. Under the General Plan, the site (4.62 acres) has the potential to develop 115 units. The Master Plan projected water demand for the site was for 115 units. The project is proposing 65 units, which is well below the demand projected by the City's Water Master Plan.

Based on the aforementioned information, the City's water supply has adequate supply to provide water to the project and depletion of groundwater supplies will not occur.

In addition, the site is located in an urbanized area that is surrounded on all sides by existing development. The site is not being used as an aquifer recharge area by the Leonard Valley Groundwater Basin so it is not anticipated that the natural aquifer recharge process will be impacted.

This response takes into account that adequate groundwater supplies exist to serve the project and that the site is not being used for aquifer recharging.

The following example does not answer the question comprehensively:

The site is currently not being used for aquifer recharging. As such, additional construction is not likely to substantially deplete groundwater supplies or interfere with groundwater recharge such that there would be a net deficit in aquifer volume or a lowering of the local groundwater table level.

This response does not discuss the water demand of the project vs. the supply of water. There is no factual data to support the conclusion other than the site is not being used for aquifer recharge.

4. Determining Significance

Following are some general factors to consider for determining significance:

- Are there any Thresholds of Significance that were formally adopted by the lead agency that are applicable to the project?

- Has the lead agency set a precedent in previously approved CEQA documents in responding to the question? If so, the Initial Study Checklist preparer should be aware of how other CEQA documents have responded to the question.

- In determining significance for this question, the Initial Study Checklist preparer should consider the following:

✓ What is the source of water for the project and to what degree is it dependent on groundwater?

✓ What are the physical characteristics of the site in terms of its ability to serve as a groundwater recharge area (e.g. location, size, soil composition, permeability)?

✓ Could the project interfere directly or indirectly with an existing aquifer recharge area that is managed by a local water agency?

Activities that could interfere directly or indirectly with an existing aquifer recharge area include: creating impervious surfaces through development that prevent absorption of water into the ground; creating surface runoff that may contaminate downstream aquifer recharge areas; and impeding the flow of water to an aquifer recharge area.

IX. HYDROLOGY and WATER QUALITY (cont.)

Would the project:

(c) Substantially alter the existing drainage pattern of the site or area, including through the alteration of the course of a stream or river, in a manner which would result in substantial erosion or siltation on- or off-site?

1. Determining the Scope of the Question

In order to determine the scope of the question, it is separated into the following parts:

Altering the Existing Drainage Pattern of the Site

Altering the existing drainage pattern of a site is common. Off-site flows that enter the site are typically redirected and collected in on-site detention/retention basins, pipes, swales, or culverts before they are discharged off-site. Thus, the existing on-site drainage pattern is altered.

However, streams or rivers cannot be altered without permission from either the U.S. Army Corps of Engineers, the California Department of Fish and Game, or the Regional Water Quality Control Board depending on who has jurisdiction over the stream or river. Thus, any alteration is addressed through the permitting process for these agencies.

Altering the Existing Drainage Pattern of the Area

Altering the existing drainage pattern of an area typically occurs as a result of creating impervious surfaces which could increase the volume of off-site flows to the extent that erosion of soil or siltation (the process of becoming clogged with fine sediments) occurs.

The alteration of the course of an existing stream or river can occur if surface water runoff from a project is directed into the stream or river causing bank erosion or siltation.

Result in Substantial Erosion or Siltation On-Site or Off-Site

In practice, off-site flows are not allowed to exceed the pre-development condition. On-site measures such as detention basins or a storm drainage system designed to slow the rate of off-site flows are intended to prevent alteration of the drainage pattern of an area.

In addition, projects are required to comply with the mandatory requirements of the National Pollution Discharge Elimination System so that off – site soil erosion and siltation are managed in a fashion that does result in negative impacts downstream.

***

Because of the aforementioned, it is unlikely that the alteration of the existing drainage pattern of an area, including through the alteration of the course of a stream or river, will result in substantial erosion or siltation on-or off-site.

2. Where to Find the Factual Data to Answer the Question

- Project hydrology (drainage) report.

- National Pollution Discharge Elimination System website located at:

  http://cfpub.epa.gov/npdes/npdesreg. cfm?program_id=45 or enter "npdes" in an Internet search engine.

- It is recommended that the California Environmental Resources Evaluation System website be consulted to see if there is any information related to this question. The website is located at:

  ceres.ca.gov or enter "ceres evaluation" in an Internet search engine.

3. Example Answers

The following example answers the question comprehensively:

Development of the project site will create impervious surfaces and increase the amount of surface runoff. According to the Hydrology Report prepared for the project, the project site receives upstream drainage from approximately 5.20 acres of land lying to the southwest which produce Q100 flows of 33.5 cfs and Q10 flows of 21.2 cfs.

These flows will be intercepted at the southerly property line and conveyed via concrete swales and/or 18-inch pipes to a new 24-inch storm drain which will connect to an existing 36-inch storm drain lying within Rogers Road. The 36-inch storm drain currently connects to an existing 60-inch culvert which crosses under Rogers Road. The existing 60-inch culvert can handle Q100 flows of 216.3 cfs.

The drainage system is designed to control the flow rate of on-site runoff so as not to exceed the pre-development condition so that the drainage pattern of the area will not be altered.

In addition, the on-site storm drain system is required to comply with the mandatory requirements of the National Pollution Discharge Elimination System to control siltation.

Therefore, both on-site and off-site erosion or siltation will not be substantial.

This response discusses the methods used to ensure that post-development off-site flows do not increase to the extent that significant erosion and siltation will occur either on-site or off-site.

The following example does not answer the question comprehensively:

The project will add substantially more pavement in the form of a building to cause additional runoff onto the streets. As part of the general requirements for industrial construction, the project will be required to comply with the National Pollutant Discharge Elimination System. Therefore, significant erosion and siltation will not occur either on-site or off-site.

The response does not discuss how increased runoff will be accommodated so that the existing drainage patterns will not be altered.

It does state that National Pollution Discharge Elimination System requirements will be implemented but that only answers one part of the question.

4. Determining Significance

Following are some general factors to consider for determining significance:

- Are there any Thresholds of Significance that were formally adopted by the lead agency that are applicable to the project?

- Has the lead agency set a precedent in previously approved CEQA documents in responding to the question? If so, the Initial Study Checklist preparer should be aware of how other CEQA documents have responded to the question.

- The key factor in determining if impacts are significant is to evaluate the difference between the pre-development surface runoff volumes vs. the post-development surface runoff volumes and how the increased volumes will be managed and treated so that the runoff does not result in erosion or siltation on or off-site.

IX. HYDROLOGY and WATER QUALITY (cont.)

Would the project:

(d) Substantially alter the existing drainage pattern of the site or area, including through the alteration of the course of a stream or river, or substantially increase the rate or amount of surface runoff in a manner which would result in flooding on- or off-site?

1. Determining the Scope of the Question

This question differs from Question IX(c) in that it deals with flooding as a result of a project instead of erosion and siltation. In the context of this question, flooding would be of a local nature because flooding on a larger scale is addressed in Question IX (i).

It the opinion of the author, this question refers to flooding caused by increased surface runoff which is not adequately controlled.

In order to determine the scope of the question, it is separated into the following parts:

Alteration in the Course of a Stream or River

A project could contribute to flooding if the course of a stream or river on the site was altered. However, this is unlikely occurrence because the alteration of a stream or river is not allowed unless reviewed and approved by the California Department of Fish and Game, U.S. Army Corps of Engineers, or the Regional Water Quality Control Board depending on whom has jurisdiction over the stream or river.

<u>Substantially Increase the Rate or Amount of Surface Runoff in a Manner Which Would Result in Flooding On-Site or Off-Site</u>

Local agencies have regulations in place that require that surface runoff be managed so that post-development volumes are the same as pre-development volumes and that downstream storm drain facilities are adequately sized and constructed to accommodate increased surface runoff.

For example, a project may not be allowed to commence construction until a downstream drainage channel is improved so that runoff entering the channel can be accommodated without flooding the local area.

***

Because of the aforementioned, it is unlikely that the alteration of the existing drainage pattern of an area, including through the alteration of the course of a stream or river, will result in substantial flooding on-or off-site.

2. *Where to Find the Factual Data to Answer the Question.*

- Project hydrology (drainage) report.

- Local flood control department or agency.

- It is recommended that the California Environmental Resources Evaluation System website be consulted to see if there is any information related to this question. The website is located at:

ceres.ca.gov or enter "ceres evaluation" in an Internet search engine.

3. Example Answers.

The following example answers the question comprehensively:

There are no streams or river on the project site. Development of the project site will create impervious surfaces and increase the amount of surface runoff. According to the Hydrology Report prepared for the project, the project site receives upstream drainage from approximately 5.20 acres of land lying to the southwest which produce Q100 flows of 33.5 cfs and Q10 flows of 21.2 cfs.

These flows will be intercepted at the southerly property line and conveyed via concrete swales and/or 18-inch pipes to a new 24-inch storm drain which will connect to an existing 36-inch storm drain lying within Rogers Road. The 36-inch storm drain currently connects to an existing 60-inch culvert which crosses under Rogers Road. The existing 60-inch culvert can handle Q100 flows of 216.3 cfs.

The drainage system is designed to control the flow rate of on-site runoff so as not to exceed the pre-development condition so that the drainage pattern of the area will not be altered to the extent flooding will occur.

This response discusses how drainage will be accommodated in a manner that will not result in flooding.

The following example does not answer the question comprehensively:

The project is adding a 45,000 square foot building to a vacant portion of a developed site. The project will not alter existing drainage patterns in a manner that would result in flooding on or offsite. No impacts would occur.

The response does not provide details as to how the increased surface runoff that will be managed so that flooding will not occur.

4. Determining Significance

Following are some general factors to consider for determining significance:

- Are there any Thresholds of Significance that were formally adopted by the lead agency that are applicable to the project?

- Has the lead agency set a precedent in previously approved CEQA documents in responding to the question? If so, the Initial Study Checklist preparer should be aware of how other CEQA documents have responded to the question.

- The key factor in determining if impacts are significant is to evaluate the difference between the pre-development surface runoff volumes vs. the post- development surface runoff volumes and how the increased volumes will be managed so that the runoff does not result in flooding.

IX. HYDROLOGY and WATER QUALITY (cont.)

Would the project:

(e) Create or contribute runoff water which would exceed the capacity of existing or planned stormwater drainage systems or provide substantial additional sources of polluted runoff?

1. Determining the Scope of the Question

In the author's opinion this question is similar to Questions IX (a), IX(c) and IX (d) in that it deals with polluted runoff and exceeding the capacity of stormwater drainage systems which could result in flooding.

Many Initial Study Checklists combine the answers into one discussion or cross reference the answers with each other.

In whatever manner this question is answered, the Initial Study Checklist preparer should include in the response:

- ✓ A discussion of the factors that contribute to increased surface runoff (e.g. creating impervious surfaces);

- ✓ How the increased runoff is managed both on-site and off-site so as not to exceed the capacity of the drainage system serving the project; and

- ✓ A discussion of the National Pollution Discharge Elimination System requirements that would control surface runoff pollutants.

319

2. Where to Find the Factual Data to Answer the Question

- Project hydrology (drainage) report.

- Local flood control department.

- National Pollution Discharge Elimination System website at:

  http://cfpub.epa.gov/npdes/npdesreg. cfm?program_id=45 or enter "npdes" in an Internet search engine.

- It is recommended that the California Environmental Resources Evaluation System website be consulted to see if there is any information related to this question. The website is located at:

  ceres.ca.gov or enter "ceres evaluation" in an Internet search engine.

3. Example Answers

The following example answers the question comprehensively:

Development of the project site will create impervious surfaces and increase the amount of surface runoff. According to the Hydrology Report prepared for the project, the project site receives upstream drainage from approximately 5.20 acres of land lying to the southwest which produce Q100 flows of 33.5 cfs and Q10 flows of 21.2 cfs.

These flows will be intercepted at the southerly property line and conveyed via concrete swales and/or 18-inch pipes to a new 24-inch storm drain which will connect to an existing 36-inch storm drain lying within Rogers Road. The 36-inch storm drain currently connects to an existing 60-inch culvert which crosses under Rogers Road. The existing 60-inch culvert can handle Q100 flows of 216.3 cfs.

The drainage system is designed to control the flow rate of on-site runoff so as not to exceed the pre-development condition so that the capacity of the existing or planned storm drain system will not be exceeded.

In addition, the on-site storm drain system is required to comply with the mandatory requirements of the National Pollution Discharge Elimination System to control polluted runoff.

Based on the aforementioned, the project would not create runoff that would exceed the capacity of the stormwater drainage system and would not provide a substantial additional source of polluted runoff.

This response incorporates the responses for Questions IX(a), IX(c) and IX (d) which adequately answers the question.

The following example does not answer the question comprehensively:

The project is adding a 45,000 square foot building to a vacant portion of a developed site. The project will not contribute run-off water which would exceed the capacity of drainage systems in a manner that would result in substantial additional sources of polluted run-off.

Construction activities will be conducted in conformance with applicable National Pollution Elimination System Best Management Practices established by the State Water Resources Control Board. No impacts would occur.

The response does not provide details as to how the increased surface runoff that will be managed so that the capacity of the storm drain system will not be exceeded.

It does state that National Pollution Discharge Elimination System requirements will be implemented, but that only answers one part of the question.

4. Determining Significance

Following are some general factors to consider for determining significance:

- Are there any Thresholds of Significance that were formally adopted by the lead agency that are applicable to the project?

- Has the lead agency set a precedent in previously approved CEQA documents in responding to the question? If so, the Initial Study Checklist preparer should be aware of how other CEQA documents have responded to the question.

- A key factor is to determine the difference between the pre-development surface runoff volumes vs. the post- development surface runoff volumes and how the increased volumes will be accommodated so that the runoff does not exceed the capacity of the stormwater drainage system.

- A significant impact may occur if the project was not in compliance with any regulations of the State Regional Water Control Board, Regional Water Quality Control Board, or any local requirements pertaining to water quality.

IX. HYDROLOGY and WATER QUALITY (cont.)

Would the project:

(f) Otherwise substantially degrade water quality?

1. Determining the Scope of the Question

In the author's opinion this question is similar to Questions IX(a), IX(c) and IX(e) in that it deals with polluted runoff. Many Initial Study Checklists combine the answers into one discussion or cross reference the answers with each other.

In whatever manner this question is answered, the Initial Study Checklist preparer should include in the response:

- ✓ A discussion of the factors that contribute to increased surface runoff (e.g. creating impervious surfaces);

- ✓ How the increased runoff is treated and managed both on-site and off-site; and

- ✓ A discussion of the National Pollution Discharge Elimination System requirements that would control surface runoff pollutants.

2. Where to Find the Factual Data to Answer the Question

- National Pollution Discharge Elimination System website at:

http://cfpub.epa.gov/npdes/npdesreg. cfm?program_id=45 or enter "npdes" in an Internet search engine.

- State Water Regional Quality Control Board website at:

  http://www.swrcb.ca.gov/ or enter "state water regional quality control board" in an Internet search engine.

- It is recommended that the California Environmental Resources Evaluation System website be consulted to see if there is any information related to this question. The website is located at:

  ceres.ca.gov or enter "ceres evaluation" in an Internet search engine.

3. Example Answers

The following example answers the question comprehensively:

Potential water pollutants that could be released from the project site include construction-related pollutants, sediment, vehicle and equipment fluids, commercial cleaning agents, trash, landscaping by-products, and other typical urban stormwater pollutants.

Impacts from these potential pollutants are adequately addressed in Questions VIII(a), VIII (c), and VII(e) of this Initial Study Checklist. Therefore, the project would not otherwise substantially degrade water quality.

This response incorporates the responses for Questions IX(a), IX(c) and IX(e) which adequately answers the question.

The following example does not answer the question comprehensively:

The project is adding a 45,000 square foot building to a vacant portion of a developed site. The proposed project will not substantially degrade water quality. No impacts would occur.

The response does not discuss pollutants associated with surface runoff or the degradation of water quality. It basically restates the question in the negative.

4. Determining Significance

Following are some general factors to consider for determining significance:

- Are there any Thresholds of Significance that were formally adopted by the lead agency that are applicable to the project?

- Has the lead agency set a precedent in previously approved CEQA documents in responding to the question? If so, the Initial Study Checklist preparer should be aware of how other CEQA documents have responded to the question.

- A significant impact may occur if the project was not in compliance with any regulations of the State Regional Water Control Board, Regional Water Quality Control Board, or any local requirements pertaining to water quality.

IX. HYDROLOGY and WATER QUALITY (cont.)

Would the project:

(g) Place housing within a 100-year flood hazard area as mapped on a federal Flood Hazard Boundary or Flood Insurance Rate Map or other flood hazard delineation map?

1. Determining the Scope of the Question

The question is asking about housing being placed within a 100-year flood hazard area which is defined as an area of land that would be inundated by a flood having a 1 percent chance of occurring in any given year.

The question refers to three (3) types of maps:

- ✓ Flood Hazard Boundary Maps prepared by the Federal Emergency Management Agency;

- ✓ Flood Insurance Rate Maps prepared by the Federal Emergency Management Agency; and

- ✓ Other flood hazard delineation map

As part of the National Flood Insurance Program, the Federal Emergency Management Agency produces the Flood Insurance Rate Maps prepared by the Federal Emergency Management Agency.

Other maps may be produced by a local agency and contained in a general plan or other planning document based on a site specific hydrologic study.

According to the Federal Emergency Management Agency, the Flood Insurance Rate Map is the most common map and most communities use this type of map to assess flood risks.

At a minimum, flood maps show flood risk zones and their boundaries, and may also show floodways.

The Flood Hazard Boundary Map is an older version of a flood map and is based on approximate data. In the opinion of the author, reliance on the Flood Insurance Rate Map is adequate to answer this question.

2. Where to Find the Factual Data to Answer the Question

- National Flood Insurance Program website located at:

  www.fema.gov/plan/prevent/fhm/index.shtm or enter "firm maps" on an Internet search engine.

- The local agency's general plan (usually under the safety element or similar element)

- It is recommended that the California Environmental Resources Evaluation System website be consulted to see if there is any information related to this question. The website is located at:

  ceres.ca.gov or enter "ceres evaluation" in an Internet search engine.

3. Example Answers

The following example answers the question comprehensively:

According to the National Flood Insurance Program, the site is located on Map Index Community-Panel No. 06081C9330E, Map Revised, March 18, 2008 and is not identified as being within a 100-year flood hazard area.

The project site is not within a flood hazard area as shown on the City's Flood Hazard Area Map. Additionally, the project is a commercial project with no residential components. Therefore, the proposed project would not place housing in a flood hazard area.

This response makes reference to the sources (i.e. maps) which show that the project is not located within a 100-year flood hazard area and states that no housing is involved in the project.

The following example does not answer the question comprehensively:

The project site is not in a Flood Hazard Zone or located in a 100-year flood plain. No impacts would result.

This response provides no reference (ie.map) to support its conclusion. It basically repeats the question in the negative.

4. Determining Significance

Following are some general factors to consider for determining significance:

- Are there any Thresholds of Significance that were formally adopted by the lead agency that are applicable to the project?

- Has the lead agency set a precedent in previously approved CEQA documents in responding to the question? If so, the Initial Study Checklist preparer should be aware of how other CEQA documents have responded to the question.

- Location of a housing project in a 100-year flood hazard area may be a significant impact.

IX. HYDROLOGY and WATER QUALITY (cont.)

Would the project:

(h) Place within a 100-year flood hazard area structures which would impede or redirect flood flows?

1. Determining the Scope of the Question

Similar to Question IX (g), this question deals with the 100-year flood hazard area. The question makes no reference to what sources are to be consulted for determination of the 100-year flood hazard area (e.g. Federal Emergency Management Agency maps).

However, Federal Emergency Management Agency maps would be an acceptable source as well as maps prepared by a local agency.

This question also uses the term "structures" which in the context of land use planning means:

"anything constructed or erected, the use of which required location on the ground or attachment to something having location on the ground; including, but not limited to, buildings, fences, walls, infrastructure, and free-standing signs."

The key to putting this question in the proper context is determining if a "structure" would "impede" or "redirect" flood flows within a 100-year flood hazard area.

Impeding or redirecting flood flows may have consequences such as:

✓ Diverting flood flows causing other areas to become flooded;

✓ Diverting floodwaters into the elevated portion of a building or into adjacent buildings; or

✓ Causing floodborne debris to strike other buildings, resulting in damage to the buildings.

Generally, new structures in flood hazard areas are required to be elevated to or above the base flood elevation. In some cases structures are constructed on open foundations (pilings, columns, or piers, and, sometimes, shear walls) that allow floodwaters to pass beneath the elevated structures. The area beneath these elevated structures must remain free of any obstructions that would prevent the free flow floodwaters during a 100-year flood event.

2. Where to Find the Factual Data to Answer the Question

- National Flood Insurance Program website located at:

  www.fema.gov/plan/prevent/fhm/index.shtm or enter "firm maps" on an Internet search engine.

- The local agency's general plan (usually under the safety element or similar element).

- Project plans and an analysis of the degree to which a structure may obstruct floodflows.

- It is recommended that the California Environmental Resources Evaluation System website be consulted to see if there is any information related to this question. The website is located at:

  ceres.ca.gov or enter "ceres evaluation" in an Internet search engine.

3. Example Answers

The following example answers the question comprehensively:

The project is the construction of a 1,200 square foot maintenance building on a 10,000 square foot site. There will be paved parking for up to 6 vehicles. No outdoor storage is allowed. According to the National Flood Insurance Program, the project site is located in Flood Zone "A" as shown on Community-Panel No. 06081C9330E, Map Revised, March 18, 2006.

The elevation of the building and the building support utility systems are elevated above the 100-year flood event according to the City Public Works Department. Therefore, flood flows will not be impeded or redirected.

This response indicates that the project is located within a 100-year flood hazard zone but that the impediment or redirection of flood flows has been mitigated by constructing the building above the 100-year flood elevation.

The following example does not answer the question comprehensively:

The project site is not in a Flood Hazard Zone or located in a 100-year flood plain. No impacts would result.

This response provides no reference (i.e. map) to support its conclusion. It basically repeats the question in the negative and makes no reference to impeding or redirecting flood flows.

4. Determining Significance

Following are some general principals to consider for determining significance:

- Are there any Thresholds of Significance that were formally adopted by the lead agency that are applicable to the project?

- Has the lead agency set a precedent in previously approved CEQA documents in responding to the question? If so, the Initial Study Checklist preparer should be aware of how other CEQA documents have responded to the question.

- If a project is located within the 100-year flood hazard area then it must meet certain design standards to ensure that flood flows are not impeded or redirected during a 100-year flood event.

IX. HYDROLOGY and WATER QUALITY (cont.)

Would the project:

(i) Expose people or structures to a significant risk of loss, injury or death involving flooding, including flooding as a result of the failure of a levee or dam?

1. Determining the Scope of the Question

Many Initial Study Checklist responses just focus on the failure of a levee or dam part of the question.

However, this question deals with all types of flooding, not just flooding as a result of the failure of a levee or dam.

Floods can also be caused by heavy rains, runoff from deep snow cover, and storm-stoked ocean swells in combination with unusually high tides in coastal areas to name a few examples.

The Initial Study Checklist preparer should address flooding caused by all types of factors in the response.

2. Where to Find the Factual Data to Answer the Question

- The location of the project site in relation to flood prone areas and dams or levees.

- National Flood Insurance Program website located at:

**www.fema.gov/plan/prevent/fhm/inde
x.shtm** or enter "firm maps" on an Internet
search engine.

- The local agency's general plan (usually
  under the safety element or similar element)
  may contain information on flood risk
  including dam inundation areas.

- The Department of Water Resources
  provides a listing of dam locations in
  California on their website at:

  **www.water.ca.gov/damsafety/damlisti
  ng/index.cfm** or enter "california dam
  safety" on an Internet search engine.

- It is recommended that the California
  Environmental Resources Evaluation System
  website be consulted to see if there is any
  information related to this question. The
  website is located at:

  ceres.ca.gov or enter "ceres evaluation" in
  an Internet search engine.

3. Example Answers

***The following example answers the question
comprehensively:***

*The project site is not within a "Flood Hazard" area
or a "Dam Inundation" area as shown on Figure S-
5 of the General Plan or in a flood hazard area as
shown on National Flood Insurance Program maps.*

In addition there are no levees, dams, or other water detention facilities upstream of the project site capable of causing flooding on the project site. Therefore, the project would not be at a significant risk from flooding, including flooding as a result of the failure of a levee or a dam.

This response takes into account the most probable factors that could cause flooding by consulting the general plan and National Flood Insurance Program Flood Hazard maps and by analyzing the location of the site relative to dams and levees.

The following example does not answer the question comprehensively:

The project site is not located within a dam inundation area. No impact would occur.

This response only focuses on flooding from a dam. It does not discuss flood hazard areas as shown on maps in a general plan or other planning documents or the National Flood Insurance Program.

4. Determining Significance

Following are some general factors to consider for determining significance:

- Are there any Thresholds of Significance that were formally adopted by the lead agency that are applicable to the project?

- Has the lead agency set a precedent in previously approved CEQA documents in responding to the question? If so, the Initial

Study Checklist preparer should be aware of how other CEQA documents have responded to the question.

- If the project site is located in a flood hazard area defined by the National Flood Insurance Program or in a flood hazard area (including risk from a dam or levee failure) by the local agency general plan or other planning document, then flood risks may be significant.

IX. HYDROLOGY and WATER QUALITY (cont.)

Would the project (expose people or structures to):

(j) Inundation by seiche, tsunami, or mudflow?

1. Determining the Scope of the Question

In order to understand the context of the question it is useful to be familiar with the terms "seiche", "tsunami" and "mudflow".

Seiche

A seiche is a free or standing-wave oscillation of the surface of water in an enclosed or semi-enclosed basin (as a lake, bay, or harbor) that varies in a period, depending on the physical dimensions of the basin, from a few minutes to several hours, and in height from several inches to a several feet.

Larger seiches can be caused by wind, earthquakes or underwater landslides. Areas located along the shoreline of a lake or reservoir are also susceptible to inundation by a seiche. The size of a seiche and the affected inundation area is dependent on different factors including size and depth of the water body, elevation, and source.

Tsunami

A tsunami is a huge ocean wave that can travel at speeds up to 600 miles per hour over hundreds of miles over open sea before it hits land. Sometimes incorrectly called a tidal wave, a tsunami is usually caused by an earthquake volcanic eruption or coastal landslide.

Mudflow

A mudflow is a downhill movement of soft wet earth and debris, made fluid by rain or melted snow and often building up great speed. Mudflows are caused by heavy and rapid precipitation, soaking into a dirt top layer.

If the dirt top layer is on a sufficient incline, as well as not having sufficient plant life to root it down, the dirt top layer will slide on top of the underlying layer resulting in mudflow.

2. Where to Find the Factual Data to Answer the Question

- **Seiche**

    The best source of information is to determine the location of the site in relation to a waterbody large enough to create a seiche.

- **Tsunami**

    The California Department of Conservation has prepared Tsunami Inundation Maps that are located at:

    www.consrv.ca.gov/cgs/geologic_hazar ds/Tsunami/Inundation_Maps/Pages/S tatewide_Maps.aspx or enter "tsunami inundation map california" in an Internet search engine.

341

California Geological Survey Tsunamis Note 55 is a good source of information on this topic. It can be located at:

www.consrv.ca.gov/cgs/information/p ublications/cgs_notes/Documents/CGS _Note_55.pdf or enter *"California Geological Survey Note 55"* in an Internet search engine.

- **Mudflows**

  Mudflows are related to the project site's proximity to an area that is susceptible to landslides or a slope area with sufficient incline.

  California Geological Survey-CGS Note 33-Hazards From Mudslides Debris Avalanches and Debris Flows in Hillside and Wildfire Areas is a good source of information on this topic. The publication can be located at:

  www.consrv.ca.gov/CGS/information/p ublications/cgs_notes/note_33/Pages/ index or enter *"california geological survey note 33"* in an Internet Search Engine.

- It is recommended that the California Environmental Resources Evaluation System website be consulted to see if there is any information related to this question. The website is located at:

  ceres.ca.gov or enter "ceres evaluation" in an Internet search engine.

3. Example Answers

The following example answers the question comprehensively:

According to the Tsunami Inundation Maps prepared by the California Department of Conservation, impacts from tsunamis are considered low.

There are no bodies of water in the vicinity of the project site that are large enough to produce a seiche that could impact the project.

Based on the geotechnical report prepared for the project, the project site is not located in an area prone to landslides, soil slips, or slumps. Therefore, the proposed project would have no impact from mudflow.

This response bases its conclusions on the project geotechnical report (for mudflows) and information from the California Department of Conservation (for tsunamis).

It also describes the site location with respect to water bodies that could create hazards from seiches.

The following example does not answer the question comprehensively:

The site is not located within any area that would expose people or structures to a significant risk of loss, including inundation by seiche, tsunami, or mudflow.

This response provides no reference (i.e. map or other information) to support its conclusion. It basically repeats the question in the negative.

4. Determining Significance

Following are some general factors to consider in determining significance:

- Are there any Thresholds of Significance that were formally adopted by the lead agency that are applicable to the project?

- Has the lead agency set a precedent in previously approved CEQA documents in responding to the question? If so, the Initial Study Checklist preparer should be aware of how other CEQA documents have responded to the question.

- Is the project site shown on the California Department of Conservation Tsunami Inundation Maps?

- How far away project site is the nearest water body capable of producing a seiche?

- What is the project site's location with respect to geologic features (i.e. slopes, areas susceptible to landslides) capable of producing mudflows?

Chapter X

Land Use and Planning

Introduction

This Chapter addresses the potential land use and planning impacts associated with a project.

It deals with the physical impacts a project may cause, such as creating barriers that would divide an established community.

It also deals with a project's compliance with the various land use plans, policies, and regulations adopted for the purpose of avoiding or mitigating an environmental effect.

345

X. LAND USE and PLANNING

Would the project:

(a) Physically divide an established community?

1. Determining the Scope of the Question

Factors that could physically divide a community include, but are not limited to:

- ✓ Construction of major highways or roadways;

- ✓ Construction of storm channels;

- ✓ Closing bridges or roadways; and

- ✓ Construction of utility transmission lines.

The key factor with respect to this question is creating physical barriers that change the connectivity between areas of a community to the extent that persons are separated from other areas of the community. Connectivity is typically provided by roadways, pedestrian paths, and bicycle paths.

The question uses the term "community" which can have a broad definition, such as a region, city, or a neighborhood.

The Initial Study Checklist preparer should determine an appropriate geographic area for analysis and take into account how a project would physically divide the geographic area.

For example, does the area contain homes, a school, a park, a shopping center that would constitute a community?

How would the project affect the roadways, pedestrian paths, or bicycle paths that connect these areas together?

2. Where to Find the Factual Data to Answer the Question

- The scope and the scale of the project and how it fits into the connectivity of the surrounding area that is considered a "community" would be the basis for analysis.

- It is recommended that the California Environmental Resources Evaluation System website be consulted to see if there is any information related to this question. The website is located at:

  ceres.ca.gov or enter "ceres evaluation" in an Internet search engine.

3. Example Answers

The following example answers the question comprehensively:

The project is the subdivision of 40 acres of vacant land into 18 residential lots. The project is located in the Orchard Heights neighborhood of the City. The Orchard Heights neighborhood is bordered by Evans Street on the north, Shannon Street on the south, by the foothills of Socorro Mountain on the east, and by Romo Avenue on the west.

This area is characterized by large lot residential sites (minimum of 2 acres) with various types of limited equine and agricultural uses such as small horse ranches and citrus groves.

There is a network of horse and pedestrian trails that provide connectivity from one part of the neighborhood to the other. The project will connect to the existing roadway and trail system and will not create any physical barriers that will divide the neighborhood.

This response describes the characteristics of the area that makes it a "community" and discusses why development of the project would not physically divide the community.

The following example does not answer the question comprehensively:

The proposed project is located within the City limits. Driveway access will be provided to Adams Avenue. Therefore the project will have no impact.

This response discusses the project at the "city limit" level and assumes because it is within the city limits no physical division of a community will occur. However, a "community" could be a geographic subpart of a city.

It states that a driveway will provide access to an existing roadway but does not discuss how the project connects into the surrounding community.

4. Determining Significance

Following are some general factors to consider for determining significance:

- Are there any Thresholds of Significance that were formally adopted by the lead agency that are applicable to the project?

- Has the lead agency set a precedent in previously approved CEQA documents in responding to the question? If so, the Initial Study Checklist preparer should be aware of how other CEQA documents have responded to the question.

- Anything that will create a physical a barrier such that persons who previously had access to an area are separated from that area may result in a physical division of a community.

X. LAND USE and PLANNING (cont.)

Would the project:

(b) Conflict with any applicable land use plan, policy, or regulation of an agency with jurisdiction over the project (including, but not limited to the general plan, specific plan, local coastal program, or zoning ordinance) adopted for the purpose of avoiding or mitigating an environmental effect?

1. Determining the Scope of the Question

This question has wide ranging implications because it involves a variety of planning mechanisms (e.g. land use plans, policies, or regulations) that are intended to avoid or mitigate an "environmental effect."

An environmental effect would basically include all of the environmental topics contained in the Initial Study Checklist from Aesthetics to Mandatory Findings of Significance.

In responding to this question, an appropriate context would be to evaluate the project against the applicable land use plans, policies, or regulations pertaining to the environmental effects of *any* agency having jurisdiction over the project. This would include federal, state, regional, and local agencies.

In the opinion of the author, if the Initial Study Checklist is completed properly, compliance with the various land use plans, policies, and regulations will be addressed.

2. Where to Find the Factual Data to Answer the Question

- The sources to answer this question would essentially be the land use plans, policies, or regulations that have been consulted to answer each of the questions in the Initial Study Checklist.

- It is recommended that the California Environmental Resources Evaluation System website be consulted to see if there is any information related to this question. The website is located at:

  ceres.ca.gov or enter "ceres evaluation" in an Internet search engine.

3. Example Answers

Author's Note: *The following is based on a city located in the Coachella Valley area of Riverside County and is used as an example only.*

Applicable land use plans, policies, or regulations will vary depending upon the project location and characteristics. For example, if the project has no impact on biological resources because the site is already paved then there is no need to address California Department of Fish and Game regulations.

In addition, a table does not have to be prepared to answer this question. A table was used in this example to illustrate the types of land use plans, policies, and regulations that could apply to a project.

The following examples answer the question comprehensively:

Example 1

The land use plans, policies, and regulations that affect the project are described in the following table.

Table X.1 Applicable Land Use Plans, Policies, or Regulations

Environmental Topic	Land Use Plan, Policy, Regulation Sources	Consistent?
I. Aesthetics	General Plan Land Use Element	YES
II. Agriculture and Forestry Resources	General Plan Conservation and Open Space Element	YES
	California Department of Conservation Farmland Mapping and Monitoring Program	YES
	Williamson Act	N/A
	State of California Department of Forestry and Fire Protection	YES
III. Air Quality	General Plan Air Quality Element	YES with mitigation
	Southcoast Air Quality Management District	YES with Mitigation
IV. Biological Resources	Coachella Valley Multiple Species Habitat Conservation Plan	YES

Environmental Topic	Land Use Plan, Policy, Regulation Sources	Consistent?
V. Cultural Resources	CEQA Guidelines Section 15064.5	YES
	Municipal Code, Chapter 12.50 (Cultural Resources Preservation)	YES
VI. Geology and Soils	Alquist-Priolo Special Studies Zone Act	YES
	California Geological Survey, Seismic Hazards Zonation Program	YES
	General Plan Public Safety Element	YES
VII. Greenhouse Gas Emissions	Office of Planning and Research OPR Technical Advisory on CEQA and Climate Change: (Published June 2008)	YES (advisory only)
	Assembly Bill 32	YES
	Senate Bill 375	YES
VIII. Hazards and Hazardous Materials	Federal Environmental Protection Agency	YES
	California Environmental Protection Agency	YES
	California Department of Toxic Substances Control	YES

353

Environmental Topic	Land Use Plan, Policy, Regulation Sources	Consistent?
	Riverside County Health Department (Certified Unified Program Agency)	YES
IX. Hydrology and Water Quality	General Plan Public Safety Element	YES
	National Pollution Discharge Elimination System	YES
X. Land Use/Planning	General Plan Land Use/Zoning Map	YES
	General Plan (all Elements)	YES
	Municipal Code Title 18, Zoning Code	YES
XI. Mineral Resources	Surface Mining and Reclamation Act	N/A
XII. Noise	General Plan Noise Element	YES with mitigation
	Municipal Code Chapter 20.06. (Noise)	YES with mitigation
XIII. Population and Housing	General Plan Housing Element	YES
XIV. Public Services	Riverside County Fire Department	YES
	Riverside County Sheriff Department	YES
	Desert Sands Unified School District	YES

Environmental Topic	Land Use Plan, Policy, Regulation Sources	Consistent?
XV. Recreation	General Plan Public Services Element	YES
XVI. Transportation/ Traffic	General Plan Circulation Element	YES
	Riverside County Congestion Management Plan-2006	YES
XVII. Utilities and Service Systems	Coachella Valley Water District	YES
	Colorado River Regional Water Quality Control Board	YES

As summarized in Table X-I and as analyzed in Sections I through XVII of this Initial Study Checklist, the project is not in conflict with any applicable land use plan, policy, or regulation of an agency with jurisdiction over the project.

This response makes reference to the analysis for each environmental topic identified in the Initial Study Checklist and provides a summary of what applicable land use plan, policy, or regulation applies to the project.

Example 2

The analysis contained in this Initial Study Checklist addressed the potential conflict with any applicable land use plan, policy, or regulation of an agency with jurisdiction over the project adopted for the purpose of avoiding or mitigating an environmental effect.

Based on this analysis, it was determined that the project could potentially have significant impacts on Air Quality and Noise. The project is located in the Southcoast Air Quality Management District and Mitigation Measures AQ-1 through AQ-7 are required to reduce air pollution emissions to below the maximum daily thresholds.

Mitigation Measures NO-1 through NO-4 are required to ensure that the project interior noise levels do not exceed the standards contained in the City's General Plan Noise Element.

Therefore, based on the analysis conducted in this Initial Study Checklist, it was determined that the project was not in conflict with any adopted land use plans, policies, or regulations adopted for the purpose of avoiding or mitigating an environmental effect.

This response provides a narrative description instead of a summary table demonstrating that the project is not in conflict with any adopted land use plans, policies, or regulations adopted for the purpose of avoiding or mitigating an environmental effect.

The following example does not answer the question comprehensively:

The proposed use is permitted by-right in the C-1, General Commercial zone. Therefore, the project will not conflict with any applicable land use plan, policy, or regulation of an agency with jurisdiction over the project adopted for the purpose of avoiding or mitigating an environmental effect.

This response assumes that consistency with the permitted uses within the applicable zone is all that is necessary to determine if a project is in conflict with any applicable land use plan, policy, or regulation of an agency with jurisdiction over the project. Compliance with zoning only is too narrow of an analysis to adequately answer the question because it excludes federal, state, regional, or local plans, polices, or regulations.

4. Determining Significance

Following are some general factors to consider for determining significance:

- Are there any Thresholds of Significance that were formally adopted by the lead agency that are applicable to the project?

- Has the lead agency set a precedent in previously approved CEQA documents in responding to the question? If so, the Initial Study Checklist preparer should be aware of how other CEQA documents have responded to the question.

- If a project is in conflict with any federal, state, regional, or local plans, polices, or regulations adopted for the purpose of avoiding or mitigating an environmental effect, impacts maybe significant.

X. LAND USE and PLANNING (cont.)

Would the project:

(c) Conflict with any applicable habitat conservation plan or natural community conservation plan?

1. Determining the Scope of the Question

In order to determine the scope of the question, it is separated into the following parts:

Habitat Conservation Plan

According to the California Department of Fish and Game website:

"Habitat Conservation Plans are long-term agreements between an applicant and the U.S. Fish and Wildlife Service. They are designed to offset any harmful effects that a proposed activity might have on federally-listed threatened and endangered species. The Habitat Conservation Plan process allows development to proceed while providing a conservation basis to conserve the species and provide for incidental take. A "No Surprises" policy provides assurances to landowners participating in Habitat Conservation Plan efforts.

A Habitat Conservation Plan can address take of federally listed, candidate and/or unlisted species. Unlisted species must be treated in the Habitat Conservation Plan as if they were listed, however, take is not authorized until the species is listed. Habitat Conservation Plan's can be prepared for any scale project (e.g., for small projects

addressing a single species or large-scale developments addressing multiple species)."
Natural Communities Conservation Plan

According to the California Department of Fish and Game website:

"The Natural Community Conservation Planning Program of the Department of Fish and Game is an unprecedented effort by the State of California, and numerous private and public partners, that takes a broad-based ecosystem approach to planning for the protection and perpetuation of biological diversity.

A Natural Community Conservation Plan identifies and provides for the regional or areawide protection of plants, animals, and their habitats, while allowing compatible and appropriate economic activity."

2. Where to Find the Factual Data to Answer the Question

- Information on Habitat Conservation Plans can be found at:

  www.fws.gov/endangered/what-we-do/hcp-overview.html or by entering "federal habitat conservation plans" in an Internet search engine.

  The U.S. Fish and Wildlife Service website has a listing of Habitat Conservation Plans for California.

  The website can be located at:

**http://ecos.fws.gov/conserv_plans/pu
blic.jsp** or enter "conservation plans and
agreements database" in an Internet search
engine. Click on the link for "Region 8,
California and Nevada" to view a list of
Plans.

- Information on Natural Community
Conservation Plans can be found at:

www.dfg.ca.gov/habcon/nccp/ or by
entering"california natural communities
conservation planning" in an Internet search
engine.

- It is recommended that the California
Environmental Resources Evaluation System
website be consulted to see if there is any
information related to this question. The
website is located at:

ceres.ca.gov or enter "ceres evaluation" in
an Internet search engine.

3. Example Answers

The following example answers the question comprehensively:

*The site is located within the boundaries of the
Western Riverside County Multi-Species Habitat
Conservation Plan ("Plan") which is considered a
Habitat Conservation Plan per the U.S. Fish and
Wildlife Service.*

*The Plan does not identify the site as being within a
Conservation Area, Cell Group, or Cell (i.e. areas*

which have been targeted for the acquisition of habitat). The site has been completely developed with a building and a paved parking lot. There are no areas on the site that would be considered as having sensitive biological resources. Therefore, the project is forecast to have no impact on a Habitat Conservation Plan or Natural Community Conservation Plan.

This response identifies that the project site is within a Habitat Conservation Plan but states the reason why the project will not be in conflict with the Plan.

The following example does not answer the question comprehensively:

The project is an infill development and there are no existing habitat conservation plans or natural community conservation plans that it could conflict with.

This response assumes that because the site is an infill development that it is not a part of a Habitat Conservation Plan or a Natural Communities Conservation Plan when in fact being an infill site has no bearing on whether or not the project site is located in such a Plan.

4. Determining Significance

- This question has only one criterion for determining significance: If a project site is located within the boundaries of a Habitat Conservation Plan or Natural Community Conservation Plan, is it consistent with the provisions of the Plan?

Chapter XI

Mineral Resources

Introduction

This question relates to "non-fuel minerals." According to the California Geological Survey, the State produces approximately 30 types of non-fuel minerals. The most commonly known are minerals such as clay, iron ore, lime, salt, Portland cement, gold, silver, sand, gravel, and crushed stone.

Sand and gravel is the leading mineral produced in the State. Combined with crushed stone, sand and gravel is used for construction aggregate which is used to construct roads, sidewalks, and building foundations for example.

In order to determine the scope of the question, it is useful to understand the regulatory framework for mineral resource mining and extraction.

The Surface Mining and Reclamation Act

Section 2790 of the Surface Mining and Reclamation Act sets for the regulatory framework for designating specific geographic areas of the state as areas of statewide or regional significance for mineral resources.

According to the *California Department of Conservation, Office of Mine Reclamation, Surface Mining and Reclamation Act and Associated Regulations,* the areas that have been designated to be of Regional Significance are identified in Sections 3550.1 through 3550.15. These resources consist of aggregate for construction purposes.

The California State Mining and Geology Board in conjunction with the California Geological Survey provides information related to the *Surface Mining and Reclamation Act.*

Local Agencies incorporate the information provided by the California State Mining and Geology Board and the California Geological Survey into their general plans, and use it in their daily land-use decisions to protect a 50-year supply of aggregate.

Any development project proposed within or near these designated areas must be evaluated in the context of causing a loss of the availability of mineral resources or creating incompatible land uses that lead to the loss of the availability of mineral resources.

Classification of mineral resource land is completed by the State Geologist in accordance with the State Mining & Geology Board's priority list into Mineral Resource Zones (called an MRZ). Classification of these areas is based on geologic and economic factors without regard to existing land use and land ownership.

The Mineral Resource Zones are described as follows:

MRZ-1-Areas where adequate geologic information indicates that no significant mineral deposits are present, or where it is judged that little likelihood exists for their presence.

MRZ-2a-Areas underlain by mineral deposits where geologic data show that significant measured or indicated resources are present.

MRZ-2b-Areas underlain by mineral deposits where geologic information indicates that significant inferred resources are present.

MRZ-3a-Areas containing known mineral deposits that may qualify as mineral resources. Further exploration work within these areas could result in the reclassification of specific localities into the MRZ-2a or MRZ-2b categories.

MRZ-3b-Areas containing inferred mineral deposits that may qualify as mineral resources.

MRZ-4—Areas where geologic information does not rule out either the presence or absence of mineral resources. The distinction between the MRZ-1 and MRZ-4 categories is important for land-use considerations. It must be emphasized that MRZ-4 classification does not imply that there is little likelihood for the presence of mineral resources, but rather there is a lack of knowledge regarding mineral occurrence.

State policy, is to include all or part of the proposed areas classified as MRZ-2a or MRZ-2b as regional or statewide significance.

However, there are two general categories of exclusion to these classifications for certain types of land:

I. Economic Exclusion, and II. Social Exclusion.

I. Economic Exclusion

A. Residential areas, and areas committed to residential development, such as approved tracts.

B. Commercial areas with land improvements (buildings).

C. Industrial areas (buildings and adjacent needed storage and parking facilities).

D. Major public or private engineering projects:

    1. Canals;

    2. Freeways;

    3. Bridges;

    4. Airports and associated developments such as parking lots;

    5. Dams;

    6. Railroads;

    7. Major pipelines; and

    8. Major power transmission lines.

E. Small areas isolated by urbanization (generally less than 40 acres)

II. Social Exclusion

    A. Cemeteries;

B. Public parks, developed historical sites and structures, and public recreation areas of all types;

C. Public or private schools, institutions, hospitals, and prisons, including adjacent developments such as parking lots; and

D. Military bases and reservations.

XI. MINERAL RESOURCES

Would the project:

(a) Result in the loss of availability of a known mineral resource that would be of value to the region and the residents of the state?

1. Determining the Scope of the Question

As noted above, minerals used in the production of construction aggregate (e.g. sand, gravel, and crushed stone) are the most widely mined minerals in the State. This is typically the context in which this question is answered.

However, the Initial Study Checklist preparer should be aware of other types of minerals that are being produced in the region (e.g. gold, silver, iron ore, clay, lime, salt, and Portland cement) and address how the project may impact those resources.

2. Where to Find the Factual Data to Answer the Question

- Local general plan.

- Useful information about the California Mineral Land Classification System can be found at:

  www.consrv.ca.gov/smgb/Guidelines/Docu ments/ClassDesig.pdf or enter "california guidelines for classification and designation of mineral lands" in an Internet search engine.

- A map showing aggregate availability in California can be found at:

  www.consrv.ca.gov/cgs/information/p ublications/ms/Documents/MS_52_ma p.pdf or enter "aggregate availability in California map" in an Internet search engine.

- The California Geological Survey webpage has information on mineral classifications available at the county level. The webpage is located at:

  www.consrv.ca.gov/cgs/information/p ublications/pub_index/Pages/products _that_we_sell.aspx or enter "cgs products that we sell" on an Internet search engine.

- It is recommended that the California Environmental Resources Evaluation System website be consulted to see if there is any information related to this question. The website is located at:

  ceres.ca.gov or enter "ceres evaluation" in an Internet search engine.

3. Example Answers

The following example answers the question comprehensively:

According to maps prepared by the California Geological Survey, the site is located in Mineral Resource Zone-1 (Areas where adequate geologic information indicates that no significant mineral _deposits are present, or where it is judged that little likelihood exists for their presence)._

In addition, according to the California Geological Survey's Aggregate Availability Map, the project is not within the vicinity of a site being used for aggregate production. The nearest aggregate production site is located in the Claremont-Upland Region which is 20 miles west of the project site.

There are no other mining sites for any type of mineral located in the vicinity of the project based on information from the California Geological Survey. Therefore, the project has no potential to result in the loss of availability of a known mineral resource.

This response makes reference to the Mineral Resource Zone in which the project site is located in and its proximity to a known aggregate resource site to support the conclusion. It also notes that there are no other mining sites for other types of minerals that are located in the vicinity of the project.

The following example does not answer the question comprehensively:

The project will not have a significant impact on mineral resources. The office building will be constructed of common materials and are required to meet all State building code requirements for energy conservation.

This response does not answer the fundamental part of the question which is whether or not the project will result in the loss of availability of a known mineral resource.

4. Determining Significance

Following are some general factors to consider for determining significance:

- Are there any Thresholds of Significance that were formally adopted by the lead agency that are applicable to the project?

- Has the lead agency set a precedent in previously approved CEQA documents in responding to the question? If so, the Initial Study Checklist preparer should be aware of how other CEQA documents have responded to the question.

- The site's Mineral Resource Zone classification and its proximity to a mineral resource extraction site are the key factors for determining significance. If a project will reduce the availability of a known mineral resource (for example by converting the site to non-mineral production uses or introducing incompatible land use prematurely in a designated mineral resource area) then impacts may be significant.

XI. MINERAL RESOURCES (cont.)

Would the project:

(b) Result in the loss of availability of a locally important mineral resource recovery site delineated on a local general plan, specific plan or other land use plan?

1. Determining the Scope of the Question

This question basically tiers off Question XI(a) because the Surface Mining and Reclamation Act is intended to provide mineral resource information for use in a local general plan, specific plan, or other land use plans.

In the author's opinion answering Question XI (a) adequately can serve as a reference in answering Question XI (b) as well. Many Initial Study Checklists often times combine this question with Question IX (a).

2. Where to Find the Factual Data to Answer the Question

- Local general plan.

- Useful information on the mineral classification system described above can be found at:

  www.consrv.ca.gov/smgb/Guidelines/Documents/ClassDesig.pdf or enter "california guidelines for classification and designation of mineral lands" in an Internet search engine.

371

- A map showing aggregate availability in California can be found at:

  www.consrv.ca.gov/cgs/information/p ublications/ms/Documents/MS_52_ma p.pdf or enter "aggregate availability in California map" in an Internet search engine.

- The California Geological Survey webpage has information on mineral classifications available at the county level. The webpage is located at:

  www.consrv.ca.gov/cgs/information/p ublications/pub_index/Pages/products _that_we_sell.aspx or enter "cgs products that we sell" in an Internet search engine.

- It is recommended that the California Environmental Resources Evaluation System website be consulted to see if there is any information related to this question. The website is located at:

  ceres.ca.gov or enter "ceres evaluation" in an Internet search engine.

3. Example Answers

As noted in the response to Question IX(a), the site is located in Mineral Resource Zone-1 (areas where adequate geologic information indicates that no significant mineral deposits are present, or where it is judged that little likelihood exists for their presence).

According to the California Geological Survey's Aggregate Availability Map, the project is not within the vicinity of a site being used for aggregate production. The nearest aggregate production site is located in the Claremont-Upland Region which is 20 miles west of the project site.

Finally, the site is not delineated on the City's General Plan, on a specific plan, or other land use plan as a mineral resource site.

Therefore, the project has no potential to result in the loss of availability of a local mineral resource recovery site.

This response makes reference to the California Geological Survey maps and aggregate production sites as well as including reference to the local agency's general plan and any applicable specific plan or other land use plan.

The following example does not answer the question comprehensively:

The activities that would be associated with the proposed project would affect a vacant area that is not being used for mineral resource production. Therefore, the project would not result in the loss of availability of locally-important minerals.

This response does not discuss whether or not the site is delineated by the local general plan, any applicable specific plan or other land use plan as a mineral resource recovery site.

4. Determining Significance

Following are some general factors to consider for determining significance:

- Are there any Thresholds of Significance that were formally adopted by the lead agency that are applicable to the project?

- Has the lead agency set a precedent in previously approved CEQA documents in responding to the question? If so, the Initial Study Checklist preparer should be aware of how other CEQA documents have responded to the question.

- The site's Mineral Resource Zone classification and its proximity to a mineral resource extraction site are the key factors for determining significance. If a project will reduce the availability of a known mineral resource (for example by converting the site to non-mineral production uses or introducing incompatible land use prematurely in a designated mineral resource area) then impacts may be significant.

- If the site is designated as a mineral resource recovery site by the local agency's general plan and/or zoning designation and the project proposes a change to another use then impacts may be significant.

Chapter XII

Noise

Introduction

The series of questions in this Chapter deals with exposure of persons to noise (both temporary and permanent), excessive groundborne vibration and related noise, and noise generated from public airports and private airstrips.

In order to determine the scope of the questions posed in this Chapter, it is useful to understand some basic noise principals and terminology.

Noise

Noise is generally defined as unwanted sound produced by human activities that interfere with communication, work, rest, recreation, or sleep.

Decibel (dB)

A decibel is a unit of measurement that indicates the relative intensity of a sound (i.e. noise). The zero point on the dB scale is based on the lowest sound level that the healthy, unimpaired human ear can detect. Audible increases in noise levels generally refer to a change of 3 dB or more, as this level has been found to be barely perceptible to the human ear in outdoor environments.

dBA

Because the human ear is not equally sensitive to all sound frequencies, a weighted scale called "Aweighting" is used because it most closely represents the range of human hearing, thus, dBA is the most common term used to describe the level of sound (i.e. noise).

Community Noise Equivalent Level (CNEL)

A noise measurement system introduced in the early 1970's by the State of California for community noise exposure. CNEL can be measured using ordinary dBA readings.

Day-Night Noise Levels (Ldn)

Another commonly used method to measure noise is the day/night average level or Ldn. The Ldn is a measure of the 24-hour average noise level at a given location. It was adopted by the U.S. Environmental Protection Agency for developing criteria for the evaluation of community noise exposure.

Significance of the Changes in Noise Levels

In general, a 3 dB change in sound pressure level is considered a barely detectable difference in most situations. A 5 dB change is readily noticeable and a 10dB change is considered a doubling (or halving) of the subjective loudness.

For each doubling of distance from a point noise source, the sound level will decrease by 6 dB. In other words, if a person is 100 feet from a machine and moves 200 feet from that source, sound levels will drop by approximately 6 dB. Moving 400 feet away, sound levels will drop approximately another 6 dB.

Noise Regulations

State

A maximum interior of 45 CNEL is mandated by the State of California Noise Insulation Standards (CCR, Title 24, Part 6, Section T25-28) for multiple family dwellings and hotel and motel rooms. A 45 dBA CNEL is also typically applied as a maximum noise exposure for single-family dwelling units.

Since typical noise attenuation within residential structures with closed windows is about 20 to 25 dBA CNEL, an exterior noise exposure of 65 dBA CNEL is generally the noise land use compatibility guideline for noise-sensitive receiver sites in California.

Local

Noise impacts are primarily regulated at the local level through the general plan noise element and noise ordinances which implement the noise goals, policies and objectives contained in the general plan noise element.

XII. NOISE

Would the project result in:

(a) Exposure of persons to or generation of noise levels in excess of standards established in the local general plan or noise ordinance, or applicable standards of other agencies?

1. Determining the Scope of the Question

This question asks about generation of noise levels in excess of standards established in the local general plan or noise ordinance, but it also refers to applicable standards of other agencies.

Many Initial Study Checklists focus on only the standards contained in the local general plan or noise ordinance, but the Initial Study Checklist preparer should be aware that there may be other noise standards that apply that may differ from the local general plan or local noise ordinance depending on the project.

Some examples of other noise standards that may be applicable to a project include the following:

- ✓ The California Department of Transportation administers several freeway noise control programs. In general, these are applied to residential and school uses that preexisted the particular freeway.

- ✓ Local airports are subject to the noise requirements of the Federal Aviation Administration and noise standards under Title 21, §5000, et seq., of the California

Code of Regulations. These standards are designed to cause the airport proprietor, aircraft operators, local governments, pilots, and the California Department of Transportation to work cooperatively to diminish noise problems. The Federal Aviation Act preempts local regulations controlling noise at airports.

✓ The U.S. Department of Housing and Urban Development has regulations that sets exterior noise standards for new housing construction assisted or supported by the Department under the Noise Abatement and Control Regulations [24 CFR 51B].

To answer this question in an appropriate context, the Initial Study Checklist preparer needs to consider noise standards that may be applicable to the project in addition to those contained in a local general plan or noise ordinance.

2. Where to Find the Factual Data to Answer the Question

- Project noise study.

- The local agency's general plan noise element.

- The local agency's noise ordinance.

- California Department of Transportation noise information can be located at:

   www.dot.ca.gov/ser/vol1/sec3/physical /ch12noise/chap12noise.htm or   enter "caltrans noise standards" in an Internet search engine.

- Federal Aviation Administration noise information can be located at:

  www.faa.gov/about/office_org/headqua rters_offices/aep/planning_toolkit/or enter "faa noise standards" in an Internet search engine.

- U.S. Department of Housing and Urban Development noise information can be found at:

  www.hudnoise.com/hudstandard.html or enter "hud noise environmental criteria" in an Internet search engine.

- It is recommended that the California Environmental Resources Evaluation System website be consulted to see if there is any information related to this question. The website is located at:

  ceres.ca.gov or enter "ceres evaluation" in an Internet search engine.

3. Example Answers

The following example answers the question comprehensively:

The project involves the construction of 82 residential condominium units. The applicable noise regulations are contained in the City's General Plan Noise Element and Municipal Code. No other agencies noise standards are applicable since the City's noise standards are the same as the State standards for residential development and the project does not involve the U.S. Department of Housing and Urban Development.

Short-Term Impacts

The City's threshold of significance for noise impacts is sound levels that reach 65 dBA for exterior and 45 dBA for interior locations for residential development. Construction noise could exceed these levels.

Pursuant to the City's Noise Ordinance, construction activity is limited to daytime hours between 7:00 a.m. and 7:00 p.m. on weekdays, and between 8:00 a.m. and 6:00 p.m. on Saturdays, and prohibited on Sundays and federal holidays. Because of the short duration of the construction noise and the fact the project has to comply with mandatory requirements in the City's Noise Ordinance. Impacts are considered less than significant. No mitigation measures are required.

Long-Term Impacts

Exterior Noise:

The long-term on-going operation of the project would result in an increase in noise levels as a result of an increase in vehicle traffic. Based on the project's noise study, traffic noise is projected to be 72 dBA CNEL at 50 feet from the centerline of Potomac Avenue. This would exceed the City standard of 65 dBA for exterior noise levels. The _following mitigation measure is proposed to reduce impacts to less than significant:_

> _NO-1: Sound walls at least five (5) feet high shall be constructed around the exposed perimeters of all first floor private patios facing Potomac Avenue._

Interior Noise:

The project's noise study shows that the exterior noise levels at the building façade will range from 45 to 69 dBA CNEL. This would exceed the City standard of 45 dBA CNEL in some cases. In order to reduce this impact to less than significant levels, the following mitigation measure is proposed:

> _NO-2: All buildings shall be constructed with the following noise attenuation features_

Panel	Construction
Exterior Wall	*Siding or stucco, 2" x 4" studs, R-13 fiberglass insulation, ½" drywall
Windows	Double pane
Sliding Glass Door	Double pane
Roof	Tile over ½" plywood, fiberglass insulation, 5/8" drywall, vented
Floor	Carpeted except kitchen and baths
*Add STC 28 glazing to all rooms with any view of Potomac Avenue.	

This response takes into account noise generated from both temporary activities (construction) and permanent activities (operation of the project). It cites the applicable noise thresholds and states that noise standards from other agencies do not apply to the project. Mitigation is recommended for long-term noise impacts.

The following example does not answer the question comprehensively:

Construction of the new 10,000 square foot annex to the existing library building will result in short-term noise impacts associated with construction activities. Construction noise levels will be controlled by conformance with the City's Noise Ordinance. Any construction noise would be less than significant.

This response only takes into account short-term construction noise and does not discuss other noise generation from operation of the building, such as from heating and cooling equipment. It also does not evaluate the projected noise generated by the project against a quantifiable noise standard.

4. Determining Significance

Following are some general factors to consider for determining significance:

- Are there any formally adopted Thresholds of Significance by the local agency that are applicable to the project?

- Has the lead agency set a precedent in previously approved CEQA documents in responding to the question? If so, the Initial Study Checklist preparer should be aware of how other CEQA documents have responded to the question.

- Exceedance of any noise standard identified in the general plan, noise ordinance, or other applicable noise standard may be a significant impact that requires mitigation.

XII. NOISE (cont.)

Would the project result in:

(b) Exposure of persons to or generation of excessive groundborne vibration or groundborne noise levels?

1. Determining the Scope of the Question

In order to determine the scope of the question, it is useful to understand the following terminology:

Groundborne Vibration

Some common sources of ground-borne vibration are trains, buses, large trucks, and construction activities such as blasting, pile-driving and operating heavy earth-moving equipment. The effects of ground-borne vibration include rumbling sounds and movement of a building, rattling of windows, and shaking of interior items such as dishes, wall pictures, etc.

Groundborne Noise

Ground-borne noise is the result of the vibration and movement of a building, rattling of windows, and shaking of interior items such as dishes, wall pictures, etc. In essence, the room surfaces project the noise so it is perceptible to ear.

2. Where to Find the Factual Data to Answer the Question

- Project noise study.

- The local agency's general plan noise element.

- The local agency's noise ordinance.

- It is recommended that the California Environmental Resources Evaluation System website be consulted to see if there is any information related to this question. The website is located at:

  ceres.ca.gov or enter "ceres evaluation" in an Internet search engine.

3. Example Answers

The following example answers the question comprehensively:

The closest land uses potentially impacted from groundborne vibration and noise (primarily from the use of heavy construction equipment) are the single-family homes and apartment homes located adjacent to the site.

The project's noise study shows that anticipated groundborne vibration from heavy equipment would be 81VdB. This vibration level is below the 100 VdB threshold level established by the City's Noise Ordinance.

In addition, the resultant noise from the groundborne vibration does not exceed the City noise standards identified in the Municipal Code according to the project's noise study.

This response identifies the sources of the groundborne vibration and evaluates the amount of vibrations against a quantified standard contained in the city's ordinance.

It also discusses the resultant noise from the groundborne vibration and evaluates it against the city's ordinance.

The following example does not answer the question comprehensively:

Development of the project is not expected to generate groundborne vibration or groundborne noise levels. However, any groundborne adverse impacts will be controlled by conformance with the City's Noise Ordinance.

This response cites no factual data to support its conclusion.

4. Determining Significance

Following are some general factors to consider for determining significance:

- Are there any formally adopted Thresholds of Significance by the lead agency that are applicable to the project?

- Has the lead agency set a precedent in previously approved CEQA documents in responding to the question? If so, the Initial Study Checklist preparer should be aware of how other CEQA documents have responded to the question.

- Exceedance of any groundborne vibration or groundborne noise standard identified in the general plan, city ordinance, or other applicable standard may be a significant impact that requires mitigation.

XII. NOISE (cont.)

Would the project result in:

(c) A substantial permanent increase in ambient noise levels in the project vicinity above levels existing without the project?

1. Determining the Scope of the Question

Ambient noise is commonly referred to as "background noise." Common examples of background noises are vehicle traffic, airplanes, trains, and noises from human activity.

The background noise is different depending on the type of environment. Obviously a commercial area near major streets is going to have more background noise than a secluded residential area.

When answering this question the Initial Study Checklist preparer needs to be aware of how a project may change the ambient noise levels in the project vicinity.

For example, a commercial project that is proposed on vacant land next to residential uses will increase the ambient noise levels in the project vicinity thus impacting the residential uses.

A residential project would not have an impact on ambient noise levels to the degree that a commercial project would.

2. Where to Find the Factual Data to Answer the Question

- Project noise study.

- The local agency's general plan noise element.

- The local agency's noise ordinance.

- It is recommended that the California Environmental Resources Evaluation System website be consulted to see if there is any information related to this question. The website is located at:

ceres.ca.gov or enter "ceres evaluation" in an Internet search engine.

3. Example Answers

The following example answers the question comprehensively:

The project is an office building on a 1 acre site. The site is located on the corner of Troy Street and Stuart Avenue both of which are 4 lane major arterial roadways. Adjacent to the project site on the east and south is an apartment complex.

Although the ambient noise level will increase, the noise study prepared for the project determined that the ambient noise levels will not increase substantially above the existing ambient noise levels in the vicinity of the project because the project is located adjacent to two major arterial roadways which have already elevated the ambient noise levels in the area.

This response compares the existing ambient noise levels against the projected ambient noise levels as a result of the project based on a noise study and states the reasons why the impacts would not be significant.

The following example does not answer the question comprehensively:

The project will be used for professional office uses. The operation and use of the building would not substantially increase ambient noise levels in the project vicinity. No impacts are expected.

This response cites no factual data to support its conclusion.

4. Determining Significance

Following are some general factors to consider for determining significance:

- Are there any formally adopted Thresholds of Significance by the lead agency that are applicable to the project?

- Has the lead agency set a precedent in previously approved CEQA documents in responding to the question? If so, the Initial Study Checklist preparer should be aware of how other CEQA documents have responded to the question.

- Exceedance of any noise standard identified in the general plan, noise ordinance, or other applicable noise standard may be a significant impact that requires mitigation.

XII. NOISE (cont.)

Would the project result in:

(d) A substantial temporary or periodic increase in ambient noise levels in the project vicinity above levels existing without the project?

1. Determining the Scope of the Question

Questions XII (d) is similar to Question XII(c) with the difference being that this question is asking about a "temporary or periodic" increase in the ambient noise levels while Question XII(c) asked about a "permanent" increase in ambient noise levels.

A temporary increase in ambient noise levels is typically associated with construction activities or a use that only generates noise on a periodic basis, such as a site used for temporary outdoor events.

2. Where to Find the Factual Data to Answer the Question

- Project noise study.

- The local agency's general plan noise element.

- The local agency's noise ordinance.

- It is recommended that the California Environmental Resources Evaluation System website be consulted to see if there is any information related to this question. The website is located at:

ceres.ca.gov or enter "ceres evaluation" in an Internet search engine.

3. Example Answers

The following example answers the question comprehensively:

The project is an office building on a 1 acre site. As discussed in Question XII(c), the project will not result in a permanent increase in the ambient noise levels in the vicinity of the project site.

The project does not involve any outdoor uses or activities that would result in the increase of the ambient noise levels on a temporary or periodic basis.

This response, by making reference to Question XII (c), compares the existing ambient noise levels with the projected temporary or periodic increase in existing ambient noise levels as a result of the project based on a noise study. In addition, it states the reasons why the impacts would not be significant.

The following example does not answer the question comprehensively:

Construction of the new development will not expose people to temporary or periodic increases in the ambient noise in excess of local standards.

This response cites no factual data to support the conclusion.

4. Determining Significance

Following are some general principals to consider for determining significance:

- Are there any formally adopted Thresholds of Significance by the lead agency that are applicable to the project?

- Has the lead agency set a precedent in previously approved CEQA documents in responding to the question? If so, the Initial Study Checklist preparer should be aware of how other CEQA documents have responded to the question.

- Exceedance of any noise standard identified in the general plan, noise ordinance, or other applicable noise standard may be a significant impact that requires mitigation.

XII. NOISE (cont.)

Would the project result in:

(e) For a project located within an airport land use plan or, where such a plan has not been adopted, within two miles of a public airport or public use airport, would the project expose people residing or working in the project area to excessive noise levels?

1. Determining the Scope of the Question

In order to determine the scope of this question, it is useful to put the following terms in an appropriate context:

Public Airport or Public Use Airport

The question uses the terms "public airport" and "public use airport." It should be noted that there is no definition for a "public airport" in the California Code of Regulations.

However, there is a definition for a "public use airport" which is defined as follows by California Code of Regulations, Title 21, Section 3527(q):

"*An airport that is open for aircraft operations to the general public and is listed in the current edition of the Airport/Facility Directory that is published by the National Ocean Service of the U.S. Department of Commerce.*"

In the opinion of the author, a "public airport" and a "public use airport" have the same meaning in the context of this question and will both be referred to as a "public use airport" in this Chapter.

It should also be noted that in California a "special use airport" can be covered by an Airport Land Use Compatibility Plan even though it is not considered a public use airport.

California Code of Regulations, Title 21, Section 3527(w) defines a Special-Use Airport as:

"An airport not open to the general public, access to which is controlled by the owner in support of commercial activities, public service operations and/or personal use."

The Kingdon Executive Airport located near Lodi in San Joaquin County is considered a special use airport and it is included in the _San Joaquin County Airport Land Use Compatibility Plan_.

Therefore, the author recommends that the response to this question should also address a special use airport.

Airport Land Use Plan

A key part of this question is whether or not the project is located within an Airport Land Use Compatibility Plan. Thus it is important to understand what is meant by the term "airport land use plan" in the context of the question.

The California Department of Transportation, Division of Aeronautics regulates public use airports. Noise impacts from a public use airport are addressed in plans called an "Airport Land Use Compatibility Plan." In the opinion of the author, an "airport land use plan" in the context of the question means an "Airport Land Use Compatibility

Plan" and will be referred to as such in this Chapter.

An Airport Land Use Compatibility Plan is prepared at the local level and is administered by an Airport Land Use Commission.

An Airport Land Use Commission serves in an advisory capacity to the lead agency's as it pertains to land uses that could be impacted by a public use airport.

Authors Note: _It should be noted that an Airport Land Use Compatibility Plan does not take precedence over a locally adopted Airport Land Use Compatibility Plan. For example, certain cities in San Bernardino and Kern Counties (and not an Airport Land Use Commission) have jurisdiction over land uses that could be impacted by a public use airport._

An Airport Land Use Compatibility Plan's primary focus is on impacts aircraft may have on the land surrounding a public use airport. These plans differ from an "Airport Master Plan" in that the primary focus of the Airport Land Use Compatibility Plan is on the land **_surrounding_** a public use airport while an Airport Master Plan focuses on the land **_within_** a public use airport and its future operational activities.

This question is asking about an Airport Land Use Compatibility Plan and not an Airport Master Plan so it is important to distinguish the difference between the two types of plans in answering the question.

The Airport Land Use Compatibility Plan will contain policies to avoid establishment of noise-sensitive land uses in the portions of airport environs that are exposed to significant levels of aircraft noise.

The Airport Land Use Compatibility Plan should identify both the current and future Community Noise Equivalent Level (CNEL) contours of an airport.

These noise contours evaluate land uses against the noise contours and provide a range of acceptability to noise exposure.

For example, the range of acceptability maybe described as: clearly acceptable; normally acceptable; marginally acceptable, normally unacceptable; and clearly unacceptable.

The Initial Study Checklist preparer should refer to the applicable Airport Land Use Compatibility Plan (if one is in place) to identify the noise compatibility contours for the particular public use airport.

If the project site is located within the area of influence of an Airport Land Use Compatibility Plan or within 2 miles of a public use airport if there is no plan, then a noise analysis should be conducted to determine potential noise impacts and mitigation measures from the operation of the airport.

Within Two Miles of a Public Airport or Public Use Airport

According to Question VIII (e), if a project is not located within the area covered by an Airport Land Use Compatibility Plan, then a two mile distance is used to evaluate impacts.

Often times this question is answered by some Initial Study Checklist preparers only in reference to a two mile distance to a public use airport.

The two mile distance criteria are **only** for circumstances where an airport land use compatibility plan **has not been** adopted.

If an airport land use compatibility land use plan has been adopted, the area impacted by noise may cover **more than two miles** so the Initial Study Checklist preparer should not restrict the analysis to a two mile distance.

2. Where to Find the Factual Data to Answer the Question

- Project noise study.

- The local agency's general plan noise element.

- The local agency's noise ordinance.

- Airport Land Use Compatibility Plan (if applicable).

- A map of public use airports in California can be found at:

  www.dot.ca.gov/hq/planning/aeronaut /documents2/pubuse07.pdf or enter "ca dot public use airports map 2007" in an Internet search engine.

- The California Office of Airports has excellent information on airports including a list of airports. The webpage can be found at:

  www.dot.ca.gov/hq/planning/aeronaut /oairport.html or enter "ca office of airports" in an Internet search engine. Click on the link "California Airports/Heliport Master Records."

- An excellent resource for airport noise is *The California Airport Land Use Planning Handbook, State of California Department of Transportation Division of Aeronautics.* The handbook can be found at:

  http://www.dot.ca.gov/hq/planning/a eronaut/documents/ALUPHComplete-7- 02rev.pdf or enter "california airport land use planning handbook" in an Internet search engine.

- It is recommended that the California Environmental Resources Evaluation System website be consulted to see if there is any information related to this question. The website is located at:

  ceres.ca.gov or enter "ceres evaluation" in an Internet search engine.

3. Example Answers

The following examples answer the question comprehensively:

For a project **within** an airport land use plan

According to the 2008 Airport Land Use Compatibility Plan for Powell Airport, a portion of Tentative Tract 94395 is within the 60 dBA CNEL noise contour. This is considered to be"marginally acceptable."

However, the noise study prepared for the project indicated that operation of the airport will not create significant noise impacts to the project and that the City's interior noise standard of 45 dBA CNEL for residential uses can be met with adherence to the noise attenuation construction methods described in the project's noise study.

This response describes the project's location relative to the applicable noise contours impacting development within the area of influence of the Powell Airport and states why impacts would be less than significant based on the noise study.

For a project ***not within*** an airport land use plan and not within 2 miles of a public airport or public use airport

The project site is located approximately 5 miles northwest of Powell Airport. According to the 2008 Airport Land Use Compatibility Plan for Powell Airport the site is not located within the Airport Referral Areas (i.e. a designated area consisting of various noise, safety, and height restrictions), therefore, aircraft noise will not significantly impact the project.

This response discusses the project's location relative to an airport. Although it is farther away than the 2 mile threshold criteria posed by the question, the response uses the Airport Referral

Area relative to noise to evaluate noise impacts as opposed to a fixed 2 mile distance.

The following example does not answer the question comprehensively:

The site is not located within an airport land use plan or within two miles of an airport.

This response states the question in the negative. It does not describe the location the project site in relation to the nearest airport. Although it may be technically correct, there is no supporting data to substantiate the conclusion.

4. Determining Significance

Following are some general factors to consider for determining significance:

- Are there any formally adopted Thresholds of Significance by the lead agency that are applicable to the project?

- Has the lead agency set a precedent in previously approved CEQA documents in responding to the question? If so, the Initial Study Checklist preparer should be aware of how other CEQA documents have responded to the question.

- Exceedance of any noise standard identified in the general plan, noise ordinance, or other applicable noise standard (e.g. airport land use plan) may be a significant impact that requires mitigation.

XII. NOISE (cont.)

Would the project result in:

(f) For a project within the vicinity of a private airstrip, would the project expose people residing or working in the project area to excessive noise levels?

1. Determining the Scope of the Question

A private airstrip is called a "personal use airport" By the California Division of Aeronautics and will be referred to as such in this section.

Section 21661.5 of the Public Utilities Code requires that the county or city approve the plan for construction of a personal use airport. Section 21661.5 of the Public Utilities Code does not apply to any temporary seaplane landing site, ultralight vehicle flightpark, or to airports owned or operated by the United States.

In order put this question in an appropriate context, it is important to consider the following:

- A personal use airport can be on either land or water.

- Unlike Question XII (e), this question uses the phrase "in the *vicinity* of a private airstrip" as opposed to "*within two miles* of a public airport or public use airport."

  Many times Initial Study Checklist preparers in responding to this question use the two mile distance to determine impacts when in fact the "vicinity" can be some other distance.

When determining what is the appropriate vicinity of a personal use airport, the Initial Study Checklist preparer should consider the relationship of a personal use airport to its surroundings with respect to aircraft takeoff and landing patterns.

- If a project is located within the vicinity of a private airstrip, a noise analysis should be prepared if the project is located within the take-off and/or landing zones of the airstrip.

2. Where to Find the Factual Data to Answer the Question

- Because personal use airports (i.e. private airstrips) are exempted from the regulations applicable to public airports pursuant to California Code of Regulations 3533, the best source of information is to check with the local agency planning department to see if a personal use airport has been permitted (typically through a conditional use permit).

- The California Division of Aeronautics maintains a document called California Airport/Heliport/Master Records" which provides information on airports. This list may contain information on personal use airports.

The website is located at:

www.dot.ca.gov/hq/planning/aeronaut /ca.html or enter "california division of aeronautics" in an Internet search engine and click on the link "california airport/heliport/master records."

- An excellent resource for airport noise is: *The California Airport Land Use Planning Handbook, State of California Department of Transportation Division of Aeronautics*. The handbook can be found at:

  www.dot.ca.gov/hq/planning/aeronaut /documents/ALUPHComplete-7- 02rev.pdf or enter "california airport land use planning handbook" in an Internet search engine.

- It is recommended that the California Environmental Resources Evaluation System website be consulted to see if there is any information related to this question. The website is located at:

  ceres.ca.gov or enter "ceres evaluation" in an Internet search engine.

3. Example Answers

The following examples answers the question comprehensively:

For a project **within** the vicinity of a Personal Use Airport (i.e. private airstrip)

A review of county records and a reconnaissance of the area surrounding the project site show that there is a personal use airport operating in the vicinity of the project site allowed under an active conditional use permit (CUP 82-15).

According to CUP 82-15 on file with the County, the airport is limited to use by one (1) light single engine propeller airplane at any time. According to the California Airport Land Use Planning Handbook, such a plane typically generates a sound level of 60 dBA upon landing or takeoff (which is the equivalent of a normal conversation at 3 feet).

The project is a residential subdivision of 35 large lot homes which is located approximately 1.7 miles north of the airport and is not within the direct path of the runway. An interior noise standard of 45 dBA CNEL can be met with building noise attenuation construction methods. Therefore, the operation of the personal use airport will not have a significant impact on either exterior or interior noise levels.

This response describes the operation of the airport and the interior and exterior noise standards and states why the project will not be negatively impacted by the private airstrip.

For a project **not within** the vicinity of a Personal Use Airport (i.e. private airstrip)

A review of county records and a reconnaissance of the area surrounding the project site show that there are no personal use airports operating in the vicinity (i.e. the area that could be impacted by aircraft take offs and landings which generate the most noise) of the project site. Therefore, impacts will be less than significant.

The response is based on a review of county records, which would show if a conditional use permit or other land use entitlement was granted for a personal use airport. It also describes the vicinity of the project with respect to the airport as opposed to fixed 2 mile distance

The following example does not answer the question comprehensively:

The site is not located within two miles of a personal use airport.

This response uses the 2 mile criteria for public airports and not the "vicinity" of a personal use airport as posed in the question. It also does not indicate if county or other agency records were consulted to see if there was a personal use airport in the vicinity of the project site.

4. Determining Significance

Following are some general factors to consider for determining significance:

- Are there any formally adopted Thresholds of Significance by the lead agency that are applicable to the project?

- Has the lead agency set a precedent in previously approved CEQA documents in responding to the question? If so, the Initial Study Checklist preparer should be aware of how other CEQA documents have responded to the question.

- If aircraft noise from a personal use airport exceeds any noise standard identified in the general plan, noise ordinance, or other applicable noise standard, impacts may be significant and requires mitigation.

Chapter XIII

Population and Housing

Introduction

This series of questions deals with a projects effect on increasing population growth either directly (developing new housing and businesses), or indirectly (by extending new infrastructure into undeveloped areas). It also deals with the displacement of housing and people that may be caused by a project.

409

XIII. POPULATION and HOUSING

Would the project:

(a) Induce substantial population growth in an area, either directly (for example, by proposing new homes and businesses) or indirectly (for example, through extension of roads or other infrastructure)?

1. Determining the Scope of the Question

In the context of this question, there are two factors that influence population growth: the first is by developing new homes and businesses that would draw people to an area; and the second is by extending infrastructure (i.e. roads, sewers, water lines, utilities etc.) into an area that is underdeveloped or undeveloped.

In both cases, the population growth would be considered "substantial" if it caused population growth that could not be supported by existing or new services (such as fire protection, police protection, schools, utilities, and other essential services).

2. Where to Find the Factual Data to Answer the Question

The information to respond to this question would most likely come through the review of the project by the local public service providers that is intended to ensure that population growth does not outpace the ability to provide public services.

Some of the information sources would include, but not be limited to:

- The local agency's general plan.

- Capital Improvement Plans prepared by the local agency.

- Growth control strategies or plans.

- Master plans for sewer, water, drainage facilities, utilities etc. prepared by the agencies that provide those services.

- It is recommended that the California Environmental Resources Evaluation System website be consulted to see if there is any information related to this question. The website is located at:

  ceres.ca.gov or enter "ceres evaluation" in an Internet search engine.

3. Example Answers

The following example answers the question comprehensively:

The project is a multiple-family residential development consisting of 65 units located in an infill development area that has all utilities and services available. The density of the project is 14 dwelling units per acre. Based on information from the California Department of Finance, there are 3.3 persons per household in the City.

This results in a population increase of 214 persons. Although the project will induce population growth, the growth is not above General Plan buildout projections because the project does not exceed the General Plan density of 25 dwelling units per acre.

Therefore, the population increase is not substantial when compared to the General Plan buildout projections and the availability of infrastructure and the necessary public services to serve the project. (Also see discussion under Section XV, Public Services and XVII, Utilities and Service Systems).

This response discusses the magnitude of the population increase and compares it to the general plan buildout projections and states the reason why the population growth will not be substantial with respect to the availability of public services.

The following example does not answer the question comprehensively:

The project proposes a new office building and is located in the Professional Office Zone. The project site is an infill development and will connect to the existing transportation network via Jefferson Avenue and thus does not require the extension of new roads. There are existing infrastructure utilities to serve the project.

This response does not address the potential of the new office building to create jobs that may indirectly lead to new population growth.

4. Determining Significance

Following are some general factors to consider for determining significance:

- Are there any formally adopted Thresholds of Significance by the lead agency that are applicable project?

- Has the lead agency set a precedent in previously approved CEQA documents in responding to the question? If so, the Initial Study Checklist preparer should be aware of how other CEQA documents have responded to the question.

- A project may be considered to have a significant impact if it caused population growth that could not be supported by existing or new services (such as fire protection, police protection, schools, utilities and other essential services).

XIII. POPULATION and HOUSING (cont.)

Would the project:

(b) Displace substantial numbers of existing housing, necessitating the construction of replacement housing elsewhere?

1. Determining the Scope of the Question

The displacement of housing can primarily occur in two ways:

- ✓ A direct physical displacement of housing (e.g. new development displaces existing housing on a project site).

- ✓ An indirect displacement of housing through a change in a land use regulation that restricts housing development in one area requiring a jurisdiction to provide for additional housing in another area to meet Housing Element goals).

In the opinion of the author, determining if housing displacement is "substantial" would have to be quantified by analyzing the existing and projected housing needs contained in the General Plan Housing Element (i.e. housing units displaced vs. housing units needed).

2. Where to Find the Factual Data to Answer the Question

- The local agency's general plan (land use and housing element).

- It is recommended that the California Environmental Resources Evaluation System website be consulted to see if there is any information related to this question. The website is located at:

  ceres.ca.gov or enter "ceres" in an Internet search engine.

3. Example Answers

The following example answers the question comprehensively:

The project is a 187 unit condominium project. The project is to be constructed on a vacant site therefore it will not displace any existing housing.

This response identifies that the project site is vacant and contains no existing housing.

The following example does not answer the question comprehensively:

The project will not displace any existing housing and no new replacement housing will be required.

This response repeats the question in the negative and does not describe the nature of the project and why existing housing will not be displaced.

4. Determining Significance

Following are some general factors to consider for determining significance:

- Are there any formally adopted Thresholds of Significance by the lead agency that are applicable to the project?

- Has the lead agency set a precedent in previously approved CEQA documents in responding to the question? If so, the Initial Study Checklist preparer should be aware of how other CEQA documents have responded to the question.

- A project that will displace substantial numbers of existing housing, necessitating the construction of replacement housing elsewhere may have a significant impact.

  Quantification of what is considered a "substantial number of existing housing" as posed in the question would have to be undertaken and would have to take into account the number of housing in the existing stock vs. the housing needs of the community.

XIII. POPULATION and HOUSING (cont.)

Would the project:

(c) Displace substantial numbers of people, necessitating the construction of replacement housing elsewhere?

1. Determining the Scope of the Question

In many Initial Study Checklists this question is answered in the same context as Question XIII(a) because the displacement of people is usually by means of displacing the housing they reside in.

2. Where to Find the Factual Data to Answer the Question

- Project plans.

- The local agency's general plan (land use and housing element).

- It is recommended that the California Environmental Resources Evaluation System website be consulted to see if there is any information related to this question. The website is located at:

   ceres.ca.gov or enter "ceres evaluation" in an Internet search engine.

3. Example Answers

The following example answers the question comprehensively:

The project is a 187 unit condominium project. The project is to be constructed on a vacant site therefore it will not displace any people.

This response identifies that the project site is vacant and contains no existing housing, and therefore, no people.

The following example does not answer the question comprehensively:

The project will not displace any people and no new replacement housing will be required.

This response repeats the question in the negative and does not describe the nature of the project and why people will not be displaced.

4. Determining Significance

Following are some general factors to consider for determining significance:

- Are there any formally adopted Thresholds of Significance by the lead agency that are applicable to the project?

- Has the lead agency set a precedent in previously approved CEQA documents in responding to the question? If so, the Initial Study Checklist preparer should be aware of how other CEQA documents have responded to the question.

- A project that will displace substantial numbers of people, necessitating the construction of replacement housing elsewhere would have a significant impact. Quantification of what is a "substantial number of people" as posed in the question would have to be undertaken and would have to take into account the number of housing units in the existing stock vs. the housing needs of the community.

Chapter XIV

Public Services

Introduction

This Chapter discusses the need for new or altered public facilities in order to maintain acceptable service ratios, response times, or other performance objectives.

The questions posed in this Chapter also deal with the physical impacts that new or altered public service facilities may cause on the environment.

XIV. PUBLIC SERVICES

Would the project:

(a) Would the project result in substantial adverse physical impacts associated with the provision of new or physically altered governmental facilities, need for new or physically altered governmental facilities, the construction of which could cause significant environmental impacts, in order to maintain acceptable service ratios, response times or other performance objectives for any of the public services:

Fire protection?

Police protection?

Schools?

Parks?

Other public facilities?

1. Determining the Scope of the Question

Often times responses to this question just focus on service ratios, response times, or other performance objectives for public services, but in fact the question also inquires about any physical adverse change that may result in providing or constructing new or altered government facilities for public services.

In the opinion of the author, the response to this question also should include an analysis that discusses if new or altered government facilities are needed to maintain acceptable service ratios, response times, or other performance objectives and what would be the physical impacts of providing or constructing such facilities.

If public services can be provided at an acceptable level without the need to construct new or altered facilities then there would be a less than significant or no impact.

If new or altered facilities are required then the physical impacts of those facilities needs to be discussed.

2. Where to Find the Factual Data to Answer the Question

- Project plans.

- Local agency general plan.

- Service providers, such as fire departments, police departments, school districts, park departments or districts, public facilities departments or districts etc.

- It is recommended that the California Environmental Resources Evaluation System website be consulted to see if there is any information related to this question. The website is located at:

  ceres.ca.gov or enter "ceres evaluation" in an Internet search engine.

3. Example Answers

Author's Note: *The following answers are based on projects of a size and scale in which public service needs can be met with existing facilities and no alterations or construction of facilities is needed. A project (e.g. a master planned community or large specific plan) that would trigger the need for new or altered facilities such as a fire station, school, or park would ordinarily require the preparation of an EIR.*

The following example answers the question comprehensively:

The project is an 82 unit detached residential subdivision with a projected population of 271 persons:

Fire

The Fire Department maintains Station No. 46 located at 12375 Mary Street which serves the project site. Currently, the station houses a Brush Engine and Engine Company staffed with six (6) personnel.

The Fire Department's review of the project has determined that adequate facilities exist in the vicinity of the project site (and if needed in conjunction with other fire facilities in the city) to maintain the required service ratios and response times mandated by the General Plan.

No new or altered fire facilities are required to meet the required service ratio or response times. There are no other performance standards required for the project in addition to service ratios or response times.

In addition, Development Impact Fees are collected for the provision of capital facilities for fire services which will provide for future facilities as the city develops.

Based on the above analysis, impacts to fire services are considered less than significant.

Police

The General Plan requires a Police Department-wide staffing ratio of one police officer per thousand residents and support personnel equal to or greater than one-half of the sworn officers. There are no required response times or other performance standards applicable to the project for police services.

A review of the project by the Police Department determined that new or altered facilities are not required to maintain this service ratio and that existing facilities/personnel can adequately respond to calls for service and to periodically monitor the project site.

In addition, Development Impact Fees are collected for the provision of capital facilities for police facilities which will provide for future facilities as the city's population increases.

Based on the above analysis, impacts to police services are considered less than significant.

Schools

The project will add additional students to the School District. The project area is served by the *following schools; Blade High School; Tyree Jr. High School; and Victoria Elementary School.*

Impacts on schools will be mitigated by the payment of mandatory school impact fees.

Based on the above analysis, impacts to schools are considered less than significant.

Parks

The nearest park is Jason Wilson Park which is located approximately one-mile west of the project site. No new or altered parks are required to provide park services to the project.

In addition, The City requires the payment of mandatory park fees to continue to provide park and recreation facilities as population increases.

Based on the above analysis, impacts to parks are considered less than significant.

Other Public Facilities

The City's library system includes a main library located within the civic center complex on Earl Drive and three branch libraries located at various locations.

Based on library usage, the existing system can adequately provide library services for the city including the addition of the projected 271 residents of the project. No new or altered library facilities are needed.

In addition, Development Impact Fees are collected for the provision of capital facilities for library facilities which will provide for future facilities as the city's population increases.

Based on the above analysis, impacts to other public facilities are considered less than significant.

The above responses describe the public services needs of the project and indicate that no new or altered governmental facilities are needed to provide these public services. Therefore, there will be no adverse physical impacts associated with providing services to the project.

The following example does not answer comprehensively for some of the identified services.

The project is an 18,200 square foot outpatient medical surgery building.

Fire

The project will have a minor impact on fire protection resulting from additional patients and employees in potential need of services. However, the County Fire Department has reviewed the design of the project to ensure adequate access is provided.

This response focuses on access instead of whether or not the project requires the need for new or altered governmental facilities to meet fire protection service ratios, response times, or other performance standards. It does not appropriately answer the question.

Police

The project will have a minor impact on police protection resulting from additional patients and hospital employees in potential need of services. The Police Department has also reviewed the project for safety.

The response does not does not define what "minor impacts" mean. It does not provide factual data to support the conclusion.

Schools

As an outpatient surgery center, the project will not impact schools but will be required to pay school fees required of a commercial building.

This is an appropriate response because it states that the project does not have a direct impact on schools and that the payment of school fees is required.

Parks

As an outpatient surgery center, the project will not impact parks but will be required to pay park fees.

Non-residential uses do not have the same degree of impact that a residential project would have on parks. However, to some extent patients and employees can use a nearby park. Therefore, the response should have discussed this.

Other Public Facilities

There are no other public facilities needed to serve the project.

This response states the question in the negative and does not provide factual data to support the conclusion.

4. Determining Significance

Following are some general factors to consider for determining significance:

- Are there any formally adopted Thresholds of Significance by the lead agency that are applicable to the project?

- Has the lead agency set a precedent in previously approved CEQA documents in responding to the question? If so, the Initial Study Checklist preparer should be aware of how other CEQA documents have responded to the question.

- If new or altered governmental facilities need to be provided or constructed in order to provide acceptable public services, then the physical impacts of those facilities needs to be analyzed to determine significance.

Chapter XV

Recreation

Introduction

This Chapter deals with the potential for a project to contribute to or accelerate the physical deterioration of recreational facilities through increased use. Responses to this question often times just focus on parks, however, other recreational facilities should also be analyzed. Other recreational facilities that may not be part of a park can include:

✓ Tennis courts;

✓ Basketball courts;

✓ Volleyball courts;

✓ Sports fields for a specific sport (baseball, football, soccer etc.);

✓ Public golf courses;

✓ Skateboard parks;

✓ Swimming pools;

✓ Picnic areas;

✓ Game rooms;

✓ Fitness centers;

✓ Walking and running paths; and

✓ Multi-purpose assembly buildings (e.g. senior centers, youth centers, etc.).

In addition, this Chapter deals with adverse physical effects on the environment as a result of constructing or expanding recreational facilities associated with a project.

XV. RECREATION

(a) Would the project increase the use of existing neighborhood and regional parks or other recreational facilities such that substantial physical deterioration of the facility would occur or be accelerated?

1. Determining the Scope of the Question

This question deals with the degree of physical deterioration that would occur on a neighborhood park, regional park, or other recreational facility as a result of a project. It basically means that a facility is being overused because it is accommodating more activities than planned for.

For example, a soccer field can deteriorate faster because it is being used for longer periods of time to accommodate the number of practices and games because of the lack of soccer fields elsewhere.

2. Where to Find the Factual Data to Answer the Question

- The local agency's department that oversees park operations and maintenance.

- It is recommended that the California Environmental Resources Evaluation System website be consulted to see if there is any information related to this question. The website is located at:

  ceres.ca.gov or enter "ceres evaluation" in an Internet search engine.

431

3. Example Answers

The following example answers the question comprehensively:

The project is a 76 unit apartment complex. It will potentially add 250 persons to the City's population.

The project of and by itself does not result in the need for new recreational facilities (i.e. parkland) because the overall ratio of parkland per person according to the General Plan is maintained even with the construction of the project.

The nearest park to the project site is Heritage Park, which is a neighborhood park that contains a large children's play area, ball field, a half basketball court, restrooms, 2 lighted tennis courts, lawn bowling green, horseshoe pits, picnic areas and large turf area for passive uses.

It was designed to accommodate the recreational needs of the neighborhood in which the project site is located. Therefore, it is not anticipated that the project will substantially contribute to the physical deterioration of the park.

In addition, the project includes on-site recreational facilities such as common open space areas, picnic and barbeque areas, and two tot lots which will to some extent reduce the need for residents to use Heritage Park or other recreational facilities.

This response describes the project's potential demand for use of a nearby park and provides

432

details explaining why the project will not substantially contribute to the physical deterioration of the park or other recreational facilities.

The following example does not answer the question comprehensively:

The project is a 123 unit apartment complex. The project will add approximately 369 persons to the City's population and some may include existing residents. The project of and by itself does not result in the need for new recreational facilities, but will be required to pay the mandatory park fee for future facilities.

This response does not discuss how the project may or may not contribute to the deterioration of existing park facilities through increased use.

4. Determining Significance

Following are some general factors to consider for determining significance:

- Are there any formally adopted Thresholds of Significance by the lead agency that are applicable to the project?

- Has the lead agency set a precedent in previously approved CEQA documents in responding to the question? If so, the Initial Study Checklist preparer should be aware of how other CEQA documents have responded to the question.

- In order to determine significance, the physical deterioration of recreational facilities caused by the project would need to be analyzed. Such factors as over use and overcrowding would contribute to physical deterioration.

XV. RECREATION (cont.)

(b) Does the project include recreational facilities or require the construction or expansion of recreational facilities which might have an adverse physical effect on the environment?

1. Determining the Scope of the Question

In order to put this question into an appropriate context, the question is separated into the following parts:

Includes Recreational Facilities Which Might Have an Adverse Physical Effect

If a project includes on-site recreational facilities then the impacts associated with those facilities would be addressed in the Initial Study Checklist prepared for the project.

Construction or Expansion of Recreational Facilities Which Might Have an Adverse Physical Effect

If a project results in the need for the construction or expansion of recreational facilities then it is likely that the project is of a size and scale that may require off-site recreational facilities to be constructed or expanded.

For example, if a project contributes to the need for a new park and the park cannot be accommodated on-site, then the construction or expansion of a park may be required off-site. In this case, there would need to be some level of

435

CEQA review for the new or expanded off-site park as well.

2. Where to Find the Factual Data to Answer the Question

- The local agency's department that oversees park operations and maintenance.

- It is recommended that the California Environmental Resources Evaluation System website be consulted to see if there is any information related to this question. The website is located at:

  ceres.ca.gov or enter "ceres evaluation" in an Internet search engine.

3. Example Answers

The following example answers the question comprehensively:

The project is a 76 unit apartment complex on a 5 acre site. The project includes on-site recreational facilities such as common open space areas, picnic and barbeque areas, and two tot lots.

The project does not require the construction or expansion of off-site recreational facilities because of its small size.

As part of the environmental review conducted in this Initial Study, it was determined that none of the on-site recreational facilities will have a physical adverse effect on the environment.

This response states that the recreational facilities included in the project were reviewed as part of the Initial Study Checklist prepared for the project and concludes there would be no physical adverse effect on the environment. It also discusses why the construction or expansion of off-site recreational facilities is not required.

The following example does not answer the question comprehensively:

Implementation of the proposed project will result in an estimated population increase of 610 new residents within the City.

The City requires the payment of a development impact fee on new development in order to provide recreational facilities. The development impact fee will be imposed as a condition of approval for the project.

The response does not address if a physical adverse effects on the environmental would occur as a result of the inclusion, construction, or expansion of recreational facilities.

Stating that payment of a development impact fee is required does not answer the question.

4. Determining Significance

Following are some general factors to consider for determining significance:

- Are there any formally adopted Thresholds of Significance by the lead agency that are applicable to the project?

437

- Has the lead agency set a precedent in previously approved CEQA documents in responding to the question? If so, the Initial Study Checklist preparer should be aware of how other CEQA documents have responded to the question.

- If any recreational facilities included within the project or constructed or expanded off-site have been determined not to have an adverse physical effect on the environment based on a CEQA analysis, then impacts would be less than significant. The key is to make sure that any proposed recreational facilities, whether on-site or off-site, have been adequately analyzed as part of the review of the project.

Chapter XVI

Transportation/Traffic

Introduction

Effective March 18, 2010, the California Natural Resources Agency made changes to the CEQA Guidelines which included changes to the questions in Appendix G for Transportation/Traffic.

Questions (a) and (b) were revised and Question (f) pertaining to parking was deleted.

The changes are summarized as follows:

✓ Question (a) was revised to change the focus from an increase in vehicular traffic at a given location (i.e. an intersection) to the effect of a project on the overall circulation system in the project area.

The change expands the need for discussion on modes of transportation other than motor vehicles (such as mass transit and non-motorized travel) and addresses a project's impact on pedestrian and bicycle paths and mass transit.

In practice, the amendments to Questions (a) and (b) would allow the lead agency to evaluate the significance of traffic impacts using other standards than level of service or volume to capacity ratios although those thresholds can still be used if so desired.

This change was made because an increase in traffic, by itself, is not necessarily an indicator of a potentially significant environmental impact.

✓ Question (b) clarifies the role of a Congestion Management Program in a CEQA analysis. Specifically, it clarifies that a Congestion Management Program contains many elements in addition to a level of service designation.

✓ Question (f) pertaining to parking was deleted because according to the Natural Resources Agency: "...*There is no statutory or case authority requiring the identification of specific measures to provide additional parking spaces in order to meet an anticipated shortfall in parking availability. The social inconvenience of having to hunt for scarce parking spaces is not an environmental impact. (Ref. San Franciscans Upholding the Downtown Plan v. City and County of San Francisco (2002) 102 Cal.App.4th 656).*

XVI. TRANSPORTATION/TRAFFIC

Would the project:

(a) Conflict with an applicable plan, ordinance or policy establishing measures of effectiveness for the performance of the circulation system, taking into account all modes of transportation including mass transit and non-motorized travel and relevant components of the circulation system, including but not limited to intersections, streets, highways and freeways, pedestrian and bicycle paths, and mass transit?

1. Determining the Scope of the Question

An appropriate context for this question is to analyze the overall performance on the circulation system in the vicinity of a project with respect to other modes of travel and not just motor vehicles (e.g. automobiles).

Prior to the 2010 amendment to Appendix G, this question focused on Level of Service and Volume to Capacity Ratio as indicators for the effective performance of the circulation system. This approach was weighted towards automobiles when in fact the circulation system involves other modes of travel such as pedestrian, bicycle and mass transit.

The author suggests reading the article published by Ronald Miliam, AICP, titled: *Transportation Impact Analysis Gets a Failing Grade When it Comes to Climate Change and Smart Growth*. The article provides an excellent discussion on this topic and can be found at:

http://opr.ca.gov/sch/pdfs/LOS_Climate_Ch ange_Smart_Growth.pdf

2. Where to Find the Factual Data to Answer the Question

- Plans, policies, or standards contained in the local agency general plan circulation element.

- Project traffic study (including traffic micro-simulation software).

- It is recommended that the California Environmental Resources Evaluation System website be consulted to see if there is any information related to this question. The website is located at:

  ceres.ca.gov or enter "ceres evaluation" in an Internet search engine.

3. Example Answers

The following example answers the question comprehensively:

The General Plan Circulation Element establishes a Peak Hour Level of Service "C" or better as generally acceptable. The Traffic Impact Assessment for the project found that for all scenarios that all intersections in the project area will continue to operate at Level of Service "C" or better.

However, in order to be consistent with new General Plan policies pertaining to greenhouse gas emissions and sustainable development such as encouraging the use of alternative transportation modes and better integration of pedestrian connectivity into the circulation system, an analysis was conducted using micro-simulation software.

The micro-simulation software modeled not only vehicle Level of Service, but also evaluated delays on persons crossing intersections and delays at intersections to buses and bicycles. In this way the overall effectiveness of the circulation system could be evaluated because a vehicle (i.e. automobile) is not the only mode of transportation using the circulation system.

The City has not adopted a threshold of significance other than Level of Service to measure transportation impacts, so no adopted quantitative standard could be applied to the results of the analysis. However, the analysis did show that the project would not substantially increase delays to persons crossing intersections or increase delays at intersections to buses and bicycles and would not be in conflict with General Plan polices.

This response recognizes the 2010 amendments to Appendix G of the CEQA Guidelines by including an analysis of impacts to other modes of transportation in addition to vehicle Level of Service.

The following example does not answer the question comprehensively:

Based on the traffic study prepared for the project, the intersections in the project area will continue to operate at Level of Service "C", which is the same as the existing conditions before implementation of the project. Therefore, impacts will be less than significant.

This response relies solely on a Level of Service analysis and does not address other modes of travel such as pedestrian, bicycles, or mass transit.

Although it is acceptable to rely solely on Level of Service, a more comprehensive approach would be to include an analysis of all modes of travel including pedestrian, bicycle, and mass transit.

4. Determining Significance

Following are some general factors to consider for determining significance:

- Are there any formally adopted Thresholds of Significance by the lead agency that are applicable to the project?

- Has the lead agency set a precedent in previously approved CEQA documents in responding to the question? If so, the Initial Study Checklist preparer should be aware of how other CEQA documents have responded to the question.

- Instead of relying solely on standards such as Level of Service and Volume to Capacity ratios to measure the performance of the circulation system impacted by a project, impacts from the project should also be evaluated against plans, policies, or ordinances that encourage or require pedestrian, bicycle, and mass transit modes of travel.

A project may have a significant impact if it was not in compliance with all the adopted standards related to performance of the circulation system.

XVI. TRANSPORTATION/TRAFFIC (cont.)

Would the project:

(b) Conflict with an applicable congestion management program, including, but not limited to level of service standards and travel demand measures, or other standards established by the county congestion management agency for designated roads or highways?

1. Determining the Scope of the Question

In order to determine the scope of this question, it is useful to separate it into the following parts:

Congestion Management Program Background

As required under 1990's Proposition 111, every county in California is required to develop a Congestion Management Program that looks at the links between land use, transportation and air quality.

By law, a Congestion Management Program must contain the following:

- ✓ A designated Congestion Management Program roadway network;

- ✓ Traffic level of service standards and a methodology for monitoring level of service on the designated Congestion Management Program roadway network;

- ✓ Transit service standards;

✓ A multimodal performance element;

✓ A land use impact analysis methodology;

✓ A seven-year multimodal Capital Improvement program; and

✓ A common database and method to analyze impacts of local land use decisions on the Congestion Management Program network.

Congestion Management Programs are typically prepared by a Congestion Management Agency that is established at the county level of government or by a council of governments.

The highway and roadway system addressed in a Congestion Management Program includes at a minimum all state highways and principal arterials.

In addition, local agencies must also adopt a transportation demand management ordinance to comply with Congestion Management Program statutes.

<u>Applicability of the Congestion Management Program to a Project</u>

All land use projects are subject to the provisions of a Congestion Management Program to some degree.

Based on the location of the jurisdiction, there are various methods and strategies to meet the intent of the Congestion Management Program legislation.

Because of the variation in methodologies and strategies, the applicability of the various components of a Congestion Management Program will vary based on the type and scale of the project and where it is located.

Authors Note: *The Initial Study Checklist preparer should consult the applicable Congestion Management Program for specific requirements.*

The following provides some examples of how the various components may apply to a project:

Congestion Management Program Roadway Network:

The highway and roadway system addressed in a Congestion Management Program includes at a minimum all state highways and principal arterials.

The Congestion Management Roadway Network is typically identified by diagram(s) contained in the document.

These types of roadways should be included in the Initial Study Checklist analysis if it is determined that the project will impact the Congestion Management Roadway Network. The Initial Study Checklist preparer should consult with the local agency's traffic engineer to determine if a Congestion Management Program Roadway may be impacted by a project.

Traffic Impact Assessments:

Congestion Management Programs contain guidelines and requirements for the preparation of a traffic impact assessment if required. In addition, the local agency's traffic impact assessment guidelines and requirements may also identify when a project needs to conduct a traffic impact assessment for a Congestion Management Program roadway.

Typically, the requirements for a traffic impact assessment are based on the number of trips generated by a project and/or the proximity of a project to a Congestion Management Program Roadway.

> **TIP.** *If a Traffic Impact Assessment is required for a project, ask that the report address the applicable Congestion Management Program.*

Trip Reduction and Travel Demand:

Section 65089(b) (3) (A) of the Government Code requires that a Congestion Management Program include a trip reduction and travel demand element that promotes alternative transportation methods.

Such methods must include, but are not limited to: carpools, vanpools, transit, bicycles, and park-and-ride lots; improvements in the balance between jobs and housing; and flexible work hours, telecommuting, and parking management programs.

449

At the local level, cities and counties have adopted transportation demand management ordinances or similar regulations to implement the provisions of the Congestion Management Program.

The Initial Study Checklist preparer should consult the local agency's municipal code to see if a transportation demand management ordinance is applicable to the project.

2. Where to Find the Factual Data to Answer the Question

- Contact the Congestion Management Agency for the county in which the project is located. The best way is to enter "*(county name) congestion management program*" in an Internet search engine. The Congestion Management Program is usually available online.

- Legislation implementing the Congestion Management Program can be found in Government Code Sections 65088-65089.10. Enter "find california codes" in an Internet search engine and click on the Government Code box and enter the code section in the appropriate box.

- It is recommended that the California Environmental Resources Evaluation System website be consulted to see if there is any information related to this question. The website is located at:

  ceres.ca.gov or enter "ceres evaluation" in an Internet search engine.

3. Example Answers

The following examples answer the question comprehensively:

Example 1

Based Traffic Impact Assessment prepared for the project, the project is projected to generate 44 trips in the AM Peak Hour and 48 trips in the PM Peak Hour. Because the number of trips is below the City's threshold of 50 peak hour trips, the City Traffic Engineer has determined that the project will not have a significant impact on the surrounding Congestion Management Program Roadways.

This response describes the number of trips and determines, based on input from the City Traffic Engineer, that Congestion Management Program Roadways will not be significantly impacted.

Example 2

As required by the Congestion Management Program, an analysis of Horizon Year (2030) freeway level of service is required for all freeway segments that carry 100 or more project trips in the peak hour.

The project contributes traffic greater than the Congestion Management Plan freeway threshold of 100 two-way trips to the I-10 and SR-60 Freeways.

The project would include on-site as well as off-site improvements and the phasing of all necessary study area transportation improvements.

Both on-site and off-site improvements are described in Table T-1 of this Initial Study Checklist and are recommended as Mitigation Measures.

Improvements include;

- ✓ *Construct additional turn lanes;*

- ✓ *Construct additional through travel lanes;*

- ✓ *Restripe eastbound dual left turn lanes to a left turn lane and a left/right turn on EB I-10;*

- ✓ *Construct an additional southbound right turn lane on WB Ramps/Auto Center Parkway (EW);and*

- ✓ *Improve various roadways ultimate to their half-section width as a Divided Arterial (120+ foot right-of-way).*

With the implementation of above described roadway improvements, impacts would be less than significant on the Congestion Management Roadway Network.

In addition, the project is required to implement applicable provisions of the City's Transportation Demand Management Ordinance because it will employ more than 100 people.

This response describes the traffic generated by the project, the project impacts on the Congestion Management Program Roadway Network, and recommends roadway improvements to ensure that impacts are less than significant.

It also describes how the project is not in conflict with other components of the Congestion Management Program (e.g. Trip Reduction and Travel Demand).

The following example does not answer the question comprehensively:

The use of the new building for offices will generate significantly less traffic than the previous light industrial usage on the site. No impacts to the level of service at surrounding intersections will result.

This response makes no reference whether or not the project is in conflict with the applicable Congestion Management Program. It also does not provide any factual data pertaining to trip generation.

4. Determining Significance

Following are some general factors to consider for determining significance:

- Are there any formally adopted Thresholds of Significance by the lead agency that are applicable to the project?

- Has the lead agency set a precedent in previously approved CEQA documents in responding to the question? If so, the Initial Study Checklist preparer should be aware of how other CEQA documents have responded to the question.

- Any project that is in conflict with the applicable Congestion Management Program may have a significant impact.

XVI. TRANSPORTATION/TRAFFIC (cont.)

Would the project:

(c) Result in a change in air traffic patterns, including either an increase in traffic levels or a change in location that results in substantial safety risks?

1. Determining the Scope of the Question.

This question deals with a project that would change air traffic patterns to the degree that safety is compromised.

In the opinion of the author, if air traffic patterns have to be changed to avoid certain types of development on the ground then air traffic may have to be increased within certain flight paths thus exposing both aircraft and persons on the ground to increased risk.

Question XVI(c) is closely related to Question VIII (e) and Question VIII(f) contained in the *Hazards and Hazardous Materials* section of the Initial Study Checklist

If the project site is located within the area of influence of an airport or in the vicinity of a personal use airport, then a compatibility analysis should be conducted to determine potential impacts as a result of increases in air traffic levels and changes in flight path locations.

2. Where to Find the Factual Data to Answer the Question

The following are excellent sources of information for this topic:

- *The California Airport Land Use Planning Handbook, State of California Department of Transportation Division of Aeronautics* can be found at:

  www.dot.ca.gov/hq/planning/a eronaut/documents/ALUPHComplete-7- 02rev.pdf or enter "california airport land use planning handbook" in an Internet search engine.

- It is recommended that the California Environmental Resources Evaluation System website be consulted to see if there is any information related to this question. The website is located at:

  ceres.ca.gov or enter "ceres evaluation" in an Internet search engine.

3. Example Answers

The following example answers the question comprehensively:

There are no airports or personal use airports within ten (10) miles of the project site according to the California Division of Aeronautics. The closest airport to the project site is the City Center Airport which is more than 20 miles away.

The project would not directly impact any airport facilities, and thus would not cause a change in air traffic patterns. Therefore, the proposed project would have no impact on air traffic patterns.

This question makes reference to the project's location with respect to an airport or airstrip and concludes that no changes to air traffic patterns will occur as a result of the project.

The following example does not answer the question comprehensively:

The project will not result in a change in air traffic patterns. Therefore, there will be no impact.

This question merely answers the question in the negative without providing any factual data to support the conclusion. In answering this question it is always best to identify the distance to the closest airport.

4. Determining Significance

Following are some general factors to consider for determining significance:

- Are there any formally adopted Thresholds of Significance by the lead agency that are applicable to the project?

- Has the lead agency set a precedent in previously approved CEQA documents in responding to the question? If so, the Initial Study Checklist preparer should be aware of how other CEQA documents have responded to the question.

457

- If the project site ***is not*** located within an airport land use plan area of influence as shown in the plan or in the vicinity of a personal use airport then there would be no impact.

- If the project site ***is*** located within an airport land use plan area of influence as shown in the plan or within 2 miles of an airport the impacts can only be evaluated by conducting a compatibility analysis based on the standards contained in the plan.

- If the project site ***is*** located within the vicinity of a personal use airport then impacts should be evaluated by having an aviation professional familiar with Federal Aviation Regulations conduct a safety compatibility analysis.

XVI. TRANSPORTATION/TRAFFIC (cont.)

Would the project:

(d) Substantially increase hazards due to a design feature (e.g., sharp curves or dangerous intersections) or incompatible uses (e.g., farm equipment)?

1. Determining the Scope of the Question

In order to determine the scope of the question, it is separated into the following parts:

Increased Hazards Due to a Design Feature (e.g. sharp curves or dangerous intersections)

Design features that may increase hazards include but are not limited to the following:

✓ Intersections that are not designed at a right angle (90°). Minor deviations from right angles are generally acceptable provided that the potentially detrimental impact on visibility and turning movements is minimal.

However, large deviations from right angles may decrease visibility, hamper certain turning operations, and will increase the size of the intersection and therefore crossing distances for bicyclists and pedestrians.

✓ Inadequate sight lines which minimize corner sight distance and the ability of drivers to judge the relative position and speed of approaching vehicles.

✓ Sharp curves that change the alignment or direction of the road.

✓ Inadequate separation distance between intersections.

✓ The width and location of medians.

✓ The proximity of lanes, shoulders, and medians to intersections.

Incompatible Uses (e.g. Farm Equipment)

As farmland is converted into urban uses there is the potential to create an interface between the remaining farmland and the new urban uses.

This has led to a substantial increase in the mix of agricultural equipment and motor vehicles on public roads.

The most common types of vehicle conflicts that can occur from the increased interface between the remaining farmland and the new urban uses includes rear-end, left-turn, passing, crossroads, and oncoming collisions.

When addressing this question, several factors to consider are:

✓ Examine how agricultural equipment can be safely moved on public roads.

✓ Examine the roadways capacity to handle increased traffic volumes.

✓ Examine design features of the existing and proposed roadways that take into account the use of the roadways by farm equipment (e.g. sufficient width of the roadway to safely handle large farm equipment machinery; roadway shoulders that are wide enough to allow farm equipment to drive totally on the shoulder; and caution signs showing a "tractor ahead warning" on roads with heavy farm traffic).

✓ Also note that uses other than agricultural production can result in an increase of traffic hazards. Some examples include equestrian uses or industrial uses that share the same roadways as the proposed project.

2. Where to Find the Factual Data to Answer the Question

• A project specific traffic study is the best source of information to evaluate this question. In the absence of a traffic study, the Initial Study Checklist preparer should refer to the local agency's roadway design standards. These are typically found in "standard drawings" maintained by the department or agency that oversees public works or engineering functions. Information may also be available in the local agency's zoning code, development code, or subdivision code.

• It is recommended that the California Environmental Resources Evaluation System website be consulted to see if there is any

information related to this question. The website is located at:

ceres.ca.gov or enter "ceres evaluation" in an Internet search engine.

3. Example Answers

The following example answers the question comprehensively:

The project is a 10 acre commercial center located on Edward Avenue.

Edward Avenue is a six-lane arterial roadway that is fully improved along the project frontage. The project does not propose any changes to the existing roadway alignment, lane configurations, or medians. The existing design of Edwards Avenue has been determined by the City Engineer to be able to safely accommodate project traffic.

The proposed driveway to the project site is proposed along Edward Avenue and is designed to have a signalized intersection. The City Traffic Engineer has determined that the location of the driveway will not result in a traffic safety hazard.

In addition, the project site is located in the central business area of the city and there are no incompatible uses (e.g. agricultural, equestrian, or industrial) that would result in a vehicle mix that could increase traffic hazards. Therefore, impacts will be less than significant.

This response describes the design features of the project in terms of traffic hazards and also discusses why there would be no conflict with vehicles associated with incompatible uses (e.g. farm equipment).

The following example does not answer the question comprehensively:

The City Engineer reviewed the project and found that it is designed in a manner that does not present hazards.

The response does not provide sufficient details as to why traffic hazards would not occur. It also does not discuss why there would be no conflict with vehicles associated with incompatible uses (e.g. farm equipment).

4. Determining Significance

Following are some general factors to consider for determining significance:

- Are there any formally adopted Thresholds of Significance by the lead agency that are applicable to the project?

- Has the lead agency set a precedent in previously approved CEQA documents in responding to the question? If so, the Initial Study Checklist preparer should be aware of how other CEQA documents have responded to the question.

- A project that does not meet the local agency's design standards for roadways or creates conflicts with other types of vehicles (e.g. farm equipment) may have a significant impact.

463

XVI. TRANSPORTATION/TRAFFIC (cont.)

Would the project:

(e) Result in inadequate emergency access?

1. Determining the Scope of the Question

This question is typically answered in the context of fire vehicle emergency access but it should include all types of emergency responders, including but not limited to, medical and police services. The type of factors that could result in inadequate emergency vehicle access includes, but is not limited to:

- ✓ Insufficient width of roadways or driveways to accommodate larger emergency vehicles (e.g. fire trucks).

- ✓ Inadequate roadway or driveway surfaces that cannot support the weight of larger emergency vehicles (e.g. fire trucks).

- ✓ Roadway or driveways that can become inaccessible if flooded.

- ✓ Roadway or driveway surfaces (e.g. dirt or gravel) that can become inaccessible due to weather conditions.

- ✓ Inadequate turning radii for larger emergency vehicles (e.g. fire trucks).

- ✓ Flag lots where the access to the property is not easily identifiable thus making it hard to locate.

✓ Too steep of a gradient on roadway and driveways.

✓ Road or driveway closure due to construction.

✓ Inadequate maneuvering space around buildings for larger emergency vehicles (e.g. fire trucks).

✓ Inadequate building or structure clearance height that restricts or prohibits access for larger emergency vehicles (e.g. fire trucks).

✓ An insufficient number of access points in relation the size of the project (e.g. secondary access may be required).

✓ Development that is located too far from emergency responders such that response times are excessive.

2. Where to Find the Factual Data to Answer the Question

- A review by the emergency responders that serve the project is the best source of information.

- It is recommended that the California Environmental Resources Evaluation System website be consulted to see if there is any information related to this question. The website is located at:

  ceres.ca.gov or enter "ceres evaluation" in an Internet search engine.

3. Example Answers

The following example answers the question comprehensively:

The project would develop an office building adjacent to Leonard Avenue.

The project site and surrounding roadway network do not have any conditions that would restrict emergency vehicle access to the project site such as insufficient width of roadways or inadequate roadway surfaces that cannot support the weight of larger emergency vehicles.

The project's ingress/egress and on-site circulation are required to meet the City Fire Department and Police Department standards, which ensure new developments provide adequate access for emergency vehicles.

In addition, Leonard Avenue will remain open during construction.

The project plans have been reviewed by the Fire and Police Departments to ensure that adequate emergency vehicle access is provided.

This response considers both long term and short term access issues in a comprehensive manner taking into account various factors that could result in inadequate emergency vehicle access.

The following example does not answer the question comprehensively:

Implementation of the project will not result in inadequate emergency access, since the project will be designed to meet the County's standards.

Although this answer may be technically correct because it states that the project will be designed to meet the County's standards, it does not provide sufficient details to support the conclusion.

4. Determining Significance

Following are some general factors to consider for determining significance:

- Are there any formally adopted Thresholds of Significance by the lead agency that are applicable to the project?

- Has the lead agency set a precedent in previously approved CEQA documents in responding to the question? If so, the Initial Study Checklist preparer should be aware of how other CEQA documents have responded to the question.

- A project that does not meet the local agency's requirements for emergency vehicle access may have a significant impact.

XVI. TRANSPORTATION/TRAFFIC (cont.)

Would the project:

(f) Conflict with adopted policies, plans, or programs regarding public transit, bicycle, or pedestrian facilities, or otherwise decrease the performance or safety of such facilities?

1. Understanding the Scope of the Question

In order to put this question into an appropriate context, the question is separated into the following parts:

<u>Public Transit</u>

The most commonly used forms of public transit in California are bus, rail (e.g. trains, and subways) and ferry. Factors that could decrease the performance or safety of public transit include, but are not limited to the following:

- ✓ Be in conflict with plans, policies or programs for public transit. An example of a public transit policy would be:

  Policy T-1: Incorporate facilities for transit and other alternative modes of transportation, such as park-and-ride lots and bus turnouts, in the design of future developments.

- ✓ Not providing bus pull-off areas.

- ✓ Creating physical barriers that make it more difficult to get to a transit stop or station.

✓ Not providing ways for people to get from the transit stop to their destinations.

Bicycle Facilities

Bicycle facilities include bicycle lanes and paths. Streets and Highway Code Section 890.4 defines a "Bikeway" as a facility that is provided primarily for bicycle travel. Bikeways are defined as follows:

✓ Class I Bikeway (Bike Path). Provides a completely separated right of way for the exclusive use of bicycles and pedestrians with crossflow by motorists minimized.

✓ Class II Bikeway (Bike Lane). Provides a striped lane for one-way bike travel on a street or highway.

✓ Class III Bikeway (Bike Route). Provides for shared use with pedestrian or motor vehicle traffic.

Factors that could decrease the performance or safety of bicycle travel include, but are not limited to the following:

✓ Be in conflict with plans, policies or programs for bicycle travel. An example of a bicycle facility policy would be:

Policy T-2: Incorporate bicycle lanes and bicycle racks in future development projects.

✓ Increasing the number of traffic lanes thus not allowing adequate room for bicycle lanes.

469

✓ Increasing traffic lane width thus not allowing adequate room for bicycle lanes.

✓ Providing dual use facilities for both pedestrians and bicycles (the two should be separated wherever possible).

Pedestrian Facilities

The most common types of pedestrian facilities include sidewalks and pedestrian paths.

Factors that could decrease the performance or safety of pedestrian facilities include, but are not limited to the following:

✓ Be in conflict with plans, policies or programs for pedestrian travel. An example of a pedestrian facility policy would be:

T-3: Encourage pedestrian travel through the creation of sidewalks and street crossings.

✓ Physical barriers such as walls that prevent convenient walking access in a community

✓ Insufficient curb ramps or the creation of steep grades or steps that prevent access for the elderly or people in wheelchairs.

✓ Placing above ground utilities within pedestrian paths.

✓ Not providing sidewalks and crosswalks.

✓ Roadway design that does not include adequate traffic control devices and lighting, for both pedestrian and vehicular movements.

✓ Providing dual use facilities for both pedestrians and bicycles (the two should be separated wherever possible).

2. Where to Find the Factual Data to Answer the Question

- Local agency general plan or other planning documents (e.g. zoning ordinances, specific plans).

- Information about federal and state transit programs is available from the California Division of Mass Transportation website at:

  www.dot.ca.gov/hq/MassTrans/# or enter "california division of mass transportation" in an Internet search engine.

- The Council of Governments that the project area is located in. Information about which Council of Governments the project area is located in can be found on the California Association of Councils of Governments website at:

  www.calcog.org/about/about.html or enter "california association of councils of governments" in an Internet search engine.

- It is recommended that the California Environmental Resources Evaluation System website be consulted to see if there is any

information related to this question. The website is located at:

ceres.ca.gov or enter "ceres evaluation" in an Internet search engine.

3. Example Answers

The following example answers the question comprehensively:

The project site is currently vacant. The project would develop a 121,000 square foot retail center adjacent to Jason Avenue. Jason Avenue is a fully improved six-lane roadway that serves as a major east-west arterial roadway in the City.

There is a Class II Bikeway within the right-of-way of Jason Avenue which provides a striped lane for one-way bike travel. In addition, there is an existing 8 foot wide sidewalk within the right-of-way of Jason Avenue

The project will provide a bus pull-off area and a transit stop adjacent to the right-of-way of Jason Avenue. This area will not use the existing right-of-way to accommodate the additional area needed for the bus pull-off area and the transit stop. The area needed to accommodate these facilities will come from the area within the project site will be dedicated to the City.

A traffic signal and crosswalk will be provided at the main project entrance off Jason Avenue that will allow for safe crossing by pedestrians and bicyclists.

Because of the above described improvements the project would not decrease the performance of existing alternative transportation facilities or be in conflict with policies, plans, or programs supporting alternative transportation.

This response provides a description of the existing and proposed alternative transportation facilities (e.g. sidewalk, bicycle lane, bus pull off area and transit stop).

It discusses why a decrease in the performance or safety of the existing facilities would not occur and why the project is not in conflict with policies, plans, or programs supporting alternative transportation.

The following example does not answer the question comprehensively:

The project is the expansion to an existing office complex, which will continue to comply with policies, plans, or programs supporting alternative transportation.

This response does not provide sufficient details to support the conclusion.

4. Determining Significance

Following are some general factors to consider for determining significance:

- Are there any formally adopted Thresholds of Significance by the lead agency that are applicable to the project?

- Has the lead agency set a precedent in previously approved CEQA documents in responding to the question? If so, the Initial Study Checklist preparer should be aware of how other CEQA documents have responded to the question.

- A project that would decrease the performance of existing alternative transportation facilities or be in conflict with policies, plans, or programs supporting alternative transportation may have a significant impact.

Chapter XVII

Utilities and Service Systems

Introduction

This Chapter involves a series of questions intended to analyze the utility service system impacts associated with a project. In some cases, the questions subject matter may appear to overlap, but there are distinct purposes for each question so the Initial Study Checklist preparer should be aware of this fact.

The utility and service systems addressed in this Chapter are wastewater, storm water drainage facilities, landfills and solid waste.

475

XVII. UTILITIES and SERVICE SYSTEMS

Would the project:

(a) Exceed wastewater treatment requirements of the applicable Regional Water Quality Control Board?

1. Determining the Scope of the Question

This question is often times narrowly interpreted to address only wastewater treated at a sewer treatment plant. However, in the opinion of the author, the question covers more than treating wastewater at a sewer treatment plant.

The Regional Water Quality Control Boards regulate wastewater discharges to both surface water (rivers, ocean, etc.) and to groundwater (via land).

Discharges to community sewer systems are typically *not* regulated by Regional Water Quality Control Boards.

However, the Regional Water Quality Control Board Water Board *does* regulate the treatment of wastewater once it reaches a sewage treatment facility.

According to the State Water Resources Control Board, wastewater can be generated by the following types of activities or land uses:

✓ Discharge of process wastewater not discharging to a sewer (e.g. factories, cooling water);

✓ Confined animal facilities (e.g., dairies);

476

✓ Waste containments (e.g. landfills, waste ponds);

✓ Construction sites;

✓ Boatyards;

✓ Discharges of pumped groundwater and cleanup (e.g. underground tank cleanup, dewatering, spills);

✓ Material handling areas draining to storm drains;

✓ Sanitary sewer overflows;

✓ Filling of wetlands;

✓ Dredging, filling and disposal of dredge wastes; and

✓ Commercial activities not discharging to a sewer (e.g. factory wastewater).

An appropriate context for answering this question would be to identify the types of wastewater discharges generated by a project and determine if the wastewater treatment requirements of the applicable Regional Water Quality Control Board are being complied with.

Chapter IX of this book, *Hydrology and Water Quality*, addresses some of the above activities which are related to surface wastewater discharges. Therefore, it is appropriate to cross-reference the answers to Questions XVII(a) with the related questions in Chapter IX.

With respect to a project connected to a sewer system where wastewater is treated at a wastewater treatment plant, the applicable Regional Water Quality Control Board monitors the ability of a wastewater treatment facility to meet the Board's treatment requirements.

Typically, if a project is connected to a community sewer system and the wastewater treatment facility is operating satisfactorily, exceeding wastewater treatment requirements is not an issue.

2. Where to Find the Factual Data to Answer the Question

- Contact the Regional Water Control Board with jurisdiction over the project if there is any potential for project activities to result in the exceedance of wastewater treatment requirements.

  Types of projects to be concerned about include, but are not limited to: agricultural uses, industrial and manufacturing uses, and golf courses.

  To find out what Regional Water Quality Control Board has jurisdiction over the project, consult the State Water Resources Control Board website at:

  www.waterboards.ca.gov/waterboards _map.shtml or enter "california state water resources control board" in an Internet

Search engine and click on the link "State Regional Water Boards' Map."

- It is recommended that the California Environmental Resources Evaluation System website be consulted to see if there is any information related to this question. The website is located at:

  ceres.ca.gov or enter "ceres evaluation" in an Internet search engine.

3. Example Answers

The following example answers the question comprehensively:

The project would develop a retail center on a currently vacant site. None of the proposed uses would generate atypical wastewater such as industrial or agricultural effluent. All wastewater generated by the project is expected to be domestic sewage.

The City is required to adhere to the requirements of the Regional Wastewater Ordinance established by the applicable water agency which requires pre-treatment regulations to prevent the introduction of pollutants into the regional sewerage system.

Any surface runoff from the project is addressed in the responses to Questions IX(a), (c), (e) and (f) of this Initial Study.

Therefore, the wastewater treatment requirements of the Regional Water Quality Control Board are not anticipated to be exceeded.

The response describes the type of wastewater the project will generate and discusses why wastewater treatment requirements should not be exceeded (e.g. discharges have to comply with pre-treatment requirements before allowed to reach the sewage treatment facility). It also cross-references the response with the water quality issues in Section IX, _Water Quality_, of the Initial Study Checklist.

The following example does not answer the question comprehensively:

The addition of a 5,000 square foot office building will not affect the wastewater treatment requirements of the Regional Water Quality Control Board. No industrial discharge into the wastewater or drainage system would occur.

This response does not provide sufficient details to justify the conclusion. It does not discuss why wastewater treatment requirements will not be exceeded.

4. Determining Significance

Following are some general factors to consider for determining significance:

- Are there any formally adopted Thresholds of Significance by the lead agency that are applicable to the project?

- Has the lead agency set a precedent in previously approved CEQA documents in responding to the question? If so, the Initial Study Checklist preparer should be aware of

how other CEQA documents have responded to the question.

- Any project that would discharge wastewater that does not go into a community sewer system and does not meet the wastewater treatment requirements of the applicable Regional Water Quality Control Board may have a significant impact.

XVII. UTILITIES and SERVICE SYSTEMS (cont.)

Would the project:

(b) Require or result in the construction of new water or wastewater treatment facilities or expansion of existing facilities, the construction of which could cause significant environmental effects?

1. Determining the Scope of the Question

In order to determine the scope of the question, it is separated into the following parts:

Require or Result in the New Construction of or the Expansion of Water Facilities

This part of the question is closely related to Question XVI(d) because it deals with water supply. Many Initial Study Checklists preparers cross-referenced these questions with each other.

That being said, in the opinion of the author this question is somewhat different because it deals with the environmental effects of constructing or expanding water facilities (e.g. delivery systems for water such as water tanks and water lines) and not just the available supply of water.

Water facilities include water treatment plants, water distribution lines, and water storage facilities.

The Initial Study Checklist preparer needs to determine what, if any, new or expanded water facilities are needed to serve the project and address the environmental impacts of constructing these facilities. These can include both on-site and off-site facilities.

<u>Require or Result in the New Construction of or the Expansion of Wastewater Treatment Facilities</u>

This part of the question is closely related to Question XVI(e) because it deals with wastewater treatment capacity. Many Initial Study Checklists preparers cross-referenced these questions with each other.

That being said, in the opinion of the author this question is somewhat different because it deals with the environmental effects of constructing or expanding wastewater treatment facilities (e.g. delivery systems for wastewater such as sewer lines and pumping stations) and not just the available capacity at a wastewater treatment plant.

Wastewater treatment facilities include wastewater collection and pumping infrastructure, wastewater treatment plants, wastewater reclamation and reuse facilities, biosolids (sludge) management, and discharge infrastructure.

The Initial Study Checklist preparer needs to determine what, if any, new or expanded wastewater treatment facilities are needed to serve the project and address the environmental impacts of constructing these facilities. These can include both on-site and off-site facilities.

2. Where to Find the Factual Data to Answer the Question

- Project plans.

- The water and/or wastewater treatment provider that serves the project area.

- It is recommended that the California Environmental Resources Evaluation System website be consulted to see if there is any information related to this question. The website is located at:

  ceres.ca.gov or enter "ceres evaluation" in an Internet search engine.

3. Example Answers

The following example answers the question comprehensively:

The project consists of 65 attached condominium units. The existing water and wastewater infrastructure was designed to accommodate this type of development and is adequately sized according to a review of the project plans by the City's Water Department.

The only water and wastewater improvements required for the project are on-site pipelines and unit connections to the existing water and wastewater infrastructure systems.

The construction of the on-site water and wastewater facilities have been addressed as part _of this Initial Study and impacts were found to be less than significant._

The project will not require or result in the construction or expansion of new water or wastewater treatment facilities off-site. Therefore, there are no significant environmental effects associated with respect to water and wastewater facilities.

This response addresses both on-site and off-site water and wastewater facilities. It indicates that based on a review of the project by the City's Water Department and the analysis contained in the Initial Study Checklist for the project, no new or expanded water or wastewater facilities will be required for the project that would result in significant environmental effects.

The following example does not answer the question comprehensively:

The project will be connected to the existing water and wastewater system via the existing lines in Troy Avenue. In order to accommodate the additional water demand and the additional wastewater flow that will be created by the project, the existing lines will be upgraded to ensure the water and wastewater treatment facilities are adequate to serve the project.

This response does not address if the upgraded water and wastewater facilities would result in significant environmental effects. It just focuses on the capacity of the wastewater treatment facilities.

4. Determining Significance

Following are some general factors to consider for determining significance:

- Are there any formally adopted Thresholds of Significance by the lead agency that are applicable to the project?

- Has the lead agency set a precedent in previously approved CEQA documents in responding to the question? If so, the Initial Study Checklist preparer should be aware of how other CEQA documents have responded to the question.

- If the construction of new or expanded water and wastewater treatment facilities is required, determining significance for this question is based on the impacts said construction or expansion may have on the environment.

XVII. UTILITIES and SERVICE SYSTEMS (cont.)

Would the project:

(c) Require or result in the construction of new storm water drainage facilities or expansion of existing facilities, the construction of which could cause significant environmental effects?

1. Determining the Scope of the Question

This question deals with the new construction of or the expansion of storm water drainage facilities.

Storm drain facilities include but are not limited to: storm drain pipes, catch basins, detention basins, retention basins, culverts, swales, gutters, and channels.

These facilities can be located on-site and off-site.

2. Where to Find the Factual Data to Answer the Question

- Project plans and hydrology study.

- Consult the flood control agency or district which serves the project area.

- It is recommended that the California Environmental Resources Evaluation System website be consulted to see if there is any information related to this question. The website is located at:

ceres.ca.gov or enter "ceres evaluation" in an Internet search engine.

3. Example Answers

The following example answers the question comprehensively:

The only storm drain improvements required for the project are on-site catch basins, gutters, and storm drain pipes which will connect to the existing storm drain system in Diana Avenue.

The construction of the storm water drainage facilities have been addressed as part of this Initial Study and impacts were found to be less than significant.

The County Flood Control District has reviewed the project and indicated that no upgrades to the existing regional storm drain system will be required to accommodate surface runoff from the project.

Therefore, the project would not require or result in the construction or expansion of new regional or off-site storm drain facilities.

This response indicates that based on a review of the project, no new or expanded storm water drainage facilities will be required for the project that would result in significant environmental effects.

The following example does not answer the question comprehensively:

The project is a 90,000 square commercial center. The project will be served by existing storm water drainage facilities. No impacts will result.

This response does not provide factual data to support the conclusion. It should discuss the capacity of the existing storm drain system and if new facilities are required.

4. Determining Significance

Following are some general principals to consider for determining significance:

- Are there any formally adopted Thresholds of Significance by the lead agency that are applicable to the project?

- Has the lead agency set a precedent in previously approved CEQA documents in responding to the question? If so, the Initial Study Checklist preparer should be aware of how other CEQA documents have responded to the question.

- If the construction of new or expanded storm water drainage facilities is required, determining significance for this question is based on the impacts said construction or expansion may have on the environment.

489

XVII. UTILITIES and SERVICE SYSTEMS (cont.)

Would the project:

(d) Have sufficient water supplies available to serve the project from existing entitlements and resources, or are new or expanded entitlements needed?

1. Determining the Scope of the Question

This question deals with the availability of water to serve a project. The term "existing entitlements" refers to the water provider's entitlements to receive water from other sources.

For example, a water provider's supply may come from several sources, including entitlements to water from the Colorado River Water and/or the State Water Project which distributes water to water suppliers in Northern California, the San Francisco Bay Area, the San Joaquin Valley, the Central Coast, and Southern California.

Entitlements to water are addressed in an Urban Water Management Plan.

In 1983, the California Legislature enacted the Urban Water Management Planning Act (Division 6 Part 2.6 of the Water Code §§10610 - 10656). The Act requires that every urban water supplier that provides water to 3,000 or more customers, or that provides over 3,000 acre-feet of water annually, should make every effort to ensure the appropriate level of reliability in its water service sufficient to meet the needs of its various categories of customers during normal, dry, and multiple dry years.

The Act describes the contents of an Urban Water Management Plan as well as how urban water suppliers should adopt and implement the plans.

Authors Note: *Be aware that Urban Water Management Plans include land uses identified in a local agency's general plan for water planning purposes. For a project that involves a general plan amendment or zone change to a use that is more intense than the use evaluated in the Urban Water Management Plan, further analysis may be required.*

Another way to determine if adequate water is available to serve a project is through a water supply assessment prepared pursuant to Senate Bill 610.

Senate Bill 610 requires that a water supply assessment be required for large projects in order to determine if adequate water supplies are available.

Authors Note: *Projects of this size would usually trigger the need for an EIR. However, it is useful for the CEQA Initial Study Checklist preparer to be aware of the requirements of Senate Bill 610.*

For purposes of Senate Bill 610, a "project" requiring a water supply assessment is defined as:

- A proposed residential development of more than 500 dwelling units;

- A proposed shopping center or business establishment employing more than 1,000 persons or having more than 500,000 square feet of floor space;

- A proposed commercial office building employing more than 1,000 persons or having more than 250,000 square feet of floor space;

- A proposed hotel or motel, or both, having more than 500 rooms;

- A proposed industrial, manufacturing, or processing plant, or industrial park planned to house more than 1,000 persons, occupying more than 40 acres of land, or having more than 650,000 square feet of floor area;

- A mixed-use project that includes one or more of the projects defined above; or

- A project that would demand an amount of water equivalent to, or greater than, the amount of water required by a 500 dwelling unit project.

- Alternately, if a public water supply has less than 5,000 service connections, the definition of a "Project" also includes any proposed residential, business, commercial, hotel or motel, or industrial development that would account for an increase of 10 percent or more in the number of the public water system's existing service connections, or a mixed-use project that would demand an amount of water equivalent to, or greater than, the amount of water required by residential development that would represent an increase of 10 percent or more in the number of public water system's existing service connections.

2. Where to Find the Factual Data to Answer the Question

- The Urban Water Management Plan prepared by the water service provider serving the project area.

- Consult with the water service provider that serves the project area.

- It is recommended that the California Environmental Resources Evaluation System website be consulted to see if there is any information related to this question. The website is located at:

  ceres.ca.gov or enter "ceres evaluation" in an Internet search engine.

3. Example Answers

The following example answers the question comprehensively:

The project is a 65 unit condominium development.

The City's water supply is provided from various sources: groundwater production from wells operated by the City's Water Department and from water entitlements from the State Water Project supplied by the Metropolitan Water District.

The Urban Water Management Plan evaluated the City's existing and planned water sources, and water distribution systems with respect to their ability to meet projected demands. The Urban Water Management Plan considered the City's General Plan Land Use Plan in determining future water demand.

The evaluation of water demands includes a comprehensive assessment of historical demands and a projection of future demands based on forecasted development of the remaining developable lands within the City's water service area. Projections were done in 5-year increments, as estimated from the status and timing of currently approved development as well as probable future development within the context of the City's General Plan.

The General Plan Land Use designation for the property is High Density Residential with a density of up to 25 dwelling units per acre. Under the General Plan, the site (4.62 acres) has the potential to develop 115 units. The Urban Water Management Plan projected water demand for the site was for 115 units. The project is proposing 65 units, which is well below the demand projected.

The maximum daily demand water supply capacity requirement for 2010 is 29.10 million gallons per day whereas the capacity available is 41.14 million gallons per day.

For 2020, a forecasted 31.25 million gallons per day is required with 48.94 million gallons per day available.

At ultimate buildout 2025, the capacity requirement will be 32.86 million gallons per day with 48.94 million gallons per day available.

Based on the aforementioned information, the City, with its present and imminent mix of water sources, possesses a significant surplus of capacity.

Therefore, sufficient water supply is available for the project.

This response provides a comprehensive description of the project's projected water demand in relation to the availability of water based on the applicable Urban Water Management Plan.

The following example does not answer the question comprehensively:

The project site is presently served by water lines that are located adjacent to the project site. As such, no significant impact on water service levels would result from the project.

This response does not address if adequate water supplies exist to serve the project. The existence of water lines adjacent to the project site is not sufficient justification that adequate water supplies are available to serve the project.

4. Determining Significance

Following are some general factors to consider for determining significance:

- Are there any formally adopted Thresholds of Significance by the lead agency that are applicable to the project?

- Has the lead agency set a precedent in previously approved CEQA documents in responding to the question? If so, the Initial Study Checklist preparer should be aware of how other CEQA documents have responded to the question.

- Any project that would create a demand for water above the water supplier's availability to provide water may have a significant impact.

XVII. UTILITIES and SERVICE SYSTEMS (cont.)

Would the project:

(e) Result in a determination by the wastewater treatment provider which serves or may serve the project that it has adequate capacity to serve the project's projected demand in addition to the provider's existing commitments?

1. Determining the Scope of the Question

This question deals with the capacity of wastewater treatment facilities to serve the project at the time of project implementation and for is future operations.

In order to determine if adequate wastewater treatment capacity is available to serve the project, the wastewater treatment provider should be consulted.

2. Where to Find the Factual Data to Answer the Question

- The wastewater treatment provider serving the project area.

- Section 10633 of the Water Code requires an Urban Water Management Plan to include, to the extent available, information on recycled water and its potential for use as a water source in the service area of the urban water supplier.

The preparation of the plan shall be coordinated with local water, wastewater, groundwater, and planning agencies that operate within the supplier's service area, and shall include a description of the wastewater collection and treatment systems in the supplier's service area, including a quantification of the amount of wastewater collected and treated and the methods of wastewater disposal.

An Urban Water Management Plan may be a good source for determining wastewater treatment capacity. The Urban Water Management Plan is usually available online from the wastewater treatment service provider's website.

- It is recommended that the California Environmental Resources Evaluation System website be consulted to see if there is any information related to this question. The website is located at:

  ceres.ca.gov or enter "ceres evaluation" in an Internet search engine.

3. Example Answers

The following example answers the question comprehensively:

The project consists of 65 attached residential condominium units. Based on generation factors for wastewater obtained from the wastewater service provider, the project is projected to generate 17,550 gallons per day of wastewater per equivalent _dwelling unit (270 gallons x 65 units = 17,550 gallons)._

The Wastewater Facilities Master Plan for the service area in which the project is located indicated that treatment capacity expansions needed to accommodate the forecasted future flows for growth in the service area through 2025 have been constructed and are in operation.

Therefore, adequate wastewater treatment capacity is available to serve the project.

This response provides a description of the project's projected wastewater generation in relation to the capacity of the wastewater treatment system based on the local wastewater treatment provider's Wastewater Facility Master Plan.

The following example does not answer the question comprehensively:

The project will be connected to the City's sewer system via the existing lines in Mary Street. Adequate capacity will be provided to serve the project's projected demand.

This response does not provide factual data to support the conclusion. The ability to connect to an existing sewer line is not an adequate indicator that capacity will exist to serve the project in the future.

4. Determining Significance

Following are some general factors to consider for determining significance:

- Are there any formally adopted Thresholds of Significance by the lead agency that are applicable to the project?

- Has the lead agency set a precedent in previously approved CEQA documents in responding to the question? If so, the Initial Study Checklist preparer should be aware of how other CEQA documents have responded to the question.

- Any project that would generate wastewater above the treatment capacity of the wastewater treatment system may create a significant impact.

XVII. UTILITIES and SERVICE SYSTEMS (cont.)

Would the project:

(f) Be served by a landfill with sufficient permitted capacity to accommodate the project's solid waste disposal needs?

1. Determining the Scope of the Question

On Jan. 1, 2010 California's recycling and waste diversion efforts were streamlined into the new Department of Resources Recycling and Recovery-CalRecycle. The agency was previously known as the California Integrated Waste Management Board.

Local Enforcement Agencies are designated by the governing body of a county or city and, upon certification by the Department of Resources Recycling and Recovery, are empowered to implement delegated programs and locally designated activities.

Local Enforcement Agencies have the primary responsibility for ensuring the correct operation and closure of solid waste facilities in the state. They also have responsibilities for guaranteeing the proper storage and transportation of solid wastes.

The following list of Local Enforcement Agencies was excerpted from the CalRecycle website in April 2010:

County of Alameda
City of Berkeley
County of Alpine

County of Amador
County of Butte
County of Calaveras
County of Colusa
County of Contra Costa
City of Pittsburg
County of Del Norte
County of El Dorado
County of Fresno
County of Glenn
County of Humboldt
County of Imperial
County of Inyo
County of Kern
County of Kings
County of Lake
County of Lassen
County of Los Angeles
City of West Covina
City of Los Angeles
Sunshine Canyon Landfill Jurisdiction
City of Vernon
County of Madera
County of Marin
County of Mariposa
County of Mendocino
County of Merced
County of Modoc
County of Mono
County of Monterey
County of Napa
County of Nevada
County of Orange
County of Placer
County of Plumas
County of Riverside
County of Sacramento

County of San Benito
County of San Bernardino
County of San Diego
City of San Diego
County of San Francisco
County of San Joaquin
City of Stockton
County of San Luis Obispo
City of Paso Robles
County of San Mateo
County of Santa Barbara
County of Santa Clara
City of San Jose
County of Santa Cruz
County of Shasta
County of Sierra
County of Siskiyou
County of Solano
County of Sonoma
County of Stanislaus
County of Sutter
County of Tehama
County of Trinity
County of Tulare
County of Tuolumne
County of Ventura
County of Yolo
County of Yuba

The Initial Study Checklist preparer should contact the Local Enforcement Agency that has jurisdiction over the project to determine the available and future capacity of a landfill that will serve the project.

2. Where to Find the Factual Data to Answer the Question

- The Local Enforcement Agency that has jurisdiction over a landfill serving a project can be found at:

  www.calrecycle.ca.gov/LEA/Directory/ or enter "local enforcement agency" in an Internet search engine.

- Information on the capacity of a landfill can be found on the Solid Waste Information System webpage located at:

  www.calrecycle.ca.gov/SWFacilities/Directory/ or enter "california solid waste information system" in an Internet search engine.

- It is recommended that the California Environmental Resources Evaluation System website be consulted to see if there is any information related to this question. The website is located at:

  ceres.ca.gov or enter "ceres evaluation" in an Internet search engine.

3. Example Answers

The following example answers the question comprehensively:

The project is a 10 acre office park.

The primary receptor of the City's solid waste is the County Area Landfill. The County Area Landfill has a total capacity of 69,700,000 cubic yards and is permitted through the year 2028.

This permitted capacity was established considering future growth in the service area including growth based on the City's General Plan buildout projections.

The buildout projections included the development of the site as a 10 acre office park in accordance with the City's General Plan.

In addition, the Local Enforcement Agency with jurisdiction over the County Area Landfill was contacted and verified that adequate capacity exists to handle the solid waste generated by the project.

Therefore, the project would be served by a landfill with sufficient permitted capacity to accommodate the project's solid waste disposal needs.

This response identifies the capacity of the applicable landfill and the project's impacts on the landfill.

The following example does not answer the question comprehensively:

The County Area Landfill serves the project site. The project will not significantly affect the volume of solid waste. Impacts will be less than significant.

This response does not provide factual data to support the conclusion.

4. Determining Significance

Following are some general factors to consider for determining significance:

- Are there any formally adopted Thresholds of Significance by the lead agency that are applicable to the project?

- Has the lead agency set a precedent in previously approved CEQA documents in responding to the question? If so, the Initial Study Checklist preparer should be aware of how other CEQA documents have responded to the question.

- Any project that would exceed the capacity of a landfill to handle its solid waste may have a significant impact. Projects that require a general plan amendment or change land uses not addressed in a landfills future growth projections would be of particular concern.

XVII. UTILITIES and SERVICE SYSTEMS (cont.)

Would the project:

(g) Comply with federal, state, and local statutes and regulations related to solid waste?

1. Determining the Scope of the Question

At the federal level, the Environmental Protection Agency is responsible for overseeing the effective disposal of non-hazardous wastes, from common household garbage to large-scale industrial wastes and materials. These wastes and materials are not specifically hazardous, and have opportunities for reduction, reuse, and recycling.

The most salient statutes and regulations in the context of the question pertain to efforts to reduce impacts from solid waste through source reduction and recycling at the state and local level.

Most Initial Study Checklists address this question in this context.

2. Where to Find the Factual Data to Answer the Question

- The Calrecycle webpage is an excellent overall resource on this topic. The webpage can be located at:

  www.calrecycle.ca.gov/ or enter "calrecycle" in an Internet search engine.

- Contact the Local Enforcement Agency that serves the project area. A list of Local Enforcement Agency contacts can be found at:

  www.calrecycle.ca.gov/LEA/Directory/ or enter "california lea directory" in an Internet search engine.

- It is recommended that the California Environmental Resources Evaluation System website be consulted to see if there is any information related to this question. The website is located at:

  ceres.ca.gov or enter "ceres evaluation" in an Internet search engine.

3. Example Answers

**The following example answers the question comprehensively:**

The California Integrated Waste Management Act requires that jurisdictions maintain a 50% or better diversion rate for solid waste. The City implements this requirement through its Source Reduction and Recycling Element, its Household Hazardous Waste Element, and Chapter 19.02, Integrated Waste Management, of the City's Municipal Code.

Section 19.02.080 of the City's Municipal Code establishes the policies for "Collection Agreements" between the City and waste disposal contractors. This section requires agreements between the City and the contracted waste disposal companies to establish procedures for complying with all state *and federal laws, rules and regulations pertaining to solid waste handling services, and for implementing state-mandated programs and the goals and policies of the City's Source Reduction and Recycling Element and Household Hazardous Waste Element.*

The City currently has a contract with Waste Recycle Inc. to provide waste disposal and recycling services.

Therefore, the project would not cause any significant impacts from conflicting with statutes or regulations related to solid waste.

This response provides a comprehensive description of the salient regulations pertaining to solid waste reduction and recycling and how the project is required to comply with them.

The following example does not answer the question comprehensively:

The project will comply with all applicable federal, state, and local statutes and regulations pertaining to solid waste. Therefore, there will be no impact.

This response does not provide factual data to support the conclusion. It should say how it will comply with all applicable federal, state, and local statutes and regulations pertaining to solid waste.

4. Determining Significance

Following are some general factors to consider for determining significance:

- Are there any formally adopted Thresholds of Significance by the lead agency that are applicable to the project?

- Has the lead agency set a precedent in previously approved CEQA documents in responding to the question? If so, the Initial Study Checklist preparer should be aware of how other CEQA documents have responded to the question.

- Any project that is not in compliance with applicable federal, state, and local statutes and regulations related to solid waste would have a significant impact. However, this is one of those instances where compliance is mandatory so having a significant impact is not likely.

Chapter XVIII

Mandatory Findings of Significance

Introduction

Certain types of impacts are defined as being significant under CEQA. These are referred to as "Mandatory Findings of Significance."

The Initial Study Checklist preparer should be aware that although the environmental resources described under the Mandatory Findings of Significance may appear to be a summary of the questions posed in Sections I through XVII of Appendix G of the CEQA Guidelines, there are some differences.

For example, Question XVIII (a) under the Mandatory Findings of Significance section asks whether a project has *"the potential to ...reduce the number or restrict the range of a rare or endangered plant or animal."* This question does not appear in Section IV *Biological Resources*. (Source: *Guide to the California Environmental Quality Act (CEQA) 11th ed.* by Remy, Thomas, Moose, and Manley).

An EIR must be prepared if based on substantial evidence; any of the questions posed in the Mandatory Findings of Significance section are answered as having a "Potentially Significant Impact."

XVIII. MANDATORY FINDINGS of SIGNIFICANCE

(a) Does the project have the potential to degrade the quality of the environment, substantially reduce the habitat of a fish or wildlife species, cause a fish or wildlife population to drop below self-sustaining levels, threaten to eliminate a plant or animal community, reduce the number or restrict the range of a rare or endangered plant or animal or eliminate important examples of the major periods of California history or prehistory?

1. Determining the Scope of the Question

The focus of this question is on Biological Resources and Cultural Resources, however, the first sentence does contain the phrase "Does the project have the potential to degrade the quality of the environment."

Therefore, all of the environmental topics in the Initial Study Checklist should be addressed in the response and not just those pertaining to Biological and Cultural Resources,

2. Where to Find the Factual Data to Answer the Question

- The Initial Study Checklist should contain all the information necessary to answer the question.

- It is recommended that the California Environmental Resources Evaluation System website be consulted to see if there is any

information related to this question. The website is located at:

ceres.ca.gov or enter "ceres evaluation" in an Internet search engine.

3. Example Answers

The following example answers the question comprehensively:

Based on the analysis contained in this Initial Study, impacts to Aesthetics, Agriculture and Forestry Resources, Air Quality, Geology/Soils, Greenhouse Gas Emissions, Hydrology/Water Quality, Land Use and Planning, Mineral Resources, Population/ Housing, Public Services, Recreation, Transportation/Traffic, and Utility/Services Systems would have a less than significant on the environment.

Impacts to Biological Resources (California Black walnut, wetlands, nesting birds) would be significant unless mitigated. Mitigation Measures, BIO-1 through BIO-3 are required of the project.

Impacts to Cultural Resources (archaeological and paleontological) would be significant unless mitigated. Therefore, Mitigation Measures CR-1 and CR-2 are required of the project.

Impacts from Noise would be significant unless mitigated. Therefore, Mitigation Measures NOI-1 and NOI-2 are required of the project

The implementation of the Mitigation Measures identified above would result in less than significant _impacts to Biological Resources, Cultural Resources, and Noise._

Therefore the project will not degrade the quality of the environment and no habitat, wildlife populations, and plant and animal communities would be impacted. All environmental topics are either considered to have "No Impact", Less Than Significant Impact", or "Less Than Significant Impact with Mitigation Incorporated."

This response addresses all environmental topics analyzed in the Initial Study checklist and makes reference that the Initial Study Checklist determined that there are either "No Impacts", "Less Than Significant Impacts", or "Less Than Significant Impacts With Mitigation Incorporated" as a result of implementing the project.

The following example does not answer the question comprehensively:

The project does not have the potential to degrade the quality of the environment and would not have a significant impact on any fish or wildlife or their habitat. The project would also not eliminate important examples of the major periods of California history or prehistory. No impacts would result.

This response does not substantiate why this conclusion was reached. The conclusion should be based on the analysis contained in the Initial Study Checklist and should identify all environmental issues that required mitigation, if any.

4. Determining Significance

- Are there any formally adopted Thresholds of Significance by the lead agency that are applicable to the project?

- Has the lead agency set a precedent in previously approved CEQA documents in responding to the question? If so, the Initial Study Checklist preparer should be aware of how other CEQA documents have responded to the question.

- A project that has impacts associated with any the environmental topics identified in Appendix G of the CEQA Guidelines that cannot be mitigated to less than significant levels would be considered to have a significant impact and as EIR is required.

XVIII. MANDATORY FINDINGS of SIGNIFICANCE (cont.)

(b) Does the project have impacts that are individually limited, but cumulatively considerable? ("Cumulatively considerable" means that the incremental effects of a project are considerable when viewed in connection with the effects of past projects, the effects of other current projects, and the effects of probable future projects)?

1. Determining the Scope of the Question

The key to answering this question is to determine how the impacts from the project relate to those of future growth and/or projects in the general area.

The Initial Study Checklist preparer should reference back to the conclusions for each of the questions posed in the Initial Study Checklist to identify those impacts that might rise to being "cumulatively considerable."

The local agency's general plan can be used as a reference. For example, the contribution of the individual project relative to the overall impact of growth (e.g. traffic from the project vs. planned buildout traffic as identified in the general plan).

2. Where to Find the Factual Data to Answer the Question

- The Initial Study Checklist should contain all the information necessary to answer the question.

- It is recommended that the California Environmental Resources Evaluation System website be consulted to see if there is any information related to this question. The website is located at:

    ceres.ca.gov or enter "ceres evaluation" in an Internet search engine.

3. Example Answers

The following example answers the question comprehensively:

Based on the analysis contained in this Initial Study Checklist, the project's land uses are consistent with the City's General Plan land use projections. These land uses have been considered with overall City growth (including increases in traffic, noise, changes to air quality etc.).

The analysis in this Initial Study Checklist demonstrated that the project is compliance with all applicable mitigation plans including but not limited to, water quality control plan, air quality maintenance plan, integrated waste management plan, habitat conservation plan, and plans or regulations for the reduction of greenhouse gas emissions such as AB 32 and SB 375.

In addition, the project would not produce impacts, that considered with the effects of other past, present, and probable future projects, would be cumulatively considerable because potential adverse environmental impacts were determined to be less than significant with implementation of mitigation measures identified in this Initial Study Checklist.

This response bases its conclusions on the fact the project is consistent with the general plan and all applicable mitigation plans. In addition, mitigation measures have been recommended to reduce certain impacts that were potentially significant to less than significant.

The following example does not answer the question comprehensively:

The proposed development will have no adverse effect on the environment, either individually or cumulatively, that cannot be properly mitigated.

This response does not provide factual data to support the conclusion.

4. Determining Significance

- In determining if the projects impacts are significant, the Initial Study Checklist preparer should be guided by CEQA Guidelines Section 15064(h) which states:

  "(1) When assessing whether a cumulative effect requires an EIR, the lead agency shall consider whether the cumulative impact is significant and whether the effects of the project are cumulatively considerable.

  An EIR must be prepared if the cumulative impact may be significant and the project's incremental effect, though individually limited, is cumulatively considerable.

  "Cumulatively considerable" means that the incremental effects of an individual project are significant when viewed in connection *with the effects of past projects, the effects of other current projects, and the effects of probable future projects.*

(2) A lead agency may determine in an initial study that a project's contribution to a significant cumulative impact will be rendered less than cumulatively considerable and thus is not significant. When a project might contribute to a significant cumulative impact, but the contribution will be rendered less than cumulatively considerable through mitigation measures set forth in a mitigated negative declaration, the initial study shall briefly indicate and explain how the contribution has been rendered less than cumulatively considerable.

(3) A lead agency may determine that a project's incremental contribution to a cumulative effect is not cumulatively considerable if the project will comply with the requirements in a previously approved plan or mitigation program (including, but not limited to, water quality control plan, air quality attainment or maintenance plan, integrated waste management plan, habitat conservation plan, natural community conservation plan, plans or regulations for the reduction of greenhouse gas emissions) that provides specific requirements that will avoid or substantially lessen the cumulative problem within the geographic area in which the project is located.

Such plans or programs must be specified in law or adopted by the public agency with jurisdiction over the affected resources through a public review process to implement, interpret, or make specific the law enforced or administered by the public agency. When relying on a plan, regulation or program, the lead agency should explain how implementing the particular requirements in the plan, regulation or program ensure that the project's incremental contribution to the cumulative effect is not cumulatively considerable.

If there is substantial evidence that the possible effects of a particular project are still cumulatively considerable notwithstanding that the project complies with the specified plan or mitigation program addressing the cumulative problem, an EIR must be prepared for the project.

(4) The mere existence of significant cumulative impacts caused by other projects alone shall not constitute substantial evidence that the proposed project's incremental effects are "cumulatively considerable."

XVIII.   MANDATORY   FINDINGS   of SIGNIFICANCE (cont.)

(c) Does the project have environmental effects which will cause substantial adverse effects on human beings, either directly or indirectly?

1. Determining the Scope of the Question

This question focuses on the environmental topics that may cause an adverse impact on human beings. These environmental topics are; Air Quality, Geology and Soils, Greenhouse Gas Emissions, Hazards and Hazardous Materials, Hydrology and Water Quality, Land Use and Planning, Noise, Population and Housing, Public Services, Recreation, Transportation and Traffic, and Utilities and Service Systems.

2. Where to Find the Factual Data to Answer the Question

- The Initial Study Checklist should contain all the information necessary to answer the question.

- It is recommended that the California Environmental Resources Evaluation System website be consulted to see if there is any information related to this question. The website is located at:

  ceres.ca.gov or enter "ceres evaluation" in an Internet search engine.

3. Example Answers

The following example answers the question comprehensively:

As discussed in Sections III, VI, VII, VIII, IX, X, XII, XIII, XVI, and XVII of this Initial Study Checklist, the project would not expose persons to adverse impacts related to air quality, seismic or geologic hazards, greenhouse gas emissions, hazards or hazardous materials, hydrology or water quality, land use and planning, noise, population and housing, or transportation/traffic hazards, and the provision of utility services to people.

These impacts were identified to have no impact, a less than significant impact, or a less than significant impact with mitigation incorporated. Therefore, the project does not have environmental effects which will cause substantial adverse effects on human beings, either directly or indirectly.

This response describes what environmental impacts were determined not to cause a substantial adverse impact on human beings based on the analysis contained in the Initial Study Checklist prepared for the project.

The following example does not answer the question comprehensively:

The project will not result in environmental effects that will cause substantial adverse effects on human beings, either directly or indirectly.

This response does not provide factual data to support the conclusion. It should reference the analysis contained in the Initial Study Checklist prepared for the project.

4. Determining Significance

- Generally, a project that has adverse impacts associated with Air Quality, Geology and Soils, Greenhouse Gas Emissions, Hazards and Hazardous Materials, Hydrology and Water Quality, Land Use and Planning, Noise, Population and Housing, Public Services, Recreation, Transportation and Traffic, and Utilities and Service Systems that cannot be mitigated to less than significant levels may have a significant impact on humans.

Chapter XIX

Other Parts of the Initial Study Checklist

At the beginning of Appendix G, there are several sections that are to be filled in. Some of the sections are to be filled in after the Initial Study Checklist analysis is completed.

Filling in these sections is fairly straightforward. However, during the course of preparing and reviewing many Initial Study Checklists, the author has encountered instances where some of these sections were not appropriately filled in.

These areas are:

✓ *Environmental Checklist Form (Item #8, Project Description);*

✓ *Environmental Factors Potentially Affected; and*

✓ *Determination.*

Suggestions and or comments for completing these sections are provided as follows:

524

ENVIRONMENTAL CHECKLIST FORM

8. Description of the Project

Preparing an accurate and complete project description is one of the most important parts of the Initial Study Checklist. It is the foundation for the analysis.

CEQA Guidelines 15378 in part defines a "Project" as the "whole of an action." The whole of an action may result in either a direct or reasonably foreseeable indirect physical change in the environment.

The project description should be comprehensive and describe all aspects of the project in sufficient detail so that the public and decision makers are adequately informed.

A project description should not simply be a brief summary. It should describe all phases of project planning, implementation, and operation.

Following are examples of a complete project description and one that is not complete:

Example of a Complete Project Description

The project proposes the development of 187 residential condominium units on a 9.8 acre site. The project site is currently designated by the City General Plan as High Density Residential (25 dwelling units per acre) and zoned High Density-2.

The proposed density is 19 dwelling units per acre, and is consistent with the General Plan and Zoning designations.

The design of the project consists of 18 three-story residential buildings. Units consist of three and four bedroom units ranging in size from 1699 square feet to 1850 square feet.

Parking for each unit is provided under the units within garages. Uncovered visitor parking is provided throughout the site.

The main entrance to the project is located off of Leonard Avenue and two secondary entrances are located off Evans Street.

The site is located in a developed area of the city and all underground utilities (e.g. sewer lines, water lines, storm drains) are available to serve the project site without any extensions or size upgrades required.

The site is relatively flat and there will be a minimal amount of grading required. Development of the site will not require the import or export of soil to balance the site.

The project proposes to mass grade the entire site over approximately 2 weeks. The infrastructure for the project will be constructed/installed immediately after mass rough grading is completed, after which construction of buildings will be initiated on the entire project simultaneously.

The construction of the project is expected to be completed in one phase and will take approximately 6 months to develop.

The project would require the following actions by the City:

- Approval of Environmental Assessment 2010-35 for the proposed Mitigated Negative Declaration;

- Approval of Tentative Tract Map 35235, consisting of one (1) lot for condominium purposes, and a Plot Plan Review 2010-35 for the layout of the buildings and site features, as well as the architectural design of the buildings;

- Approval Tree Removal Permit 2010-03 authorizing the removal of one or more protected trees; and

- Issuance of grading, encroachment, and building permits in order to construct the project.

Example of an Incomplete Project Description

The subdivision of approximately 14.77 gross acres into 91 residential lots (4,000 s.f. minimum) and 4 lots for open space and drainage, developed pursuant to the Planned Residential Development standards.

ENVIRONMENTAL FACTORS POTENTIALLY AFFECTED

The environmental factors checked below would be potentially affected by this project, involving at least one impact that is "Potentially Significant Impact" as indicated by the checklist on the following pages.

□ Aesthetics

□ Agriculture and Forestry Resources

□ Air Quality

□ Biological Resources

□ Cultural Resources

□ Geology/Soils

□ Greenhouse Gas Emissions

□ Hazards & Hazardous Materials

□ Hydrology & Water Quality

□ Land Use and Planning

□ Mineral Resources

□ Noise

□ Population and Housing

□ Public Services

□ Recreation

□ Transportation/ Traffic

□ Utilities/Service Systems

□ Mandatory Findings of Significance

Comment: *A "Potentially Significant Impact" response is used when the project has the potential to have an effect on the environment that is considered to be significant and adverse. These boxes **should not** be checked unless an EIR is required.*

DETERMINATION

On the basis of this initial evaluation

☐ I find that the proposed project COULD NOT have a significant effect on the environment, and a NEGATIVE DECLARATION will be prepared.

Comment: *This determination is made when no mitigation measures are required. In practice, this determination is usually used for Initial Study Checklists that are prepared for a proposed ordinance or similar regulatory action.*

■ I find that although the proposed project could have a significant effect on the environment, there will not be a significant effect in this case because revisions in the project have been made by or agreed to by the project proponent. A MITIGATED NEGATIVE DECLARATION will be prepared.

Comment: *This is the most common determination for a development project.*

☐ I find that the proposed project MAY have a significant effect on the environment, and an ENVIRONMENTAL IMPACT REPORT is required.

Comment: *This determination would be made if any of the boxes under "Environmental Factors Potentially Affected" (See Page 524) were checked. This means that an environmental factor could not be mitigated to a less than significant level even with the imposition of mitigation measures.*

☐ I find that the proposed project MAY have a "potentially significant impact" or "potentially significant unless mitigated" impact on the environment, but at least one effect 1) adequately analyzed in an earlier document pursuant to applicable legal standards, and 2) addressed by mitigation measures based on the earlier analysis as described on the attached sheets. An ENVIRONMENTAL IMPACT REPORT is required, but it must analyze only the effects that remain to be addressed.

Comment: *This determination would be for a Mitigated Negative Declaration or EIR tiered off a previous Mitigated Negative Declaration or EIR so that the subsequent document does not have to be so detailed (i.e. it relies on a previous certified CEQA document for its support of findings).*

☐ I find that although the proposed project could have a significant effect on the environment, because all potentially significant effects (a) have been analyzed adequately in an earlier EIR or NEGATIVE DECLARATION pursuant to applicable standards, and (b) have been avoided or mitigated pursuant to that earlier EIR or NEGATIVE DECLARATION, including revisions or mitigation measures that are imposed upon the proposed project, nothing further is required:

Comment: *This determination is often used to support the use of an Addendum to a previous Mitigated Negative Declaration or EIR.*

Appendix A

Internet Webpage References

Appendix A is a listing off all the information sources cited throughout the book. They are arranged by environmental topic for easy reference. All links were active as of June 1, 2010.

GENERAL CEQA INFORMATION

- Governor's Office of Planning and Research

  www.opr.ca.gov/

- The California Environmental Quality Act

  ceres.ca.gov/ceqa/

- California Land Use Planning Information Network

  ceres.ca.gov/planning/

- Association of Environmental Professionals

  www.califaep.org/

- Find California Codes

  www.leginfo.ca.gov/calaw.html

- Environmental Database of the State Clearinghouse

www.ceqanet.ca.gov/

AESTHETICS

- It is recommended that the California Environmental Resources Evaluation System website be consulted to see if there is any information related to this topic. The website is located at:

  ceres.ca.gov or enter "ceres evaluation" in an Internet search engine.

AGRICULTURE AND FORESTRY RESOURCES

- It is recommended that the California Environmental Resources Evaluation System website be consulted to see if there is any information related to this topic. The website is located at:

  ceres.ca.gov or enter "ceres evaluation" in an Internet search engine.

- The Farmland Mapping and Monitoring Program has an excellent website which addresses this topic. It contains interactive maps that can be used to determine if a site is mapped as agricultural land. The website is located at:

  www.consrv.ca.gov/dlrp/FMMP or enter "farmland mapping and monitoring program" in an Internet search engine.

- The Natural Resource Conservation Service Web Soil Survey provides soil data and information produced by the National Cooperative Soil Survey. The website can be located at:

  http://websoilsurvey.nrcs.usda.gov/app/ or enter "nrcs web soil survey" in an Internet Search engine.

- The Land Evaluation Site Assessment Model is recommended by the California Department of Conservation to determine the suitability of land for agriculture use. The website can be located at:

  www.consrv.ca.gov/DLRP/Pages/qh_lesa.aspx or enter "land evaluation site assessment" in an Internet search engine.

- The California Department of Conservation has an excellent website which addresses Williamson Act contracts. The website is located at:

  www.conservation.ca.gov/dlrp/lca or enter "williamson act contract" in an Internet search engine.

- The California Department of Forestry and Fire Protection has an excellent website which addresses this topic. The website is located at:

  www.fire.ca.gov/ and click on the "Resource Management" link or enter "california department of forestry" in an Internet search engine.

- The California Department of Conservation has an excellent website about farm land. The website can be located at:

- **www.conservation.ca.gov/**. Click on the link "Land Protection" or enter "california department of conservation" in an Internet search engine.

AIR QUALITY

- It is recommended that the California Environmental Resources Evaluation System website be consulted to see if there is any information related to this topic. The website is located at:

  ceres.ca.gov or enter "ceres evaluation" in an Internet search engine.

- The best source of information is the Air Quality Control District/Air Quality Management District in which the project is located in. A list of Districts can be found at:

  www.arb.ca.gov/capcoa/roster.htm or enter "california local air district directory" in an Internet search engine.

- The Urban Emissions Model" (URBEMIS) is a modeling tool used to estimate air quality impacts from land use projects. Many Air Quality Control Districts/Air Quality Management Districts recommend using

URBEMIS. The most recently updated version of the model (URBEMIS, Version 9.2.4), can be downloaded from the following sites:

www.aqmd.gov/ceqa/urbemis.html or **www.urbemis.com** or enter "urbemis 2007" in an Internet search engine.

- ICF Jones and Stokes (now ICF International) has prepared an excellent guide titled: *Software User's Guide: URBEMIS2007 for Windows* that can help in using URBEMIS. The guide can be located at:

  www.urbemis.com/support/manual.ht ml or enter "urbemis users manual" in an Internet search engine.

- Information on Federal and State Ambient Air Quality Standards can be found on the California Air Resources Board webpage located at:

  www.arb.ca.gov/research/aaqs/aaqs.h tm or enter "california ambient air quality standards (aaqs)" in an Internet search engine.

- The *Air Quality and Land Use Handbook: A Community Health Perspective* adopted by the California Air Resources Board, has some tools to assist in conducting assessments of cumulative emissions. The handbook's webpage is located at:

www.arb.ca.gov/ch/landuse.htm or enter "air quality land use handbook" in an Internet search engine.

- *The Community Health Air Pollution Information System* is a user friendly, Internet-based system for displaying information on emissions from sources of air pollution in an easy to use mapping format.

  The system contains information on air pollution emissions from selected large facilities and small businesses that emit criteria and toxic air pollutants. The webpage is located at:

  www.arb.ca.gov/ch/chapis1/chapis1.htm or enter "chapis emission maps" in an Internet search engine.

- *The Hot Spots Analysis and Reporting Program* is a software database package that evaluates emissions from one or more facilities to determine the overall health risk posed by the facility(-ies) on the surrounding community.

  Proper use of the software package ensures that the risk assessment meets the latest risk assessment guidelines published by the State Office of Environmental Health Hazard Assessment. *The Hot Spots Analysis and Reporting Program* is designed with air quality professionals in mind and is available from the Air Resources Board. The webpage is located at:

www.arb.ca.gov/toxics/harp/harp.htm
or enter "arb harp" in an Internet search engine.

- The California Air Pollution Control Officers Association has an excellent publication titled: *Health Risk Assessments for Proposed Land Use Projects* which deals with this issue. The document can be found at:

www.capcoa.org/wp-content/uploads/downloads/2010/05C APCOA_HRA_LU_Guidelines_8-6-09.pdf. or enter "capcoa" in an Internet search engine and click on the link to the publication.

- The California Air Pollution Control Officers Association has general information on the effects of air pollution on human health. The webpage is located at:

www.capcoa.org/health-effects/

BIOLOGOCAL RESOURCES

- It is recommended that the California Environmental Resources Evaluation System website be consulted to see if there is any information related to this topic. The website is located at:

ceres.ca.gov or enter "ceres evaluation" in an Internet search engine.

- Information on endangered species can be found on the U.S. Fish and Wildlife Service website located at:

  www.fws.gov/endangered/ or enter "us endangered species program" in an Internet search engine.

- Information on endangered species can be found on the California Department of Fish and Game website located at:

  www.dfg.ca.gov/habcon/ or enter "dfg habitat conservation" in an Internet search engine.

- The California Natural Diversity Database is a program that inventories the status and locations of rare plants and animals in California. California Natural Diversity Database staff work with partners to maintain current lists of rare species as well as maintain database of GIS-mapped locations for these species. The website is located at:

  www.dfg.ca.gov/biogeodata/cnddb/ or enter "cnddb" in an Internet search engine.

- Information on Natural Communities can be found on the CDFG website located at:

  http://www.dfg.ca.gov/biogeodata/veg camp/natural_communities.asp or enter "cdfg biological information natural communities" in an Internet search engine.

- The _Protocols for Surveying and Evaluating Impacts to Special Status Native Plant Populations and Natural Communities_ published by the California Department of Fish and Game may help Initial Study Checklist preparers review environmental documents, determine when a botanical survey is needed, how field surveys may be conducted, what information to include in a survey report, and what qualifications to consider for surveyors. The document can be located at:

  www.dfg.ca.gov/biogeodata/cnddb/pdf s/Protocols_for_Surveying_and_Evaluat ing_Impacts.pdf or enter "dfg protocols for surveying natural communities" in an Internet search engine.

- The California Department of Fish and Game Biogeographic Data Branch has a webpage that identifies vegetation mapping, rare species tracking, and species range mapping that can assist in identifying wildlife movement corridors and nursery sites. The webpage is located at:

  www.dfg.ca.gov/biogeodata/ or enter "dfg biogeographic data branch" in an Internet search engine.

- In 2007 the State Legislature required the Department of Fish and Game to identify high priority areas for vegetation mapping and to map known wildlife corridors in the state.

A report was prepared titled: *Legislative Analyst's Office Supplemental Report of the 2007 Budget Act 2007-08 Fiscal Year*. This report contains an excellent overview on wildlife corridors. It can be found on the California Department of Fish and Game Biogeographic Data Branch webpage. The webpage is located at:

www.dfg.ca.gov/biogeodata/ or enter "dfg biogeographic data branch" in an Internet search engine. The webpage contains a link to the report located at:

www.dfg.ca.gov/biogeodata/vegcamp/pdfs/WCB_Veg-Mapping_LAO_Supplemental_Report_2007.pdf or enter "legislative analyst's office supplemental report item 3640-301-6051" in an Internet search engine.

- The U.S. Environmental Protection Agency has an excellent website that provides information on wetlands. It is located at:

  www.epa.gov/owow/wetlands/or enter "wetlands us epa" in an Internet search engine.

- The U.S. Fish and Wildlife Service, National Wetlands Inventory webpage contains a mapping system for wetlands. It is located at:

  www.fws.gov/wetlands/Data/Mapper.html or enter "national wetlands inventory" in an Internet search engine or enter "usfws wetlands inventory" in an Internet search engine.

- The U.S. Fish and Wildlife Service website has a listing of Habitat Conservation Plans for California. The website is located at:

  http://ecos.fws.gov/conserv_plans/ser vlet/gov.doi.hcp.servlets.PlanSelect or enter "usfws conservation plans and agreements" in an Internet search engine. Click on the link for "Region 8, California and Nevada" to view a list of Plans.

- The California Department of Fish and Game website has information about the Natural Community Conservation Planning Program. The website is located at:

  www.dfg.ca.gov/habcon/nccp/ or enter "california natural community conservation planning" in an Internet search engine. Click on the link "Summary Table" to view a list of Plans.

CULTURAL RESOURCES

- It is recommended that the California Environmental Resources Evaluation System website be consulted to see if there is any information related to this topic. The website is located at:

  ceres.ca.gov or enter "ceres evaluation" in an Internet search engine.

- National Register of Historic Places

The National Park Service website has a listing of properties that are listed in the National Register of Historic Places. The website can be located at:

www.nationalregisterofhistoricplaces.com/or enter "national register of historic places listings" in an Internet search engine.

- A good resource to consult with respect to cultural resources is: *California State Law and Historic Preservation Statutes, Regulations & Administrative Policies Regarding the Preservation and Protection of Cultural and Historical Resources*. The document can be located at:

  www.parks.ca.gov/pages/1069/files/10%20comb.pdf or enter "california historic preservation statutes" in an Internet search engine.

- The California Historic Research Information System (CHRIS) maintains the statewide Historical Resources Inventory database which provides current archaeological and historical resource information for the entire State of California.

  As a standard practice, a records search should be requested from the applicable Regional Information Center in the county in which the project is located.

  A Regional Information Center Roster can be located at:

www.parks.ca.gov/pages/1068/files/ic %20roster.pdf or enter "california ic roster" in an Internet search engine and click on the "IC Roster" link.

GEOLOGY AND SOILS

- It is recommended that the California Environmental Resources Evaluation System website be consulted to see if there is any information related to this topic. The website is located at:

  ceres.ca.gov or enter "ceres evaluation" in an Internet search engine.

- Alquist-Priolo Earthquake Fault Zones

  Division of Mines and Geology Special Publication 42 which is titled: *Fault-Rupture Hazard Zones in California, Alquist-Priolo Earthquake Fault Zoning Act with Index to Earthquake Fault Zone Maps.*

  The most recent publication is the Interim 2007 edition. It is available from the California Department of Conservation website located at:

  ftp://ftp.consrv.ca.gov/pub/dmg/pubs /sp/Sp42.pdf or enter "dmg special publication 42" in an Internet search engine.

  Alquist-Priolo Earthquake Fault Zone Maps and related information are available from the California Department of Conservation website located at:

www.consrv.ca.gov/cgs/rghm/ap/Page s/index.aspx or enter "alquist-priolo fault maps" in an Internet search engine.

- Strong Seismic Ground Shaking

  Probabilistic Seismic Hazard Maps can be found on the California Department of Conservation website located at:

  www.conservation.ca.gov/cgs/rghm/ps ha/Pages/index.aspx or enter "seismic hazard shaking maps of california" in an Internet search engine

  Author's Note: *These maps are not intended for site-specific hazard analysis, but only provide a regional perspective of earthquake hazard in California.*

  Overall information on seismic shaking hazards can be found under the California Department of Conservation Seismic Hazard Zonation Program Data Access Page located at:

  http://gmw.consrv.ca.gov/shmp/MapP rocessor.asp?Action=SHMP&Location=A ll&Version=8&Browser=IE&Platform=W in or enter "seismic hazard zonation program data access page" in an Internet search engine. (In addition, please see information under Landslides below)

- Seismic-related Ground Failure, Including Liquefaction

  The California Department of Conservation website has maps that are intended to assist cities and counties in fulfilling their responsibilities for protecting the public from ground failure caused by earthquakes.

Maps showing liquefaction and landslide hazard areas for **Northern California** can be found at:

http://gmw.consrv.ca.gov/shmp/html/ pdf_maps_no.html or enter "seismic hazards zonation program" in an Internet search engine and click on the "Quickview/Download PDF Maps" link.

Maps showing liquefaction and landslide hazard areas for **Southern California** can be found at:

http://gmw.consrv.ca.gov/shmp/html/ pdf_maps_so.html or enter "seismic hazards zonation program" in an Internet search engine and click on the "Quickview/Download PDF Maps" link.

- Landslides

The California Department of Conservation has a program called the Seismic Hazard Zonation Program. The program prepares maps that identify existing landslides and designates landslide zones of require preparation of site-specific studies and reports that recommend measures to mitigate impacts from landslides. Information on the program can be found at the California Department of Conservation website located at:

www.conservation.ca.gov/cgs/shzp/Pa ges/Index.aspx or enter "seismic hazard zonation program" in an Internet search engine.

In addition, please note that *California Geological Survey Special Publication 117* states:

"The fact that a site lies outside a zone of required investigation does not necessarily mean that the site is free from seismic or other geologic hazards, regardless of the information shown on the Seismic Hazard Zone Maps.

The zones do not always include landslide or lateral spread run-out areas. Project sites that are outside of any zone may be affected by ground failure runout from adjacent or nearby sites. Finally, neither the information on the Seismic Hazard Zone Maps, nor in any technical reports that describe how the maps were prepared nor what data were used is sufficient to serve as a substitute for the required site-investigation reports called for in the Act."

Special Publication 117 can be found at:

www.conservation.ca.gov/smgb/Guidel ines/Documents/SP117-091508.pdf or enter "*California Geological Survey Special Publication 117*" in an Internet search engine.

- An excellent source of information for Geology is the California Department of Conservation website located at:

  www.conservation.ca.gov/ and click on the "Geology" link and then click on the "California Geological Survey" link.

- The Natural Resources Conservation Agency has prepared manuscripts and soils maps for California counties that are available online at:

  http://soils.usda.gov/survey/Online_S urveys/California/ or enter "california online soil survey manuscripts"

  Another source of maps provided by the Natural Resources Conservation Agency show soil classification. The Initial Study Checklist preparer will have to know what types of soils are considered to have expansive characteristics. These are generally clay soils.

  The maps can be found at:

  http://websoilsurvey.ncrs.usda.gov/ap p/ or enter "nrca web soil survey" in an Internet search engine.

GREENHOUSE GAS EMISSIONS

- It is recommended that the California Environmental Resources Evaluation System website be consulted to see if there is any information related to this topic. The website is located at:

ceres.ca.gov or enter "ceres evaluation" in an Internet search engine.

- The best source of information would be from a technical report prepared consistent with CEQA Guidelines Sections 15064.4(a) and (b) and 15126.4 (c) and guidance from Governor's Office of Planning and Research Technical Advisory on Climate Change. The document can be found at:

  www.opr.ca.gov/ceqa/pdfs/june08-ceqa.pdf or enter "opr technical advisory ceqa and climate change" in an Internet search engine.

- The Office of Planning and Research website also provides information on Greenhouse Gases. The website is located at:

  www.opr.ca.gov/. Click on the link "CEQA GUIDELINES AND GREENHOUSE GASES." or enter "opr ghg emissions" in an Internet search engine and follow the above links.

  The Office of Planning and Research website also has links to other websites that deal with greenhouse gases in California.

- The Natural Resources Agency's *Final Statement of Reasons for Regulatory Action, Amendments to the State CEQA Guidelines Addressing Analysis and Mitigation of Greenhouse Gas Emissions Pursuant to SB97, December 2009* provides an excellent overview of greenhouse gas emissions as they pertain to CEQA. The document can be found at:

http://ceres.ca.gov/ceqa/docs/Final_S tatement_of_Reasons.pdf or enter "final statement of reasons for regulatory action ghg" in an Internet search engine.

- *CEQA and Climate Change, Evaluating and Addressing Greenhouse Gas Emissions from Projects Subject to the California Environmental Quality Act, June 2008* published by the California Air Pollution Control Officers Association is an excellent resource on this topic. The publication can be found at:

  www.capcoa.org/or enter "capcoa" in an Internet search engine.

- The AB 32 Scoping Plan can be found at:

  www.arb.ca.gov/cc/scopingplan/scopin gplan.htm or enter "ab 32 scoping plan" in an Internet search engine.

HAZARDS AND HAZARDOUS MATERIALS

- It is recommended that the California Environmental Resources Evaluation System website be consulted to see if there is any information related to this topic. The website is located at:

  ceres.ca.gov or enter "ceres evaluation" in an Internet search engine.

- The best source to consult is the local Certified Unified Program Agency which oversees hazardous materials at the local level. They work closely with local agencies through the project review process to ascertain the impacts from hazardous materials. Consult the Cal Certified Unified Program Agency for information.

  Information about where to locate the Certified Unified Program Agency for a region can be found at:

  www.calepa.ca.gov/CUPA/Directory/def ault.aspx or enter "cupa directory search" in an Internet search engine.

- Additional information can be found at the following websites:

  U.S. Environmental Protection Agency website at **www.epa.gov/** or enter "us epa" in an Internet search engine.

  California Environmental Protection Agency website at **www.calepa.ca.gov/** or enter "cal epa" in an Internet search engine.

  Department of Toxic Substance Control website at **www.dtsc.ca.gov/** or enter "ca dtsc" in an Internet search engine.

- For naturally occurring asbestos, the following sources provide good information:

  The Office of Planning and Research publication titled: *CEQA AND ASBESTOS:*

Addressing Naturally Occurring Asbestos in CEQA Documents can be located at:

www.opr.ca.gov/planning/publications /asbestos_advisory.pdf or enter "naturally occurring asbestos in ceqa documents" in an Internet search engine.

The California Air Resources Board has state wide maps showing areas likely to contain naturally occurring asbestos. The website is located at:

www.arb.ca.gov/toxics/asbestos/geninfo.htm or enter "areas likely to contain naturally occurring asbestos california" in an Internet search engine.

- The best source of information for hazardous emissions is the applicable Air Pollution Control District/Air Quality Management District. A list of districts can be found at:

  www.arb.ca.gov/capcoa/roster.htm or enter "california air districts" in an Internet search engine.

Cortese List

- List of Hazardous Waste and Substances Sites from Department of Toxic Substances Control EnviroStor database.

- List of Leaking Underground Storage Tank Sites by County and Fiscal Year from Water Board GeoTracker database.

- List of solid waste disposal sites identified by Water Board with waste constituents above hazardous waste levels outside the waste management unit.

- List of "active" Cease and Desist Orders and Cleanup and Abatement Orders from the Water Board.

- List of hazardous waste facilities subject to corrective action pursuant to Section 25187.5 of the Health and Safety Code, identified by Department of Toxic Substances Control.

  For more information on where to find these lists, consult the Cortese List website at:

  www.calepa.ca.gov/SiteCleanup/Cortes eList/default.htm or enter "cortese list" in an Internet search engine.

- A list of public use airports in California can be found at:

  www.dot.ca.gov/hq/planning/aeronaut /documents2/pubuse07.pdf or enter "california public use airports-2007 and military fields" in an Internet search engine.

- *The California Airport Land Use Planning Handbook, State of California Department of Transportation Division of Aeronautics* can be found at:

  www.dot.ca.gov/hq/planning/aeronaut /documents/ALUPHComplete-7-

02rev.pdf or enter "california airport land use planning handbook" in an Internet search engine.

- Airport Land Use Commission Contacts by County can be found at:

www.dot.ca.gov/ha/planning/aeronaut /documents2/ALUC3-2-09.pdf or enter "aluc contact list 3-2-09" in an Internet search engine.

- For specific guidance concerning airports in an area contact "Airport Land Use Compatibility Guidance" at:

www.dot.ca.gov/hq/planning/landuse. html or enter "airport land use compatibility guidance" in an Internet search engine.

- The California Department of Forestry and Fire Prevention, Fire Hazard Severity Zones Maps identify wildland fire hazard areas. The webpage is located at:

www.fire.ca.gov/fire_prevention/fire_p revention_wildland_zones.php

The webpage has links to county and city level maps. The webpage can also be found on an internet search engine by entering "california fire hazard severity zone maps" in an Internet search engine.

- The Office of Planning and Research publication titled: *Fire Hazard Planning* is an excellent source of information on wildland fires. The document can be located at:

www.opr.ca.gov/planning/publications /Fire_Hazard_Planning- Final_Report.pdf or enter "fire hazard planning california technical advice" in an Internet search engine.

- Information of California Wildland Urban Building Codes can be found at:

  www.fire.ca.gov/fire_prevention/fire_p revention_wildland_codes.php or enter "california's wildland urban interface code information" in an Internet search engine.

HYDROLOGY AND WATER QUALITY

- It is recommended that the California Environmental Resources Evaluation System website be consulted to see if there is any information related to this topic. The website is located at:

  ceres.ca.gov or enter "ceres evaluation" in an Internet search engine.

- The Water Education Foundation has a webpage titled: "Where Does My Water Come From" that provides general information on water supply. The webpage is located at:

  www.ater-ed.org/watersources/ or enter "where does my water come from" in an Internet search engine.

- The issue of future water supply reliability is discussed in the California Department of Water Resources' update to the State Water Plan, which can be viewed at:

  www.waterplan.water.ca.gov or enter" california state water plan" in an Internet search engine.

- Visit this U.S. EPA web site to learn more about the surface water resources in your region. The webpage is located at:

  http://cfpub.epa.gov/surf/locate/index .cfm or enter "us epa surf your watershed" in an Internet search engine.

- The Office of Planning and Research has an excellent Technical Advisory on hydrology and water quality titled: *CEQA and Low Impact Development Stormwater Design: Preserving Stormwater Quality and Stream Integrity Through California Environmental Quality Act (CEQA) Review.* The document can be found at:

  www.opr.ca.gov/ceqa/pdfs/Technical_ Advisory_LID.pdf or enter "ceqa low impact development storm water design" in an Internet search engine.

- National Pollution Discharge Elimination System website at:

  http://cfpub.epa.gov/npdes/npdesreg. cfm?program_id=45 or enter "npdes" in an Internet search engine.

- State Water Regional Quality Control Board website at:

  www.swrcb.ca.gov/ or enter "State Water Regional Quality Control Board" in an Internet search engine.

- National Flood Insurance Program website located at:

  www.fema.gov/plan/prevent/fhm/inde x.shtm or enter "firm maps" in an Internet search engine.

- The Department of Water Resources provides a listing of dam locations in California on their website at:

  www.water.ca.gov/damsafety/damlisti ng/index.cfm or enter "california dam safety" on an Internet search engine.

- The California Department of Conservation has prepared Tsunami Inundation Maps that are located at:

  www.consrv.ca.gov/cgs/geologic_hazar ds/Tsunami/Inundation_Maps/Pages/I ndex_Maps.aspx or enter "tsunami inundation map california" in an Internet Search Engine.

  California Geological Survey Tsunamis Note 55 is a good source of information on this topic. It can be located at:

**www.consrv.ca.gov/cgs/information/p
ublications/cgs_notes/Documents/CGS
_Note_55.pdf** or enter "California
Geological Survey Note 55" in an Internet
search engine.

- **Mudflows**

  *California Geological Survey -CGS Note 33-
  Hazards From Mudslides Debris Avalanches
  and Debris Flows in Hillside and Wildfire
  Areas* is a good source of information on this
  topic. The publication can be located at:

  **www.consrv.ca.gov/cgs/information/p
  ublications/cgs_notes/note_33/Pages/
  index.aspx** or enter "california geological
  survey note 33" in an Internet Search
  Engine.

LAND USE AND PLANNING

- It is recommended that the California
  Environmental Resources Evaluation System
  website be consulted to see if there is any
  information related to this topic. The website
  is located at:

  ceres.ca.gov or enter "ceres evaluation" in
  an Internet search engine.

- Information on Habitat Conservation Plans
  can be found at:

  **www.fws.gov/endangered/what-we-
  do/hcp-overview.html** or by entering

"federal habitat conservation plans" in an Internet search engine.

The U.S. Fish and Wildlife Service website has a listing of Habitat Conservation Plans for California, which is located in Region 8.

The website can be located at:

http://ecos.fws.gov/conserv_plans/pu blic.jsp or enter "conservation plans and agreements database" in an Internet search engine. Click on the link for "Region 8, California and Nevada" to view a list of Plans.

- Information on Natural Community Conservation Plans can be found at:

  www.dfg.ca.gov/habcon/nccp/ or by entering"california natural communities conservation planning" in an Internet search engine.

MINERAL RESOURCES

- It is recommended that the California Environmental Resources Evaluation System website be consulted to see if there is any information related to this topic. The website is located at:

  ceres.ca.gov or enter "ceres evaluation" in an Internet search engine.

- Useful information on the California Mineral Land Classification System can be found at:

**www.consrv.ca.gov/smgb/Guidelines/D
ocuments/ClassDesig.pdf** or enter
"california guidelines for classification and
designation of mineral lands" in an Internet
search engine.

- A map showing aggregate availability in
  California can be found at:

  **www.consrv.ca.gov/cgs/information/p
  ublications/ms/Documents/MS_52_ma
  p.pdf** or enter "aggregate availability in
  California map" in an Internet search engine.

- The California Geological Survey webpage
  has information on mineral classifications
  available at the County level. The webpage
  is located at:

  **www.consrv.ca.gov/cgs/information/p
  ublications/pub_index/Pages/products
  _that_we_sell.aspx** or enter "cgs products
  that we sell" on an Internet search engine.

NOISE

- It is recommended that the California
  Environmental Resources Evaluation System
  website be consulted to see if there is any
  information related to this topic. The website
  is located at:

  ceres.ca.gov or enter "ceres evaluation" in
  an Internet search engine.

- California Department of Transportation noise information can be located at:

  www.dot.ca.gov/ser/vol1/sec3/physical /ch12noise/chap12noise.htm or enter "caltrans noise standards" in an Internet search engine.

- Federal Aviation Administration noise information can be located at:

  www.faa.gov/about/office_org/headqua rters_offices/aep/planning_toolkit/or enter "faa noise standards" in an Internet search engine.

- U.S, Department of Housing and Urban Development noise information can be found at:

  www.hudnoise.com/hudstandard.html or enter "hud noise environmental criteria" in an Internet search engine.

- A map of public use airports in California can be found at:

  www.dot.ca.gov/hq/planning/aeronaut /documents2/pubuse07.pdf or enter "ca dot public use airports map 2007" in an Internet search engine.

- The California Office of Airports has excellent information on airports including a list of airports. The webpage can be found at:

www.dot.ca.gov/hq/planning/aeronaut /oairport.html or enter "ca office of airports" in an Internet search engine. Click on the link "California Airports/Heliport Master Records."

- An excellent resource for airport noise is: *The California Airport Land Use Planning Handbook, State of California Department of Transportation Division of Aeronautics.* It can be found at:

www.dot.ca.gov/hq/planning/aeronaut /documents/ALUPHComplete-7- 02rev.pdf

- The California Division of Aeronautics maintains a document called "California Airport/Heliport/Master Records" which provides information on airports (including private airports). This list may contain information on personal use airports (i.e. private airstrips). The website is located at:

www.dot.ca.gov/hq/planning/aeronaut /ca.html or enter "california division of aeronautics" in an Internet search engine and click on the link "california airport/heliport/master records."

POPULATION AND HOUSING

- It is recommended that the California Environmental Resources Evaluation System website be consulted to see if there is any information related to this topic. The website is located at:

ceres.ca.gov or enter "ceres evaluation" in an Internet search engine.

PUBLIC SERVICES

- It is recommended that the California Environmental Resources Evaluation System website be consulted to see if there is any information related to this topic. The website is located at:

  ceres.ca.gov or enter "ceres evaluation" in an Internet search engine.

RECREATION

- It is recommended that the California Environmental Resources Evaluation System website be consulted to see if there is any information related to this topic. The website is located at:

  ceres.ca.gov or enter "ceres evaluation" in an Internet search engine.

TRANSPORTATION/TRAFFIC

- It is recommended that the California Environmental Resources Evaluation System website be consulted to see if there is any information related to this topic. The website is located at:

  ceres.ca.gov or enter "ceres evaluation" in an Internet search engine.

- The author suggests reading the article published by Ronald Miliam, AICP, titled: *Transportation Impact Analysis Gets a Failing Grade When it Comes to Climate Change and Smart Growth.* The article provides an excellent discussion on this topic and can be found at:

  http://opr.ca.gov/sch/pdfs/LOS_Climat e_Change_Smart_Growth.pdf or enter the title of the article in an Internet search engine.

- *The California Airport Land Use Planning Handbook, State of California Department of Transportation Division of Aeronautics* can be found at:

  www.dot.ca.gov/hq/planning/a eronaut/documents/ALUPHComplete-7-02rev.pdf or enter "california airport land use planning handbook" in an Internet search engine.

- Information about federal and state transit programs is available from the California Division of Mass Transportation website at:

  www.dot.ca.gov/hq/MassTrans/# or enter "california division of mass transportation" in an Internet search engine.

- The Council of Governments that the project area is located in has information on mass transit. Information about which Council of Governments the project area is located in can be found on the California Association of Councils of Governments website at:

www.calcog.org/about/about.html or enter "California Association of Councils of Governments" in an Internet search engine.

UTILITIES AND SERVICE SYSTEMS

- It is recommended that the California Environmental Resources Evaluation System website be consulted to see if there is any information related to this topic. The website is located at:

  ceres.ca.gov or enter "ceres evaluation" in an Internet search engine.

- To find out what Regional Water Quality Control Board has jurisdiction over the project, consult the State Water Resources Control Board website at:

  www.waterboards.ca.gov/waterboards _map.shtml or enter "california state water resources control board" in an Internet Search engine and click on the link "State Regional Water Boards' Map."

- Information on the capacity of a landfill can be found on the Solid Waste Information System webpage located at:

  www.calrecycle.ca.gov/SWFacilities/Dir ectory/ or enter "california solid waste information system" in an Internet search engine.

- The Calrecycle webpage is an excellent overall resource on this topic. The webpage can be located at:

  www.calrecycle.ca.gov/ or enter "calrecycle" in an Internet search engine.

- The Local Enforcement Agency that has jurisdiction over a landfill serving a project can be found at:

  www.calrecycle.ca.gov/LEA/Directory/ or enter "local enforcement agency" in an Internet search engine.

Appendix B

Preliminary Biological Assessment Format

TASK 1: PRE-FIELDSURVEY INVESTIGATIONS: Pre-field survey records search of the current California Natural Diversity Database for the applicable United States Geological Survey Quadrangles in the project area to identify any sensitive plant or animal species or habitat recorded onsite or adjacent to the project site which could be impacted by the project.

TASK 2: FIELD SURVEY: Perform a single field survey of the entire project site and areas immediately adjacent to ascertain the presence or absence of any sensitive plant or animal species or habitat that supports such species which could be impacted by the project. In addition, identify any jurisdictional wetlands or watercourses that could be impacted by the project.

TASK 3: WRITTEN FINDINGS: As a result of Tasks 1 and 2, written findings will be provided which either:

1. State the ***absence*** of any sensitive plant or animal species or habitat that supports such species observable within the boundaries of the project site, or immediately adjacent to the project site, which could be impacted by the project. The written findings will also state that there is no need for further studies and state the time period for which the findings are valid (i.e. one year etc.).; or

2. State the ***presence*** of any sensitive plant or animal species or habitat that supports such

species observable within the boundaries of the project site, or immediately adjacent to the project site, which could be impacted by the project. The written findings will make recommendations specifying which, **future** focused and/or protocol biological field surveys will be necessary and the time frame in which each survey(s) are to be conducted (e.g. May-August).

Three copies of the written findings will be "wet signed" and submitted to the Lead Agency.

Appendix C

Preliminary Geologic Report Format

1. PURPOSE & INTENT: A Preliminary Geotechnical Report is a Mandatory Submittal Requirement for most development projects. The Planning Division will advise you if it is not required under certain circumstances.

In order to meet the requirements of the California Environmental Quality Act (CEQA) in the preparation of an Initial Study, the City is required to answer a series of questions that are contained in Appendix "G" of the CEQA Guidelines. The responses to these questions assist in determining the significance of the environmental effects caused by a project and whether a Negative Declaration, Mitigated Negative Declaration, reliance on a previous environmental document(s), or an Environmental Impact Report is required.

According to CEQA, the determination of whether a project may have significant effect on the environment calls for careful judgment on the part of the City, based to the extent possible on scientific and factual data. [Ref. CEQA Guidelines Section 15064(b)]. The City uses the information contained in the technical studies and other project application information as the factual basis to make this determination.

Therefore, it is important that any technical studies or information submitted for a project be prepared in such a manner that they include information necessary to assist the City in answering the questions based on Appendix "G" of the CEQA Guidelines.

2. CEQA APPENDIX "G" QUESTIONS: With respect to Geology and Soils, the City uses the following information to satisfy the requirements of Appendix "G":

Would the project expose people or structures to risk or loss as a result of one or more of the following occurrences? (Potential impacts must be described and mitigation measures recommended, where applicable. Detailed analyses should be provided for all geotechnical issues where there is a significant risk to either people or structures).

1) Earthquake Fault Rupture – evaluation of rupture potential must be presented per the requirements of the Alquist-Priolo Earthquake Fault Zoning Act (CDMG Special Publication 42) (AP Act) and all subsequent revisions. Site-specific fault investigations will be required per the AP Act and associated Earthquake Fault Zone maps.

2) Secondary Seismic Hazards – evaluation of secondary seismic hazards should include, at a minimum, seismic shaking, liquefaction, lateral spreading, seismic settlement, seismically-induced landsliding, tsunami, and seiche potential. Evaluation should be presented per the requirements of the AP Act and the Guidelines for Evaluating and Mitigating Seismic Hazards in California (CDMG Special Publication 117).

3) Landslides – evaluation of existing and potential landslides and other mass movements identified on

published geologic documents and/or based on site-specific geologic evidence.

4) Erosion – evaluation of erosion must include, at a minimum, qualitative review and/or analysis of the potential for soil erosion or loss of topsoil.

5) Soil and Geologic Unit Stability – evaluation of the site must include analysis of unstable and potentially unstable soil and geologic units encountered, and must include an opinion as to landsliding, settlement, collapse, and the above listed seismic hazards (Paragraph 2 above).

6) Expansive Soils – evaluation of soil expansion potential must be based on the currently adopted California Building Code.

7) On-site Sewage Disposal – evaluation of any on-site sewage or waste water disposal systems must include opinion on the potential impacts of the planned system to both on-site as well as off-site properties based on the site-specific geotechnical conditions.

8) Groundwater – evaluation of groundwater must include regional and site-specific data as to depth of groundwater.